I0812856

IMAGES
of America

AROUND ESSEX
ELEPHANTS AND RIVER GODS

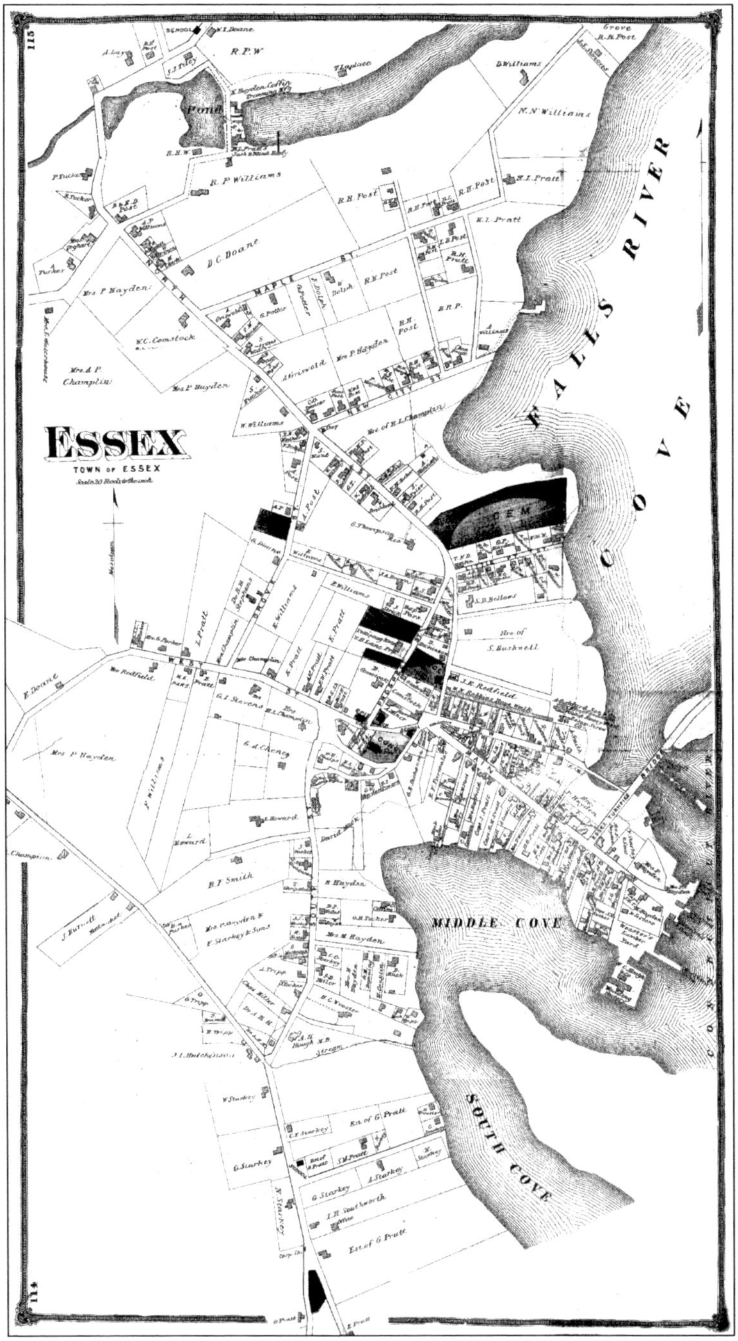

A MAP OF ESSEX VILLAGE. This map was published by F.W. Beers & Company, New York, New York, 1874.

On the cover: **COMSTOCK, CHENEY & COMPANY EMPLOYEES.** Comstock, Cheney & Company in Ivoryton employed hundreds of people in 1900. The workers included a mixture of Yankees, followed by Swedish and German and then Italian and Polish immigrants. This factory was representative of much of the workforce in the industrial sector of the United States.

IMAGES of America

AROUND ESSEX
ELEPHANTS AND RIVER GODS

Robbi Storms and Don Malcarne
Ivoryton Library Association

ARCADIA PUBLISHING

ISBN 978-0-7385-0931-0

Published by Arcadia Publishing
Charleston, South Carolina

Printed in the United States of America

Library of Congress Catalog Card Number: 2001091711

For all general information contact Arcadia Publishing at:
Telephone 843-853-2070
Fax 843-853-0044
E-mail sales@arcadiapublishing.com
For customer service and orders:
Toll-Free 1-888-313-2665

Visit us on the Internet at www.arcadiapublishing.com

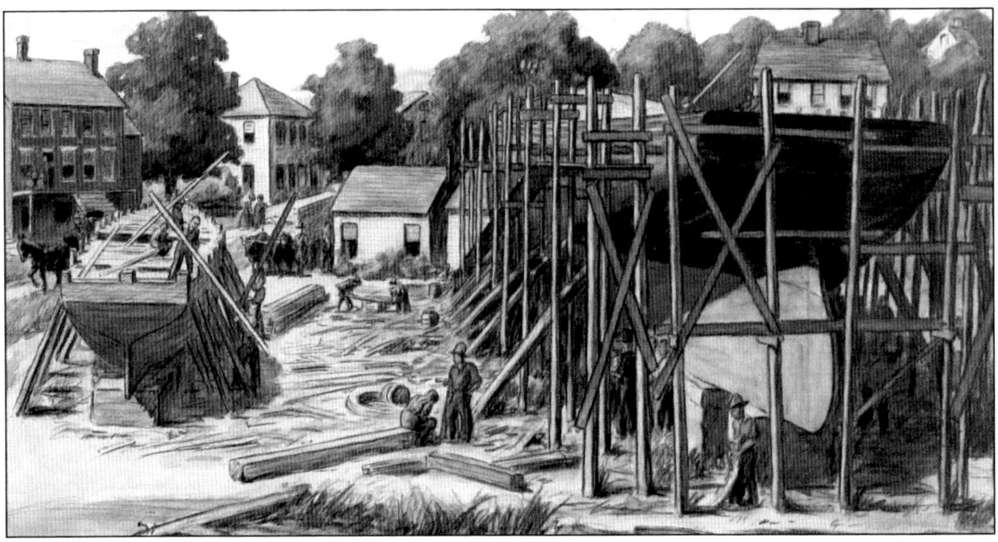

SHIPBUILDING C. 1815, MAIN STREET, ESSEX. This painting shows the area near Robert Lay's 1660 wharf, the first wharf built in Potapoug. The wharf signaled the advent of an activity that would one day bring fortune to many Potapoug families. On the left is the 1809 Hayden Chandlery. The Connecticut River has been very important in the growth of Essex village. Whether it was yachting in the 20th century or shipbuilding in the 18th and 19th centuries, Essex has always had a focus on the water. The painting portrays Essex as it was before the area at the foot of Main Street between the Steamboat Dock and the Dauntless Club was filled. (Photograph courtesy of Connecticut River Museum.)

CONTENTS

Acknowledgments

This collection of pictorial and written history would not have been possible without the contribution of Don Malcarne, Essex town historian, who spent years researching the history of the three villages. I am infinitely grateful for the contribution and guidance from Brenda Milkofsky, director emeritus of the Connecticut River Museum, who created the exhibit "Combs to Keyboards," and for the support of Elizabeth Alvord, the president of the Ivoryton Library Association, and and to each of the association's trustees. Most of the photographs in the book have been borrowed from the Essex Historical Society and the Connecticut River Museum, and I especially appreciate the help of Elizabeth Cook and Alison Guinness. I am indebted to Ann K. Thompson, Daniel A. Nesbett, Bill Nelson, Shirley Malcarne, and Paula Feder. I appreciate the efforts of Charlotte T. Comstock, Max Miller, James Garlinghouse, and Patrick Jonynas. The library was fortunate to have the support of the Lions Club, the Hermes Foundation, the Essex Savings Bank, Mr. and Mrs. Merritt M. Comstock, Evelyn Comstock Carlisle, and Mr. and Mrs. Harwood Comstock. I would like to give special thanks to Hanford Johnson for his donation of the Peter Comstock postcard collection of Ivoryton and Centerbrook, Mr. and Mrs. Merritt Comstock for the eight scrapbooks of Bessie and Laura Comstock, Beatrice Fox McLean for the diaries of her mother, Amelia Miller Fox, and to the members of the community who have generously loaned the library parts of their own collections and parcels of their time.

—Robbi Storms

This book is dedicated to Edith DeForest, curator of the Deep River Historical Society and, for many years, curator of the Pratt Read & Company Museum, and to the elephants that were killed before our communal consciousness was raised.

INTRODUCTION

For roughly 300 years, Essex has been a vital link in the evolution of the lower Connecticut River Valley. It consists of three villages, Essex, Centerbrook, and Ivoryton, spread over 11.8 square miles.

The area was officially laid out as Potapoug Quarter in 1648 and, for the next 20 years, only three families, the Pratts, Lays, and Hides, lived there, owning all the land along the river and engaging in subsistence farming. Subsequently, people who moved into Potapoug settled in the Centre Brooke area. The combination there of rich farmland and the potential for waterpower from the steep drop on the Falls River was attractive. After 1700, Charles Williams, from neighboring Rhode Island Colony, was invited to operate an ironworks there. Also, a new gristmill and sawmill were established.

Soon, there was a large enough population in Potapoug Quarter (Deep River, Chester, and Essex today) to apply for the establishment of a Congregational church. The Colonial Court of Connecticut granted this in 1722, and the Second Ecclesiastical Society was created. The new church building was erected in Centre Brooke, the part of Potapoug where most people lived.

By 1770, the Point (Essex village) was supplanting Centre Brooke as the apex of Potapoug Quarter. The building of large sailing vessels would govern the economic and social life for almost a century beginning in the 1760s. This thriving settlement became part of the global scene, as the great sailing ships built here brought back cargo, ideas, and inspirations from around the world. This was an era of pre-industrialization, and it brought riches to an enterprising class of people. This growing affluence and influence spelled the end of the Puritan era and ushered in the Connecticut Yankee.

The Industrial Revolution doomed wooden shipbuilding, and Essex village suffered. The western part of town, however, later called Ivoryton, was emerging as the new economic center of Essex. Economic and social changes swept in as the shipbuilding culture began to fail. A few small companies were manufacturing combs, toiletries, billiard balls, and sewing implements from elephant tusks by 1850. During the Victorian period, a national demand for a piano in every parlor created unprecedented growth. These small ivory shops began manufacturing piano actions and keyboards. Interchangeable parts, consistent power sources, and a dependable workforce replaced the artisan culture of shipbuilding.

Comstock, Cheney & Company, founded by one of the leading local entrepreneurs of the day, Samuel Merritt Comstock, became the ultimate beneficiary of the new trend. From a small shop employing a few workers in 1849, this factory became very large by the beginning of the 20th century, employing up to 900 workers. For almost 100 years, starting in 1850, 90 percent of all the ivory imported to the United States from Africa was shipped to the factory in Ivoryton or the nearby Pratt Read & Company in Deep River. Ivoryton remained economically dominant among the three villages up to the Great Depression. By 1920, almost two-thirds of the taxes collected by the town of Essex came from Ivoryton.

Comstock, Cheney & Company and the Comstock family encouraged or helped finance a Congregational church, an Episcopal mission, a Swedish Lutheran church, a library, and a new grammar school in Ivoryton.

The Depression of 1929 and World War II brought changes to the company. Comstock, Cheney & Company merged with its competitor from Deep River in 1936, and the new firm was known as Pratt Read & Company. U.S. government contracts to make gliders during the war expanded the product line and financially strengthened the company. After World War II, Pratt Read & Company opened a factory in the south and diversified its product line. The company disbanded in the late 1980s, with the exception of one division, which manufactures screwdrivers. Ironically, this is the product that Samuel M. Comstock made in 1832, before entering the ivory comb business.

—Don Malcarne

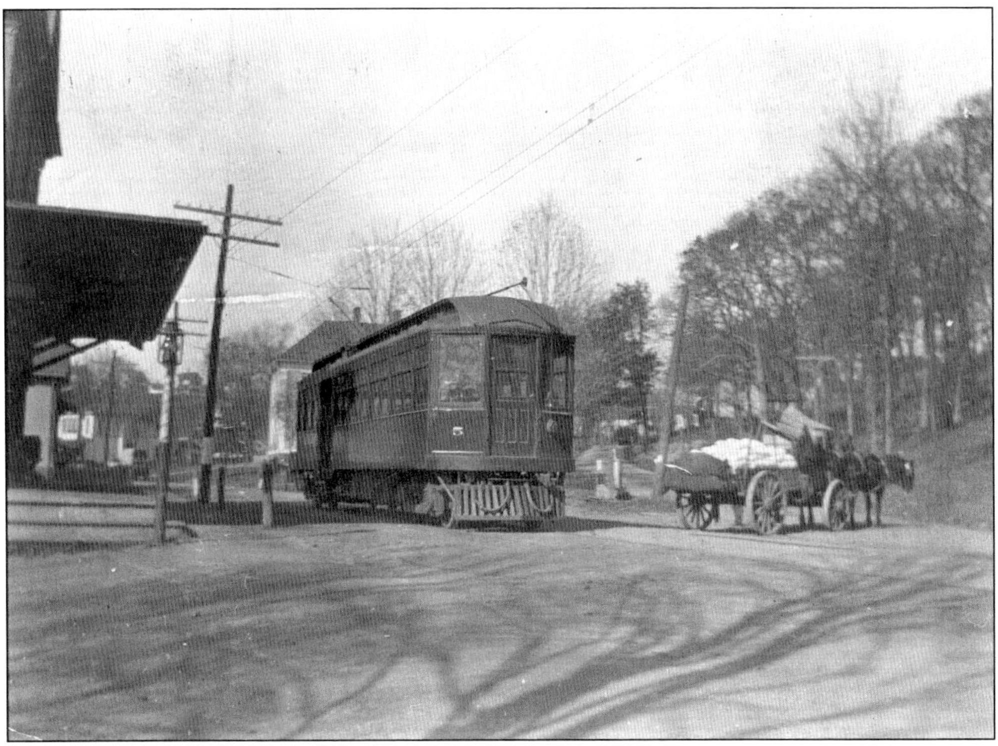

IVORYTON CENTER, C. 1910. Pictured here is Ivoryton at the beginning of the 20th century, when it was a company town controlled by Comstock, Cheney & Company. On the left is Rose's store, essentially the company store, and behind the trolley is the 1900 Ivoryton Grammar School, built primarily by Comstock, Cheney & Company. A buggy loaded with tusks is on its way to the ivory vault, waiting for the trolley to pass. The trolley only operated from 1910 to 1918. (Photograph courtesy of Mary Bowers.)

One

Dawn at Potapoug Quarter

It was 1648 when English colonists in Saybrook Colony surveyed the northern section of the colony. They divided the colony into four sections, which included Eight Mile Meadow, also known as Potapoug Quarter. The word Potapoug, which refers to the peninsula-like outcropping that is now Main and Pratt Streets, came from the Nehantic tribe. The Great Meadow north of the Point swarmed with wildlife: beaver, otters, deer, marsh wrens, hawks, ospreys, and bald eagles.

The surveying committee, charged with finding new settlements, included William Hide; William Pratt, a formidable leader in the Pequot War; and a Mohegan guide, Attawanahood (called Joshua), the son of Mohegan chief Uncas. A few years before Potapoug was settled, a treaty was signed by Gov. John Winthrop, forcing the Pequots to give up their rights to the land along the river. This was partially responsible for the Pequot War (1636–1638). In a surprise attack, John Mason, Lt. William Pratt, and a group of volunteers torched the Pequot village near Mystic and killed between 400 and 600 Pequots. Uncas, Joshua, and the Mohegans allied themselves with the Connecticut and Saybrook Colonies throughout this war.

The eight men from Saybrook Colony who held ownership rights to the newly opened Eight Mile Meadow area (Essex, Deep River, and Chester) were George Fenwick, Nathaniel Eldred, John Clarke, Thomas Birchard, William Hide, William Parker, William Pratt, and William Waller. Together they paid for the right to purchase property in Potapoug. Two of these original owners, Pratt and Hide, had established temporary residences on the Point by 1660. A third settler, John Lay, purchased Waller's rights and then moved there. The three set claim to all the waterfront property. Lay took the northern section, Pratt the middle section, and the southern section went to Hide. Lay built his home on the water just west of what is now the Connecticut River Museum. Pratt lived south of Essex Square near the site of what became the Osage Inn. Hide built his home near the intersection of South Main Street and Route 154.

Pratt, Hide, and Lay's main occupation was farming corn, wheat, oats, and flax. The treasures of the valley along the river were endless. The depths were rich with fish and crabs, and the waters spread fertile sediments onto the floodplains. The river offered the farmers a local transportation and trade route.

Of the original landowners, only William Pratt has been considered a founding father of Essex. He remained in Potapoug and died in his family homestead approximately 28 years after his arrival. John Lay purchased land across the river and sold his share of the Point to his brother Robert Lay. William Hide joined others in founding Norwich in 1659.

A wharf was built by 1664 in front of Robert Lay's house, and a small amount of trade with the West Indies commenced. The ship *Diligence* carried agricultural products and a horse to Barbados at this time. Shipping out of Potapoug would not become significant for almost another 80 years. Those ships that did arrive from the Indies usually carried rum and sugar.

Beginning in 1987, Dr. John Pfeiffer led an archaeological dig with Wesleyan University graduate students at the foot of Main Street. What began as a teaching exercise to define the bank of the Connecticut River as it existed in 1635 lasted three summers because Pfeiffer and his crew uncovered Robert Lay's Wharf behind the Steamboat Dock. Because the wharf was buried, its oak and conifer beams were intact and arranged in Lincoln-log style. It was approximately 328 years old when uncovered. Some experts said this was the oldest wharf yet discovered in the United States.

The building of ships, originally developed to facilitate trade, soon became an end in itself. The Williams, Tooker, Hayden, Post, and Starkey families dominated this field locally in becoming entrepreneurs and pioneers of the sea.

—Robbi Storms

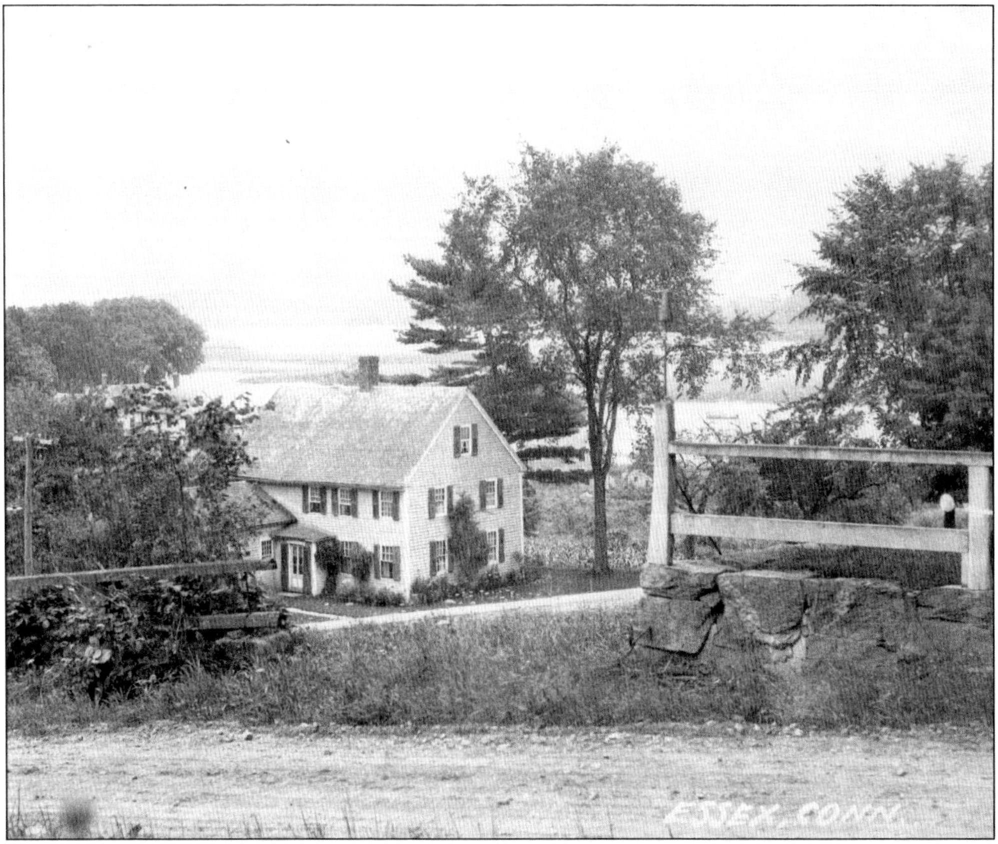

THE c. 1730 NATHANIEL PRATT HOUSE, SOUTH MAIN STREET (EAST), PHOTOGRAPH 1920. Nathaniel Pratt, the youngest son of William Pratt, built this house *c.* 1730 near the site of his father's house. Prior to 1670, William Pratt, a founder of Essex, had built a much smaller structure, which was one of the first three houses in Potapoug. He owned much of the southern part of town, specifically the property on the south side of the current Main Street. In the mid-1930s, this homestead became a restaurant known as the Osage Inn, which operated for more than 20 years. (Photograph courtesy of Don Malcarne.)

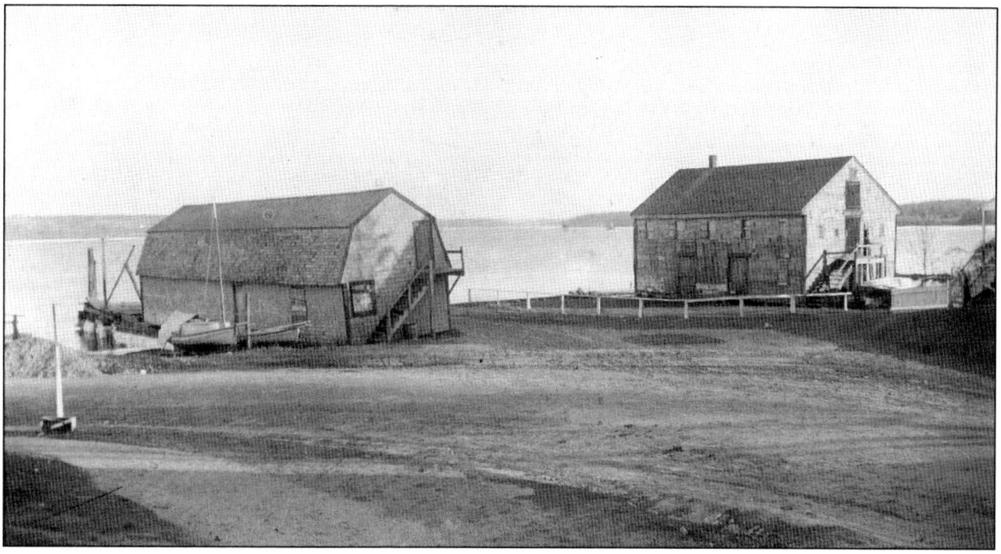

The Old Dock and Hayden Dock, the Foot of Main Street, Photograph Before 1898. This view, looking south down the river toward Saybrook, shows the Abner Parker loft. Captain Parker built this place in 1753 but went bankrupt shortly thereafter. All of Parker's nearby property was sold to Uriah Hayden, including his house at the site of the present Dauntless Club. This building was the first local warehouse for vessels picking up or dropping off cargo. The building on the right is the Uriah Hayden sail loft and chandlery, built *c.* 1775. Both were demolished by 1918. (Photograph courtesy of Essex Historical Society.)

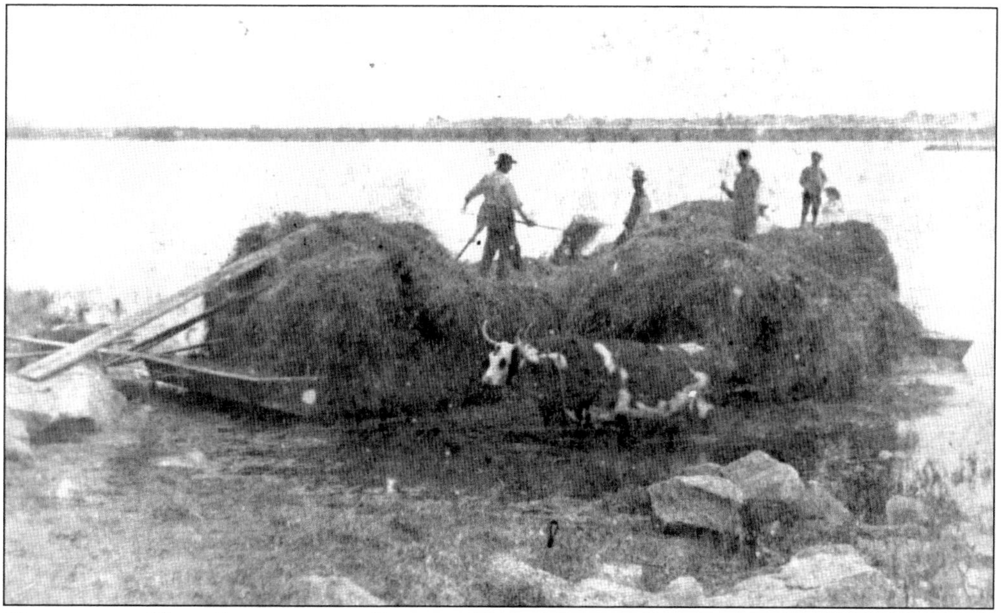

Unloading Hay, Photograph Before 1900. The hay that grew in the Great Meadows around North Cove and on Thatchbed Island near South Cove provided food and bedding for farm animals. This hay was harvested, brought across the coves, and unloaded at places such as Little Point, Denison's Point, and Potapoug Point. During the early settlement of Potapoug, this natural product was a valuable resource. (Photograph courtesy of Florence Griswold Museum.)

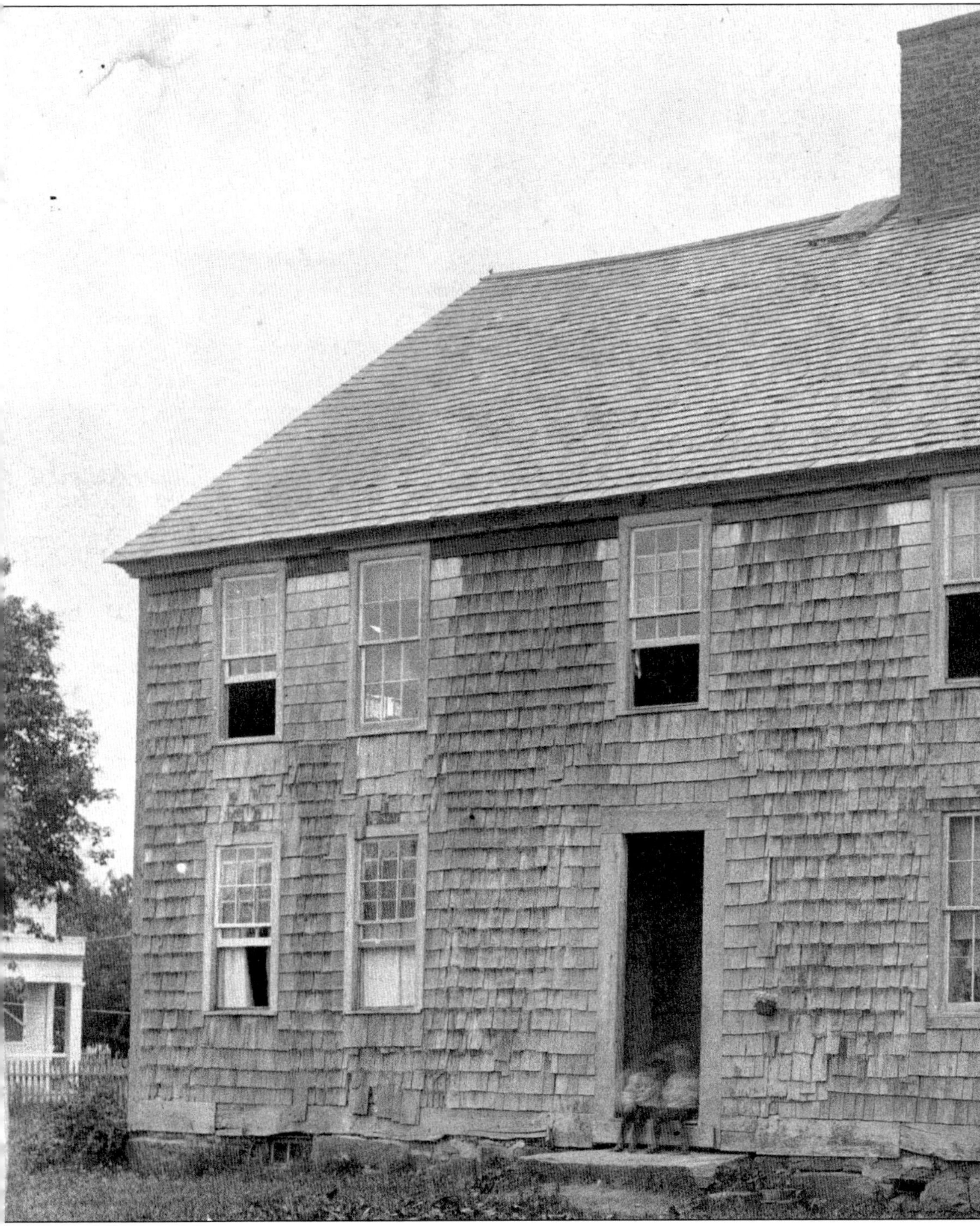

The 1730 Samuel Lay House, Photograph 1897. Samuel Lay built this house near the site of the original Robert Lay house. Standing behind the current Steamboat Dock, it is one of the three oldest houses on Potapoug Point. The unkempt-looking house was known as "the Beehive" in 1897 because so many rooms were rented. After the decline of shipbuilding,

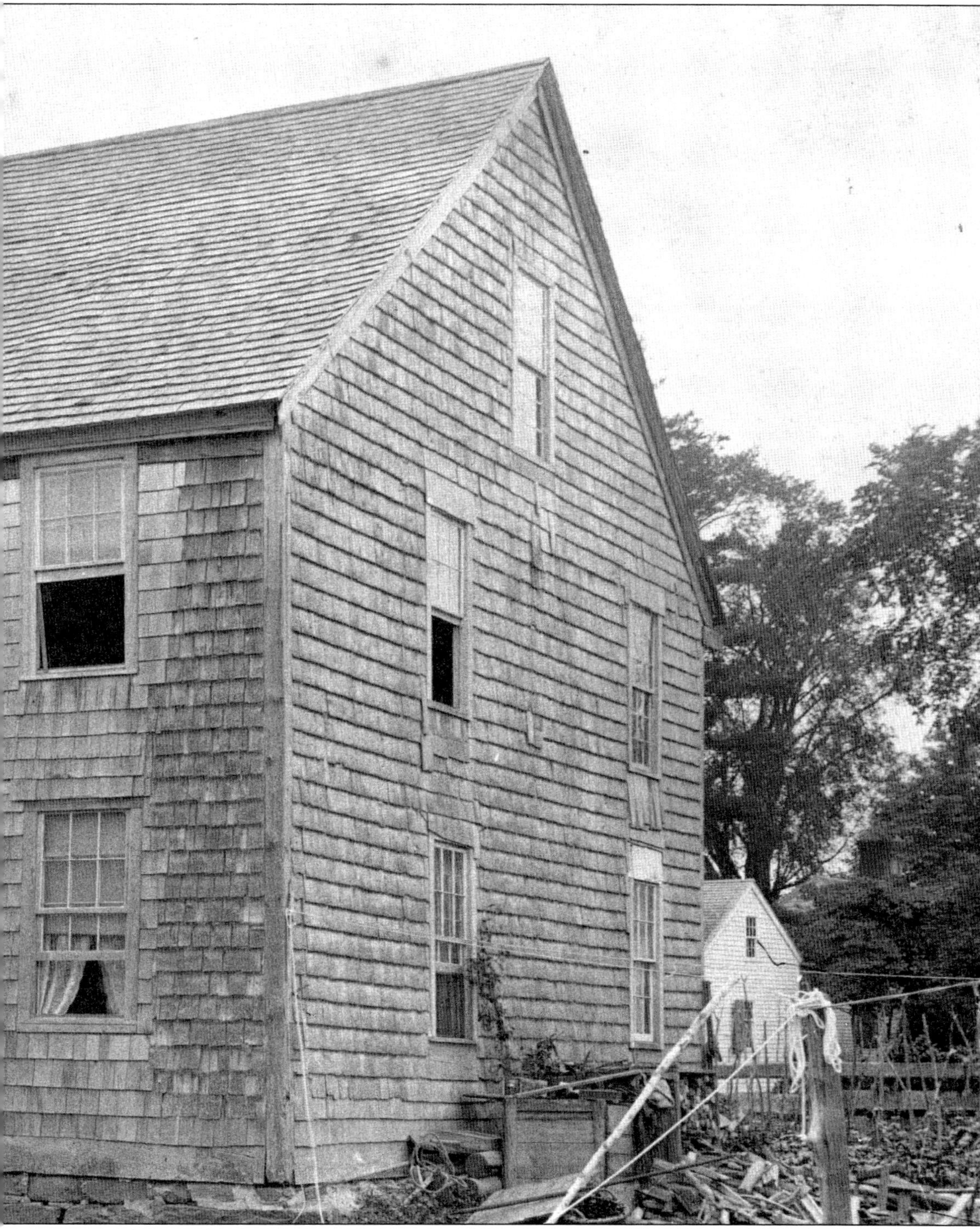

tenement houses dominated Essex village. Essex, which had flourished on the strength of the shipbuilding industry, due to its decline, had fallen into much more difficult times. This building housed the Dauntless Club in the early part of the 20th century. (Photograph courtesy of Connecticut River Museum.)

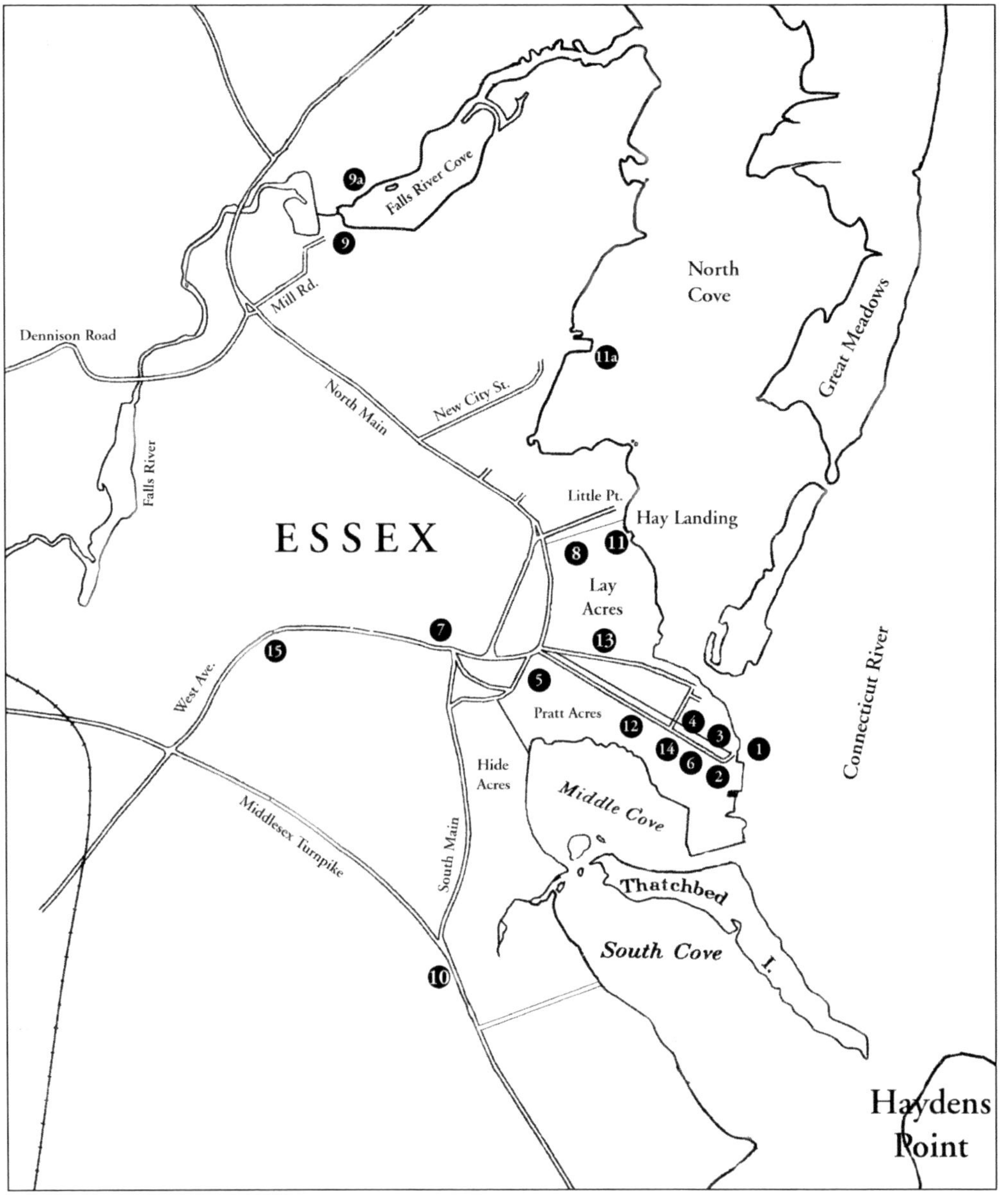

AN EARLY MAP OF ESSEX VILLAGE. The key to the map is as follows: (1) Abner Parker Loft and Uriah Hayden Loft and Chandlery, (2) Uriah Hayden House, (3) Samuel Lay House, on the site of the John Lay House, (4) Timothy Starkey House, (5) Nathaniel Pratt House, (6) Hayden-Starkey Store, (7) John Pratt Jr., (8) Lay's Cart Path, (9) Williams Gristmill, (9A) Williams Shipyard, (10) Noah Starkey House, (11) Abner Parker Williams House, (11A) Second Williams Shipyard, (12) site of the original Ropewalk Company, (13) site of the second Ropewalk Company, (14) Ebenezer Hayden II House, and (15) Ebenezer Hayden House.

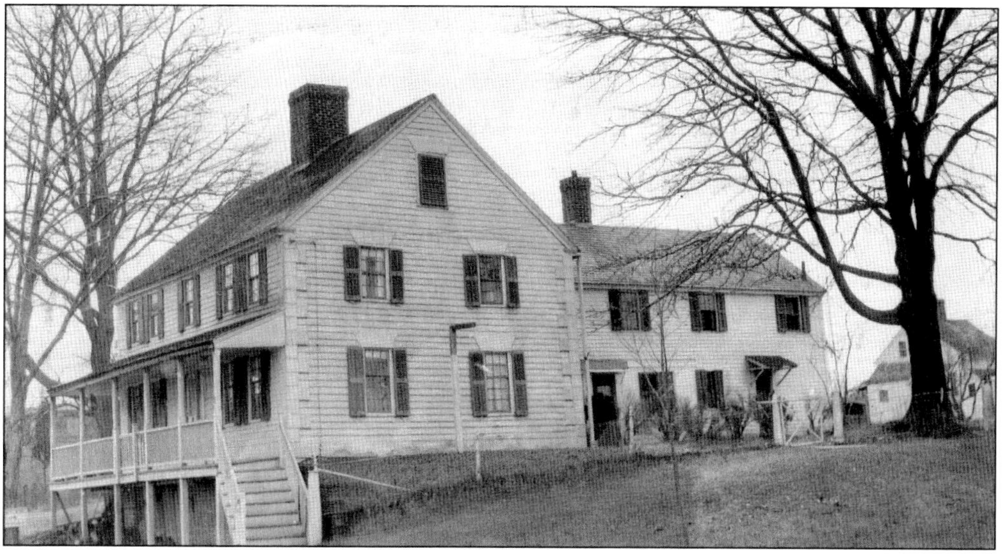

THE 1767 URIAH HAYDEN HOUSE, MAIN STREET (SOUTH), PHOTOGRAPH 1922. A section of the rear ell of this house is slightly older than the main part of the house and was built by Capt. Abner Parker as early as 1755. Capt. Uriah Hayden built the main house into the riverbank with a walkout basement. It featured quoins and was the first new home built on the Point in 20 years. With this action, Hayden was establishing a maritime lineage. He soon opened a tavern in the basement of this building and later purchased what is now Hayden's Point. Along the side of the house is where the *Oliver Cromwell* was built, setting the stage for shipbuilding in Essex from 1775 forward. In 1918, this building became the Dauntless Club and has been so for more than 80 years. (Photograph courtesy of Don Malcarne.)

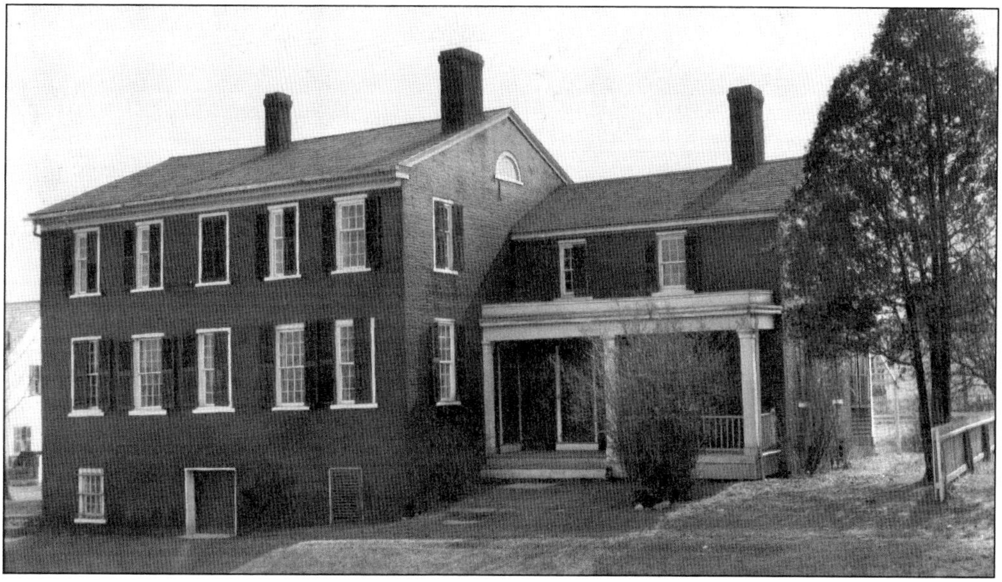

THE 1809 HAYDEN-STARKEY STORE, MAIN STREET (SOUTH), PHOTOGRAPH 1922. Samuel Hayden and Ebenezer Hayden II, sons of Uriah Hayden, and their brother-in-law, Timothy Starkey Jr., owned the Hayden-Starkey Store at the foot of Main Street. It was conveniently located near their homes on the Point. During the attack by the British in 1814, rope stored in the cellar was destroyed. (Photograph courtesy of Don Malcarne.)

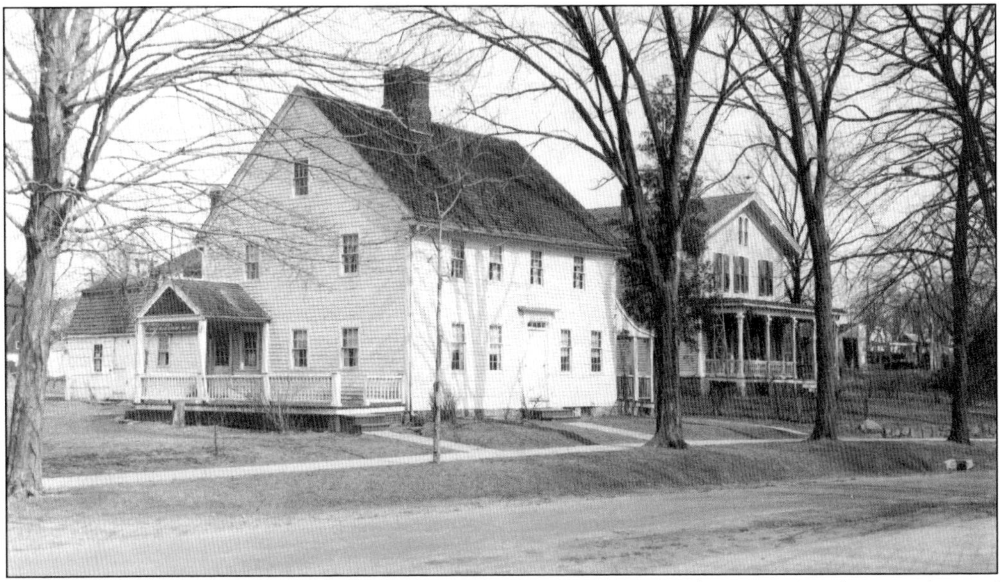

THE EARLY-1700S JOHN PRATT JR. HOUSE, WEST AVENUE. John Pratt Jr., the grandson of William Pratt, built the rear ell of this house in 1701 and started the front section in 1732. He constructed a smithy adjacent to his home. He was the second of nine generations of Pratts to operate a smithy. The original smithy was torn down in 1845, when the brick smithy replaced it. At the time of its demise in the 1940s, Pratt's Village Smithy was considered the oldest continuously run family business in the United States. (Photograph courtesy of Don Malcarne.)

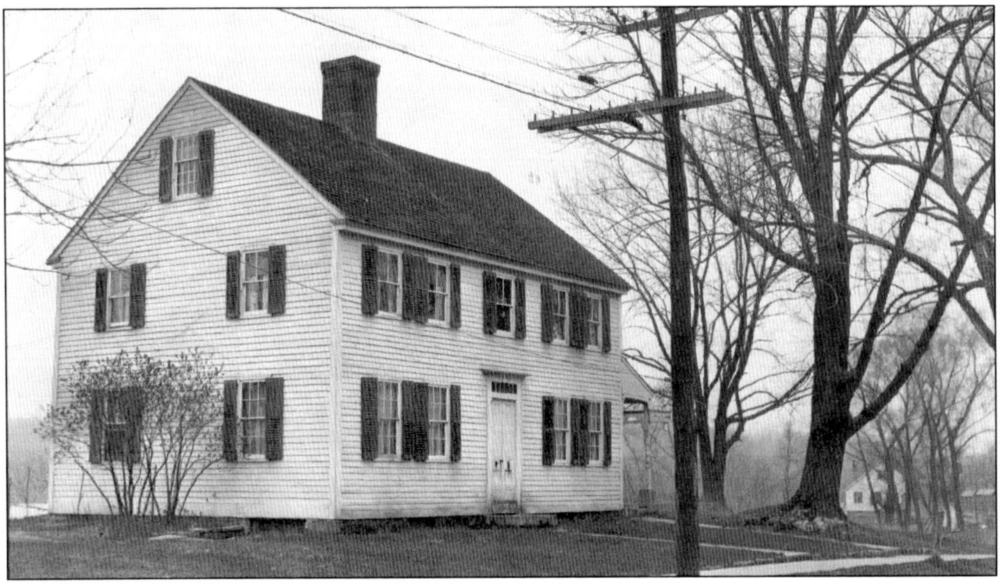

THE 1719 (1773) PARKER-BULL HOUSE, EAST MAIN STREET, IVORYTON. This house, partially built by Jonathan Parker in 1719, is the oldest house in Ivoryton still standing. It was rebuilt by Edward Bull in 1773. The Bull family lived in it over a span of 175 years. At this site, the Bulls operated a gristmill, a sawmill, a cider mill, and a fulling mill. Along with these small operations, the Bulls owned 220 acres of farmland and two ships, the *Columbia* and the *Manilla*, which sailed out of Potapoug. Few houses were built in Ivoryton before 1830. (Photograph courtesy of Don Malcarne.)

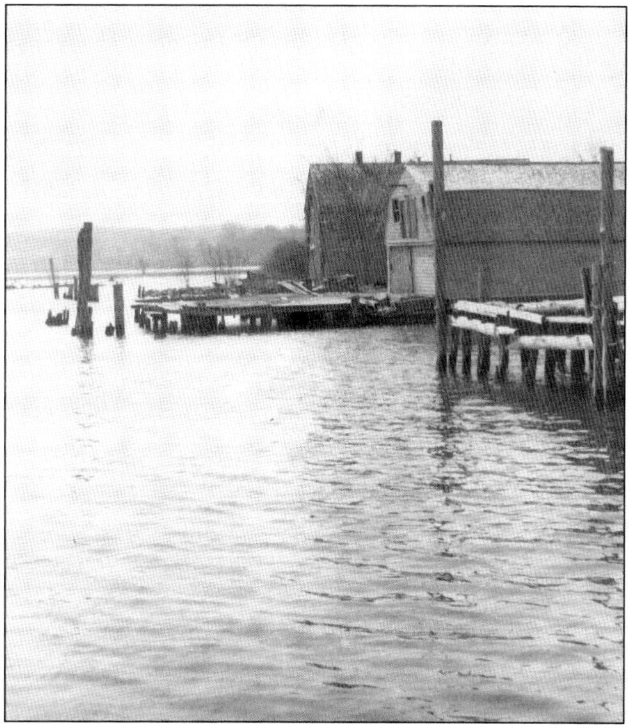

THE C. 1775 URIAH HAYDEN CHANDLERY AND THE 1753 ABNER PARKER WAREHOUSE, PHOTOGRAPH C. 1895. On the riverfront are the Uriah Hayden Chandlery (left) and the gambrel-roofed Abner Parker warehouse. The 1753 warehouse (current site of the E.E. Dickinson boathouse) became the original steamboat landing from 1823 until the new steamboat stop was built in 1878. (Photograph courtesy of Connecticut River Museum.)

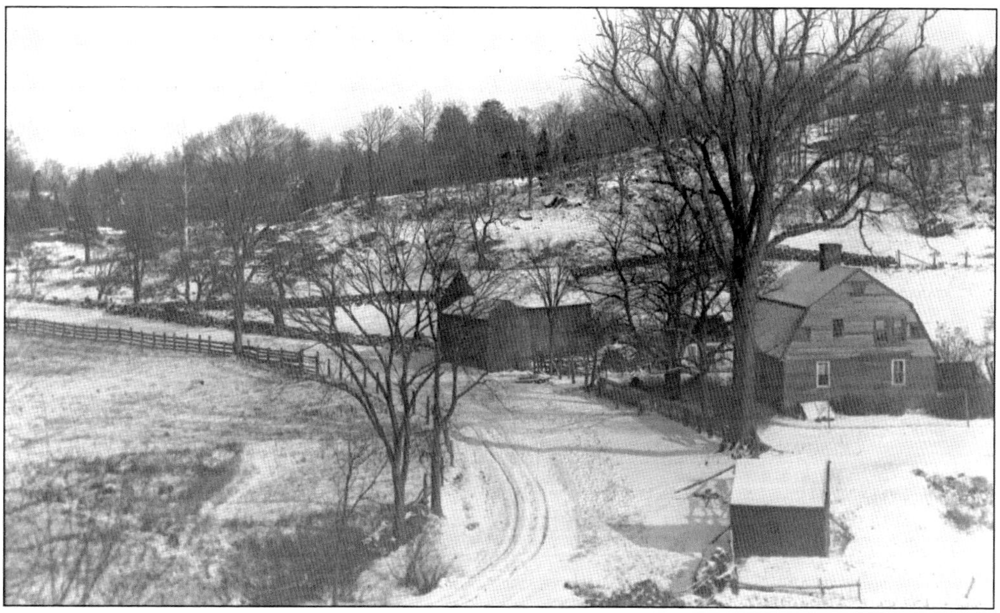

JOSEPH HILL FARM, INGHAM HILL ROAD, C. 1824. This view, looking north on Ingham Hill Road, shows the large-acre farm built by one of the wealthiest men ever to live in Essex, Col. Joseph Hill. Hill lived on North Main Street and, like many other businessmen in Essex, kept a farm in the Scotch Plains area of Centerbrook, on Ingham Hill, the main road from Essex to Westbrook. He was an attorney whose sister married into the Hayden family. The cemetery on Grove Street was built for the Hayden family by Hill, and he is buried there. Hills Academy is named for him. (Photograph courtesy of Essex Historical Society.)

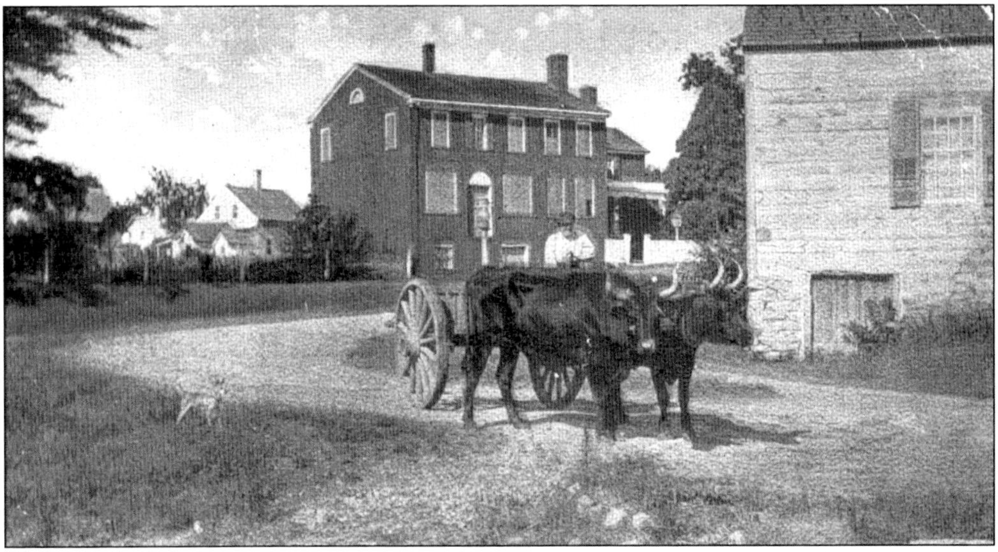

THE OLD WAY OF TRANSPORTATION. In 1748, as the need for a road to the river became more pressing, settlers in the area reached an agreement. Samuel Lay and the Saybrook Colony traded land in the area that is now Main Street to provide road access to the wharf. The western end of Main Street changed direction slightly in 1815, making it the straight highway it is today. (Photograph courtesy of Connecticut River Museum.)

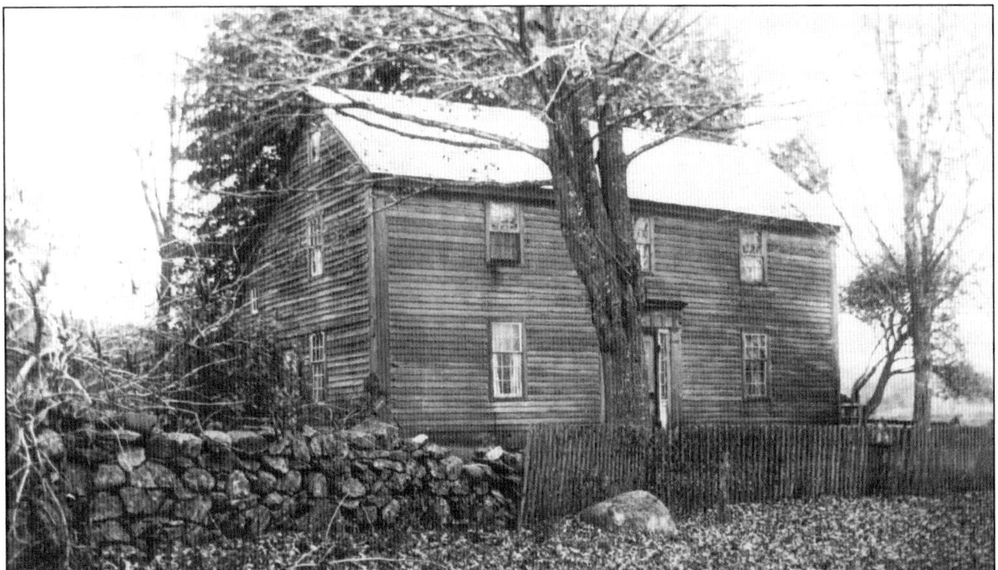

THE C. 1757 JOSIAH NOTT HOUSE, WESTBROOK ROAD, CENTERBROOK. Josiah Nott, grandson of Abraham Nott, who was the first pastor of the Second Ecclesiastical Society of Saybrook (Centerbrook Congregational Church), built this three-bay saltbox c. 1757. The first church in Potapoug, it was founded because the settlers, having increased in number, found it a hardship to travel to the southern part of Saybrook as often as twice a week for worship. Centre Brooke had many families living there and was the focal point of town until 1775. The main thoroughfare was through here to Saybrook via Bokum Road. (Photograph courtesy of Essex Historical Society.)

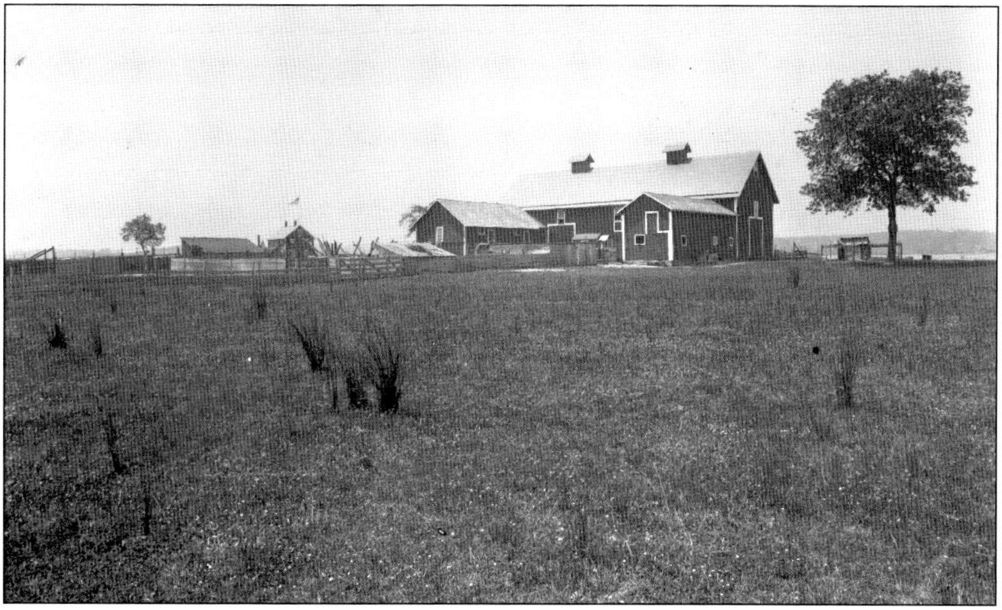

THE NOTT ISLAND FARM, ESSEX-OLD LYME. Nott Island Farm, directly across from the Steamboat Dock, was destroyed by fire in the late 1940s. The farm dates back to the founding of Saybrook Colony, when Potapoug settler Robert Lay tended it for Lord Fenwick, who owned the property. In the 20th century, Thomas MacWhinney, a contractor and former first selectman of Essex, purchased the farm from Peter H. Comstock. It is now owned by the state. This photograph was taken *c.* 1918. (Photograph courtesy of Essex Historical Society.)

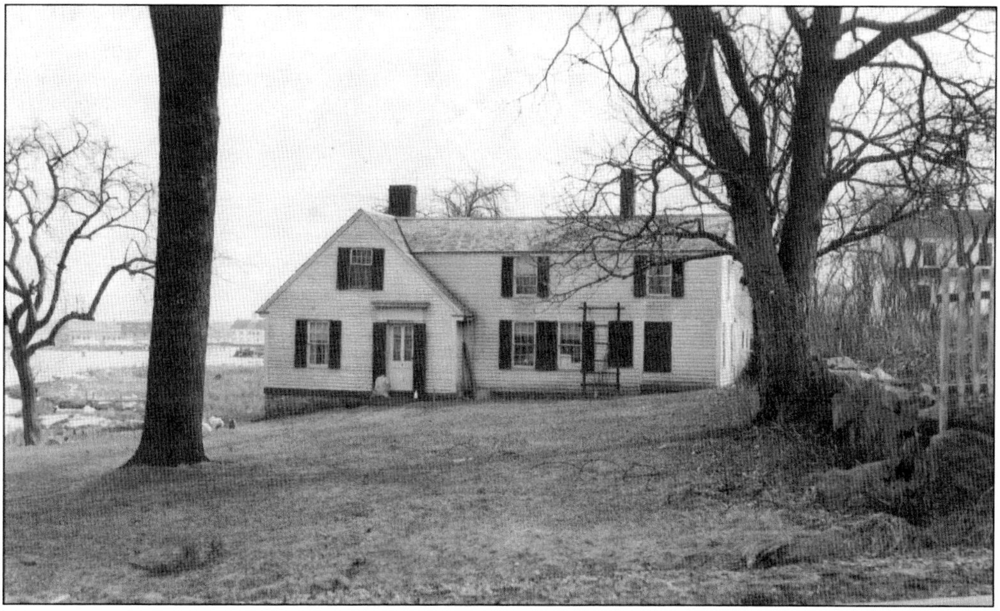

THE 1798 ABNER PARKER WILLIAMS HOUSE, LITTLE POINT STREET (SOUTH), PHOTOGRAPH 1922. In the background can be seen the 1878 Steamboat Dock, built by Phebe Hayden for use by the Hartford and New York Transportation Company. Abner Parker Williams, a sea captain, built the house facing North Cove in 1798. It was conveniently located on the cove near the shipbuilding industry. (Photograph courtesy of Don Malcarne.)

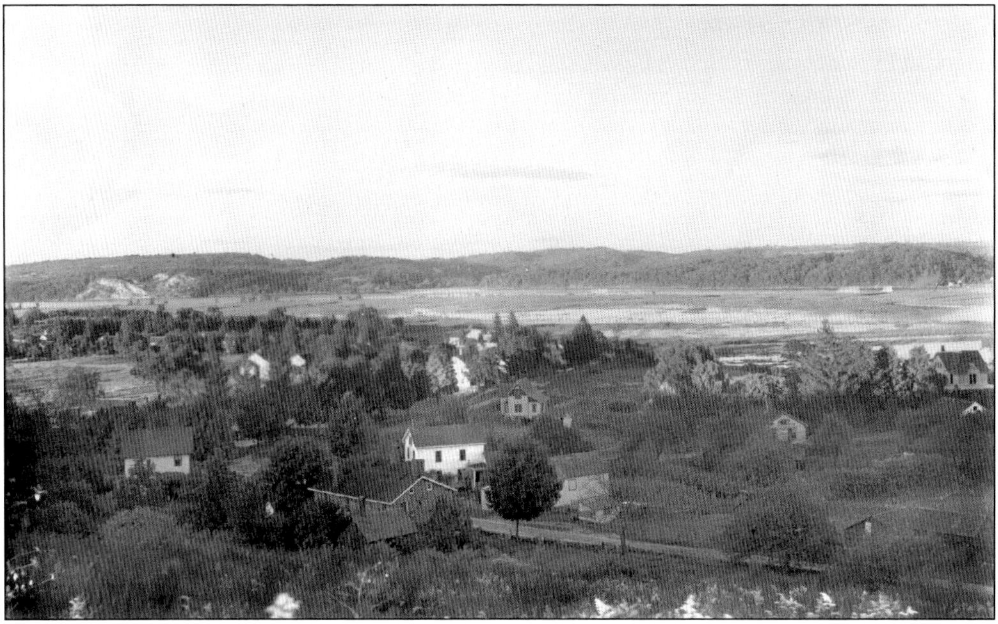

A BIRD'S-EYE VIEW. This view was taken from the top of Stone Pit Hill looking east toward Lyme. The stone house on Grove Street built by Ambrose Post can be seen in the foreground. The Great Meadows, the Connecticut River, and Joshua's Rock (upper left) can be seen in the background. (Photograph courtesy of Essex Historical Society.)

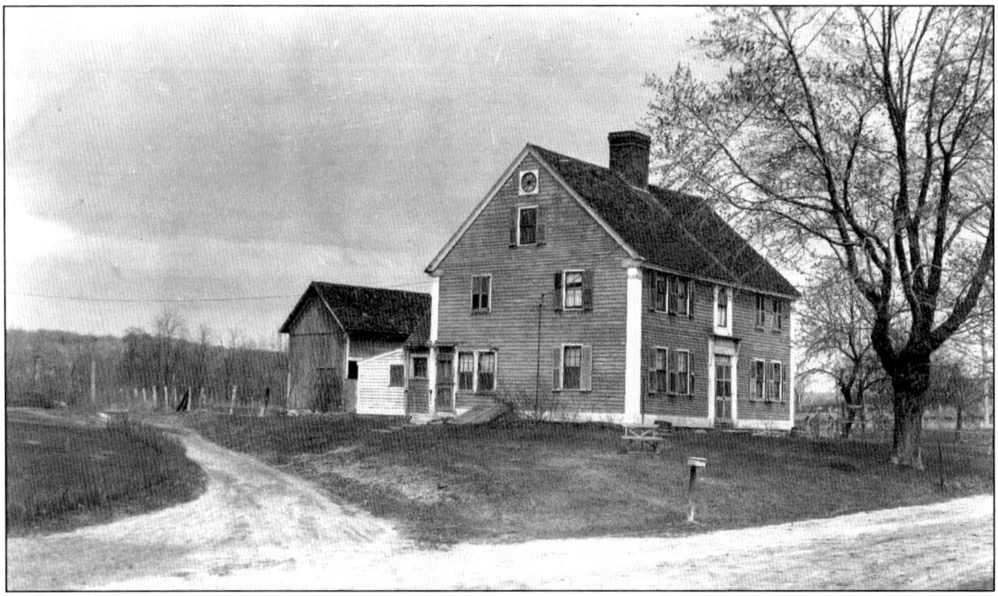

THE MATHER HOUSE, C. 1787. Dr. Elisha Mather lived in this house on Old Denison Road, which at the time was the main thoroughfare between Centerbrook and Potapoug Point. The house doubled as a medical office and pharmacy. Centre Brooke was the center of town until the Revolutionary War. One of Mather's sons, Ezra Mather, also a doctor, moved to Main Street in Essex in 1815 when Essex village had replaced Centre Brooke as the center of town. Another son, Ulysses Mather, was a local doctor as well, but he died at an early age. (Photograph courtesy of Don Malcarne.)

Two

WAKING THE RIVER GODS

The term "river god" is a coined phrase, usually referring to merchants and entrepreneurs north of Middletown. These people often maintained their economic and social power through marriage into ministers' families, which combined business success with Puritan spirituality. While this was not as prevalent among the pioneers of the Potapoug shipbuilding industry, a few did follow this formula. The factors of kinship and marriage were of vital importance in maintaining economic control.

Potapoug Point was virtually unpopulated in the 1650s when Robert Lay built the settlement's first wharf in front of his house on the west side of the Great River, several miles upstream from Long Island Sound. This was the first venture into what would ultimately become the town's livelihood. Surrounded by the river and fringed with coves and harbors, Potapoug was among the first Connecticut settlements to turn to the sea in quest of maritime pursuits. By 1732, Noah and Richard Tooker would build the first ships in Potapoug on South (now Middle) Cove, just south of the present public landing.

By 1795, Samuel Williams, a mill owner on the Falls River, took advantage of his sawmill's location and created a major shipyard where the Falls River empties into North Cove. Waterpower from the Falls River allowed Williams to forge iron and fabricate the wooden parts necessary for his shipbuilding enterprise. Up until 1840, an average of one ship per year was produced at the Williams shipyard. He and his son Calvin Williams had an interest in the landing, dock, and shipyard at the foot of New City Street, and Richard P. Williams, another son, turned this into a thriving shipyard. Calvin Williams married into a prominent shipbuilding family in nearby Deep River.

Uriah Hayden was the first of Potapoug's river gods, by virtue of the fact that he owned a great deal of waterfront property and was instrumental in bringing the Episcopal church to town. His family connections certainly helped him achieve his goals. His aunt was married to Samuel Lay, grandson of an original Potapoug founder, and his daughters, Mary Ann and Esther, married Timothy and Felix Starkey of the shipbuilding Starkeys.

The Hayden shipyard, established *c.* 1770 on all the land east of Scholes Lane and south of Main Street, dominated the local shipbuilding trade. Uriah Hayden had acquired the Tooker and Parker family holdings in this area. In 1776, the colony of Connecticut chose Hayden to construct the largest ship ever built in the Connecticut River valley up to that time. The *Oliver Cromwell*, a 300-ton battleship, carried 20 guns and had a crew of 125. Under Capts. Seth Harding and Timothy Parker, the *Oliver Cromwell* fought in the Revolutionary War, capturing five British ships before the British seized it in 1779. The *Oliver Cromwell's* fame and Potapoug as a fine shipbuilding site were two reasons that wealth came to the community.

The United States, moving toward becoming an industrial power, badly needed ships for trade. Although commerce with the West Indies, Europe, and along the east coast from the Connecticut River was important, it was the building of the ships that was most profitable for Potapoug. Between 1788 and 1870, more than 600 ships were built there, and many local shipyards became well known. Ships launched in this period commonly had names that were closely associated with people or places in Potapoug. A 1799 schooner was named *Prudence* for Ebenezer Hayden's deceased wife. The ship *Six Brothers*, built at the Williams yard in 1821, was named for the sons of Capt. Samuel Williams.

In 1823, when steamboats started plying the Connecticut River, the end of shipbuilding in Potapoug was in sight. These vessels traveled between Hartford and New York City until 1931, making stops along the way. Abner Parker's 1753 warehouse, at the foot of Main Street, had been the stop in Potapoug for the steamboats. In 1878, Phebe Hayden built the Steamboat Dock, now the Connecticut River Museum, to pick up and let off passengers and cargo.

The largest vessel built in Potapoug was the *Middlesex*, a 1,424-tonner launched in 1851 near the site of today's Essex Boat Works. Shortly before their demise, these shipyards produced some of the most ornate and spectacular ships ever built in the area. The Williams yard turned out some of the larger ones, including the 682-ton *Orphan* in 1845, the 785-ton *Seine* in 1849, and the 1,081-ton *Connecticut*, also in 1849. One of the most noteworthy was the *Osage*, built by a merchant for the East Indies trade. It was destroyed by the British in 1814 and has laid in the Falls River Cove mud for over 100 years. The Tiley family raised it in the early 20th century, and its salvageable parts were made into furniture. The mantle in the Essex Yacht Club, built in 1936, was made of material from the *Osage*. The *Elisha Denison*, built in 1827, sailed out of New York for the Hurlburt Line for many years. It was destroyed in 1853 in a gale off Galveston, Texas.

By 1840, the Williams family operation at the Falls River was in bankruptcy, but the New City yard continued to produce wooden sailing vessels into the 1850s. However, the sunset of the old way of building boats had arrived and the dawn of metal steam-driven boats was here. The Industrial Revolution was in place.

One cannot understate the importance of this industry for Essex. It fueled the growth of a new class of entrepreneur—the full-time business financier—and ignited the explosion of the grand and stately homes that still stand today.

—Don Malcarne

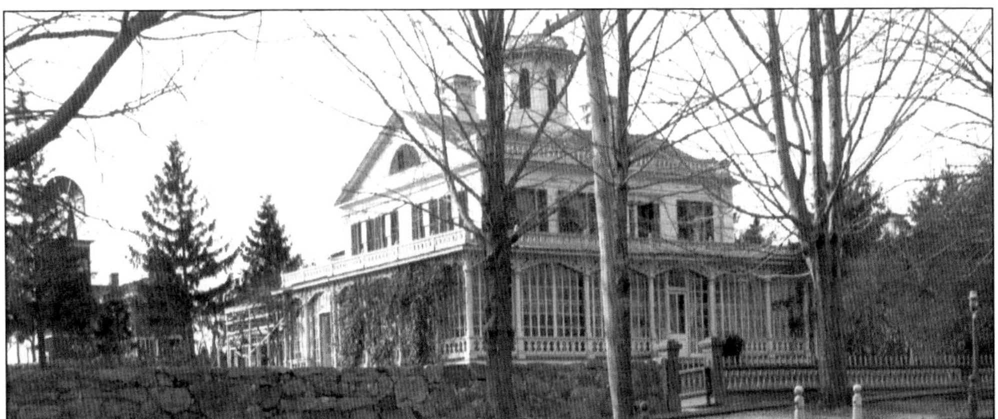

THE C. 1819 CHARLES URIAH HAYDEN HOMESTEAD, PHOTOGRAPH 1908. This house across from the town hall was the home of Charles Uriah Hayden, who was the grandson of one of the wealthiest persons to live in the lower valley, Ebenezer Hayden. Ebenezer Hayden dominated shipbuilding in Potapoug. He had no direct heirs when he passed away in 1818, his wife and children having predeceased him, so he left his money to his grandchildren. Five of the houses on West Avenue and at Champlin Square reflect this family's wealth. (Photograph courtesy of Essex Historical Society.)

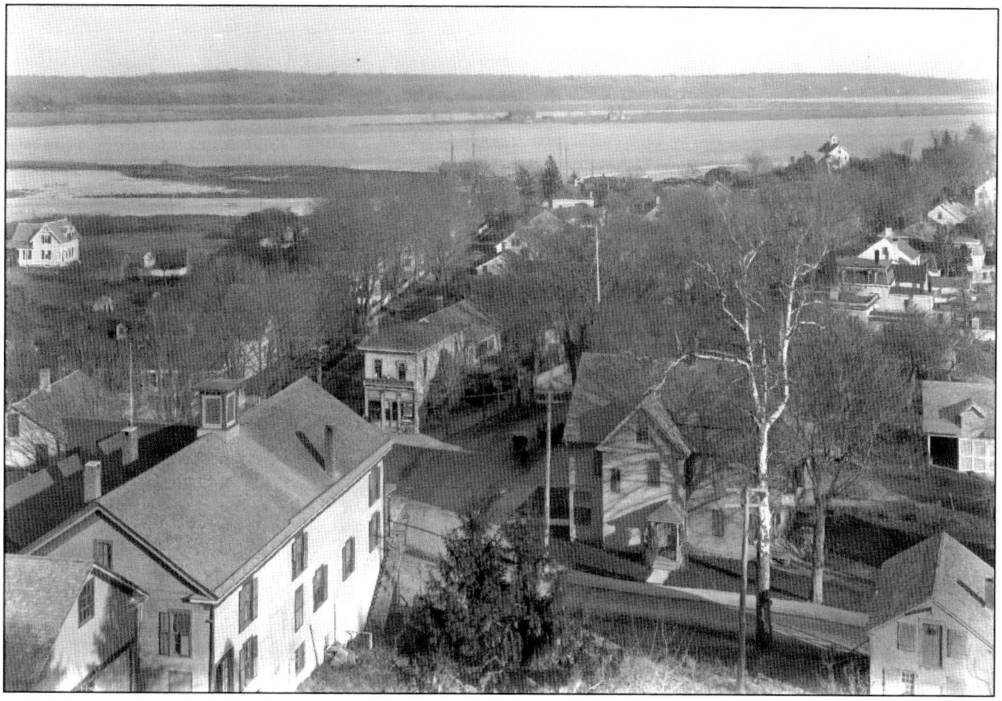

A VIEW EAST FROM METHODIST CHURCH STEEPLE. This 1900s photograph was taken from the steeple of the Methodist church. It is said that from this location in the early 1800s as many as 30 vessels could be seen on the stocks in the yards. At one time, 2,000 tons of wooden ships were built in Potapoug annually. Visible in the background are two double-masted schooners and the farm on Nott Island. The farm was originally owned by Lord Fenwick and tended by Robert Lay. (Photograph courtesy of Essex Historical Society.)

A MODEL OF THE *OLIVER CROMWELL*, BY JOHN COMSTOCK. The *Oliver Cromwell*, the first vessel financed by the colony of Connecticut, was built at the Hayden shipyard in 1776. From 1776 to 1778, it captured five British vessels. In its final battle against the HMS *Daphne*, which was assisted by the HMS *Delaware* and HMS *Union*, its captain and crew were taken prisoner. Three of the crew were killed, and four died of wounds. Captain Parker and the remaining crew were held on the prison ship *Jenny*. Nine escaped; some were forced to serve on British ships; others died. The British later renamed the ship the *Restoration*. (Photograph courtesy of Connecticut River Museum.)

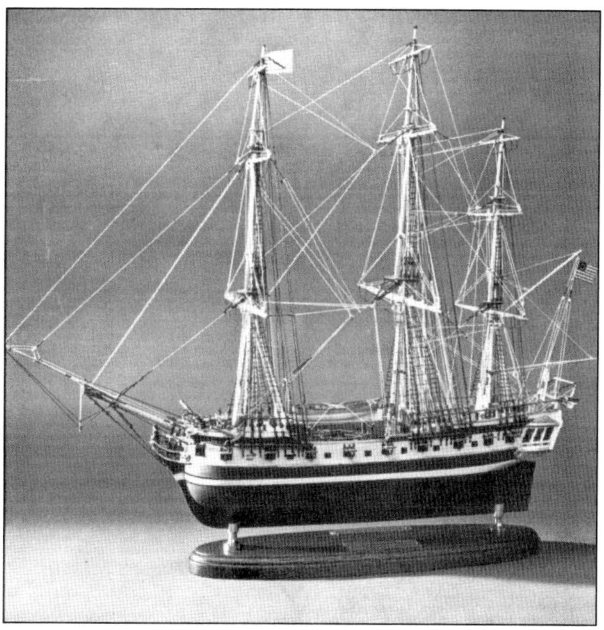

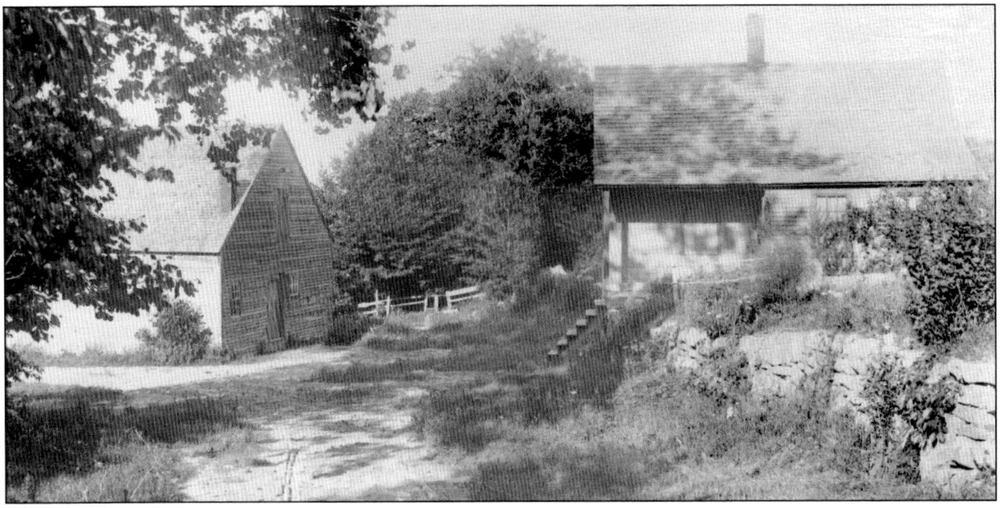

THE OLD GRISTMILL, MILL ROAD, PHOTOGRAPH C. 1890. Mill Road, at the intersection of Denison Road and North Main Street, reflects the legacy of the famous Williams complex on the first Falls River dam at a point where that waterway empties into Falls River Cove. On the left is the 1777 gristmill, which burned down in the early 1890s. This original gristmill, run by Samuel Williams, later became the Essex Woodturning Shop. On the right is a 19th-century house, which was torn down in the middle of the 20th century. Initially, it served as a warehouse and later as a homestead. The Doane family purchased much of this property in the late 19th century and farmed it for many years. After 1960, this Doane farm was subdivided and new homes were built. Mill Road in front of the gristmill crossed the dam and entered River Road. (Photograph courtesy of Essex Historical Society.)

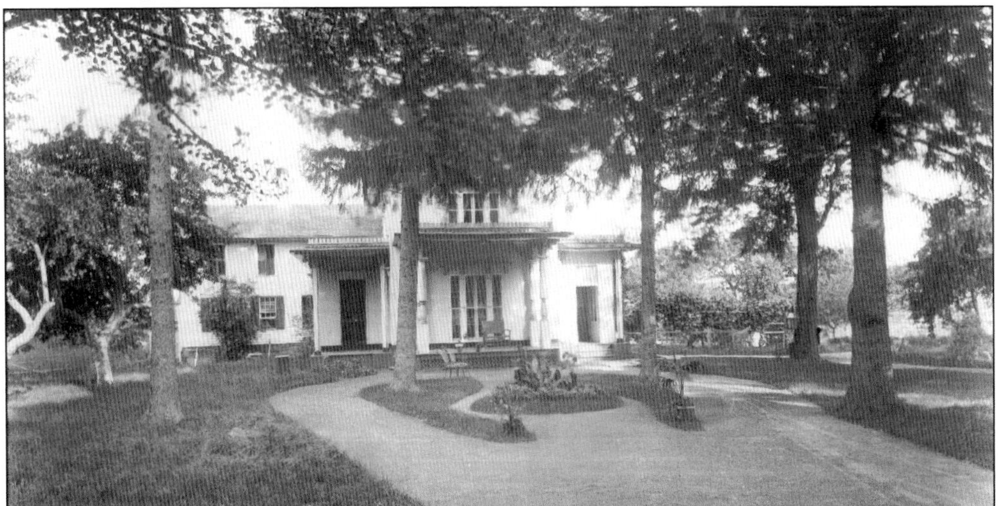

THE 1849 HENRY WOOSTER HOMESTEAD, PHOTOGRAPH EARLY 1900S. Built on land owned by Capt. William Williams, this house was prestigious in its time. It was located on South Main Street, where the Williams family had owned 14 acres for over 70 years. Daughter Jane Williams married Henry Wooster, a prominent lumberman, whose shop was on the Williams complex on Mill Lane. This was the well-known Wooster-Gladwin Lumber Yard, which later moved to the end of Novelty Lane, where the Essex Yacht Club is now located. (Photograph courtesy of Essex Historical Society.)

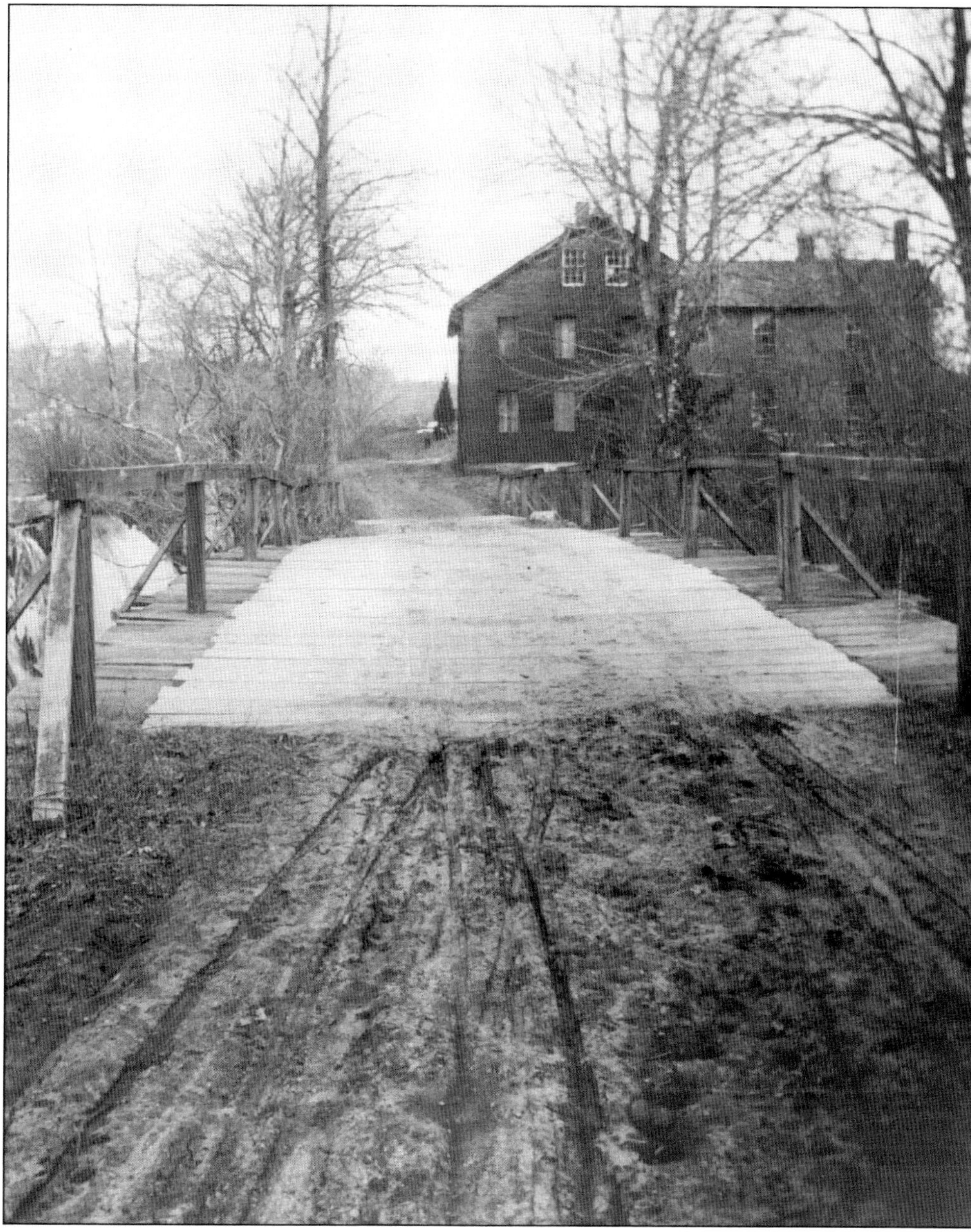

THE C. 1830 WILLIAMS MILL, PHOTOGRAPH C. 1895. This picture shows not only the Williams Mill but also the wooden bridge over the Falls River, with the Williams dam on the left. Capt. Samuel Williams had seven sons. One of them, David Williams, ran the famous Williams Shipyard after the death of his father and built the mill on the site of his father's sawmill. The dam powered a sawmill, a gristmill, a bone-and-ivory-cutting operation, and a forge, as well as the shipyard. Among the most famous of the ships built there were the *Osage* and the *Six Brothers*. The latter vessel was named for six sons of Samuel Williams. Two sons, Richard and David Williams, became master shipbuilders, and all six sons became sea captains. (Photograph courtesy of Essex Historical Society.)

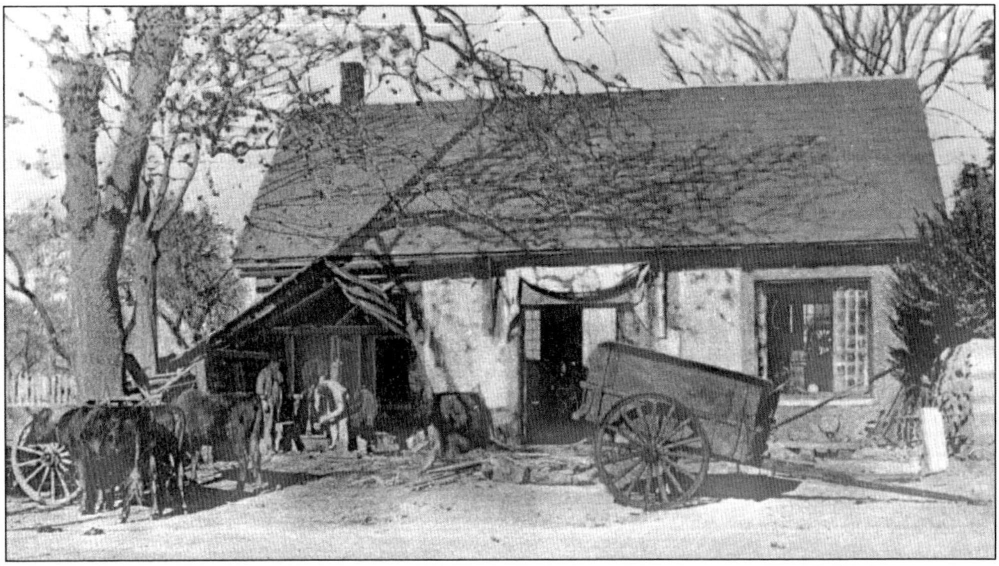

Pratt's Village Smithy, Photograph c. 1910. This business was established in 1678 in Saybrook and moved to Potapoug Point after 1700. It remained in the Pratt family for nine generations, a period of 268 years. John Pratt, son of Essex founder William Pratt, built a wooden shop at this site. The shop lasted until 1845, when it became too small, and Elias Pratt built the present brick structure, later covered with ivy, to replace it. The photograph is a quaint picture of the blacksmith's yard, located on Champlin Square in Essex village. (Photograph courtesy of Connecticut River Museum.)

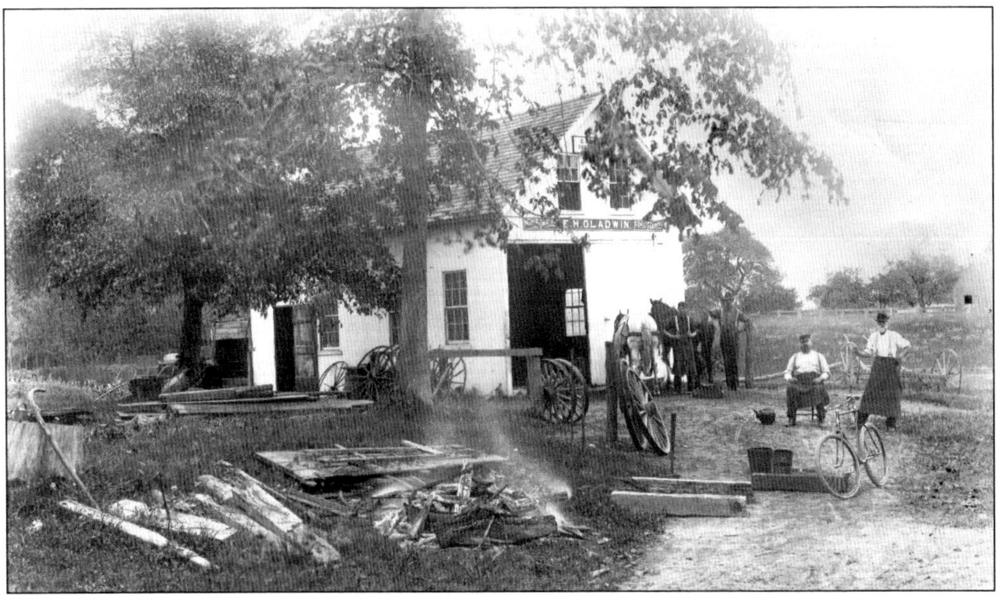

The Gladwin Smithy, Centerbrook. Gladwin's blacksmith shop exists today as the Essex ambulance barn. The blacksmith, himself, lived in the house immediately west of the shop, known as the Robert Pratt House. In the 1800s, there were seven blacksmiths forging a living in Potapoug, not only repairing wagons and shoeing horses but also hammering out the iron nails and fastenings for the shipbuilders and carpenters. (Photograph courtesy of Essex Historical Society.)

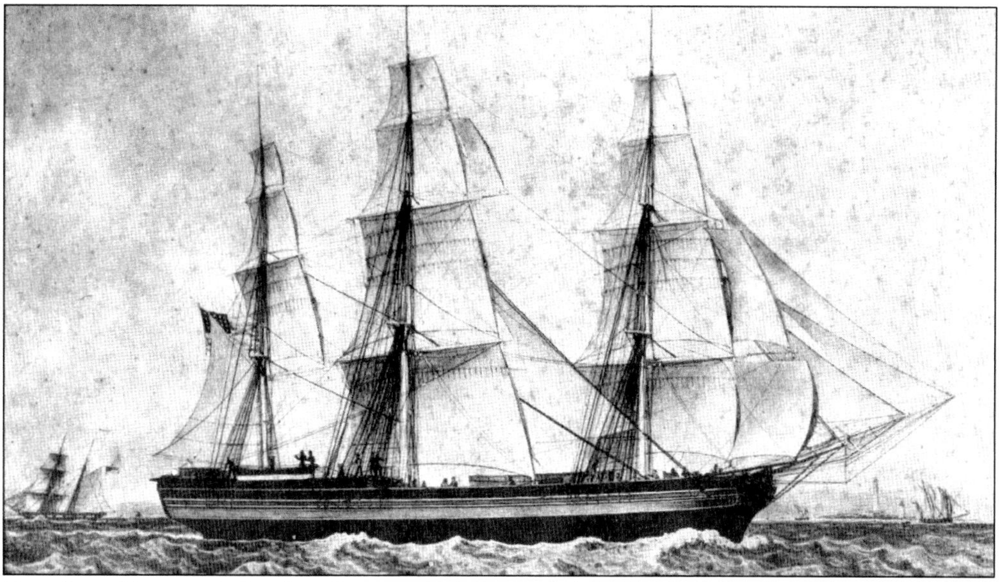

THE SHIP *HECTOR*. The ship *Hector* was commanded first by Joseph Post (1789–1878), who helped found Hills Academy, and later by his brother, David Post (1807–1849). Noah Starkey built it in his shipyard on South Cove in 1833. At the time of its construction, it weighed 557 tons and was 134 feet long. By the end of the 1840s, the number of locally produced vessels was dropping, while their size was increasing. Later, when shipbuilding had practically come to a halt, the 1,400-ton *Middlesex* was built by Nehemiah Hayden in the Redfield & Parmelee Shipyard. Capt. Hosmer Parmelee was the only commander of this ship until it was lost at sea in 1861. (Photograph courtesy of Essex Historical Society.)

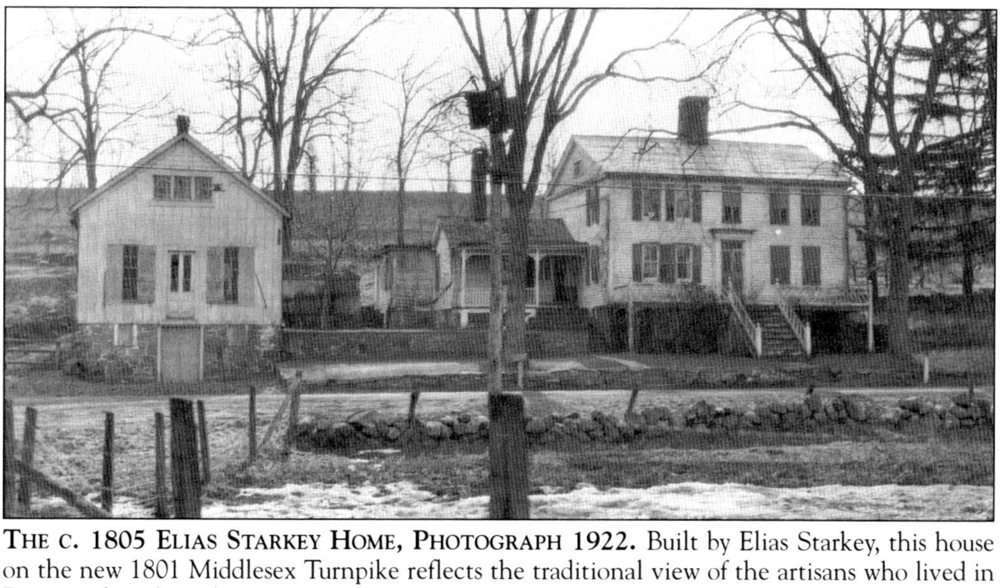

THE C. 1805 ELIAS STARKEY HOME, PHOTOGRAPH 1922. Built by Elias Starkey, this house on the new 1801 Middlesex Turnpike reflects the traditional view of the artisans who lived in Essex, rather than the more Georgian or Federal forms of architecture. The four houses that flank this house were all Starkey homes. Noah Starkey owned a shipyard in nearby South Cove and was the patriarch of the Starkey family in this area. This photograph shows that in 1922, the hill in the background was pasture. Today, it is forest and homes. (Photograph courtesy of Don Malcarne.)

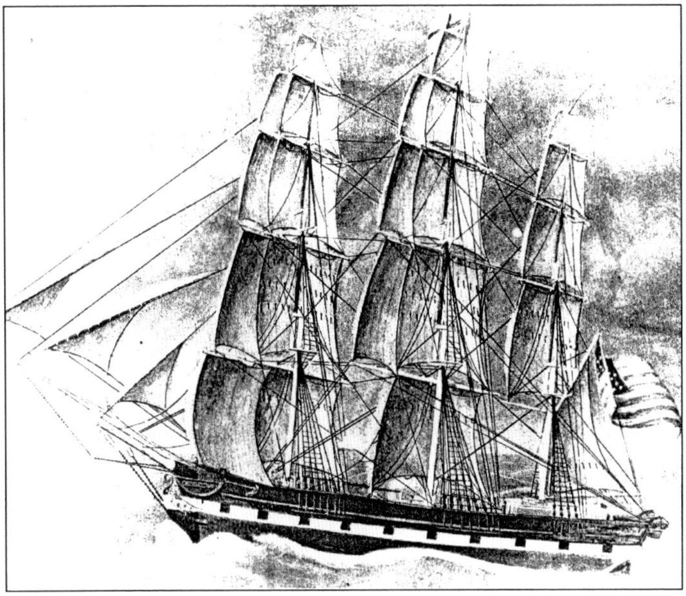

THE COTTON PLANTER. The *Cotton Planter,* built in East Haddam, was partially owned by Cornelius Doane of Essex. Doane, a pioneer in the Mobile packet and cotton trade, lived across the street from what is now the post office in Essex. In 1852, when the shipping industry began to fail, he handed over his last command to his brother, William H. Doane, and focused on making Essex a retail center. (Photograph courtesy of Essex Historical Society.)

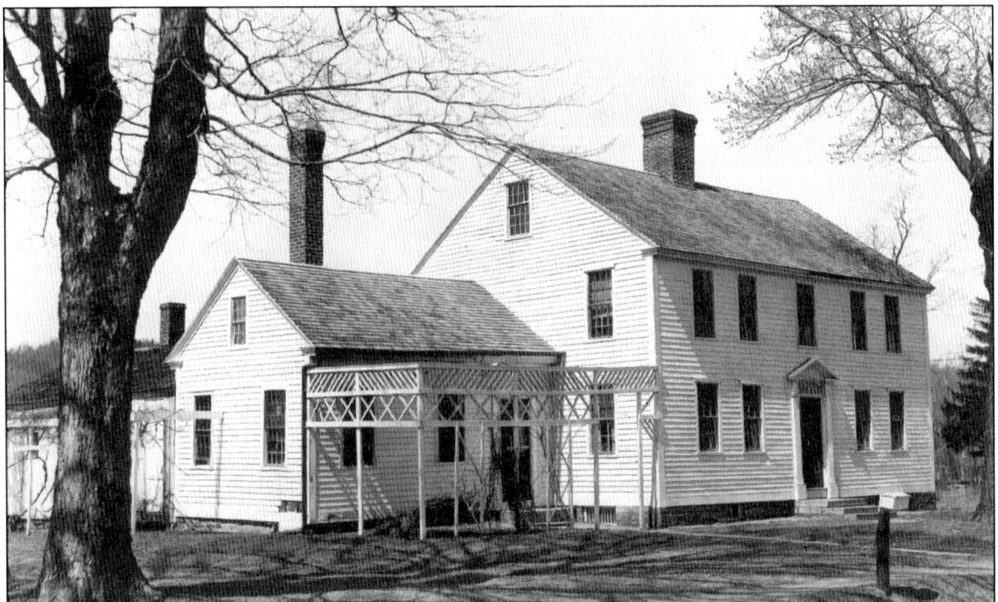

THE TABOR TOOKER HOUSE, DENISON ROAD, C. 1806. Tabor Tooker built this house on Denison Road, which at the time was still the main thoroughfare. He was a shipbuilder and a sea captain. His progeny became famous mariners and chose to live near one another on Denison Road, River Road, and North Main Street. The Tooker name changed to Tucker in the middle of the 19th century. This particular house was later owned by Capt. Calvin Williams of the Williams shipyard fame and John Urquhart (1805–1846), who owned a packet line out of New York. Urquhart's sons, William and John Urquhart, both graduated from the local Hills Academy. William Urquhart became a well-known sea captain in his own right and was involved in several sea rescues in 1873 and 1879. (Photograph courtesy of Don Malcarne.)

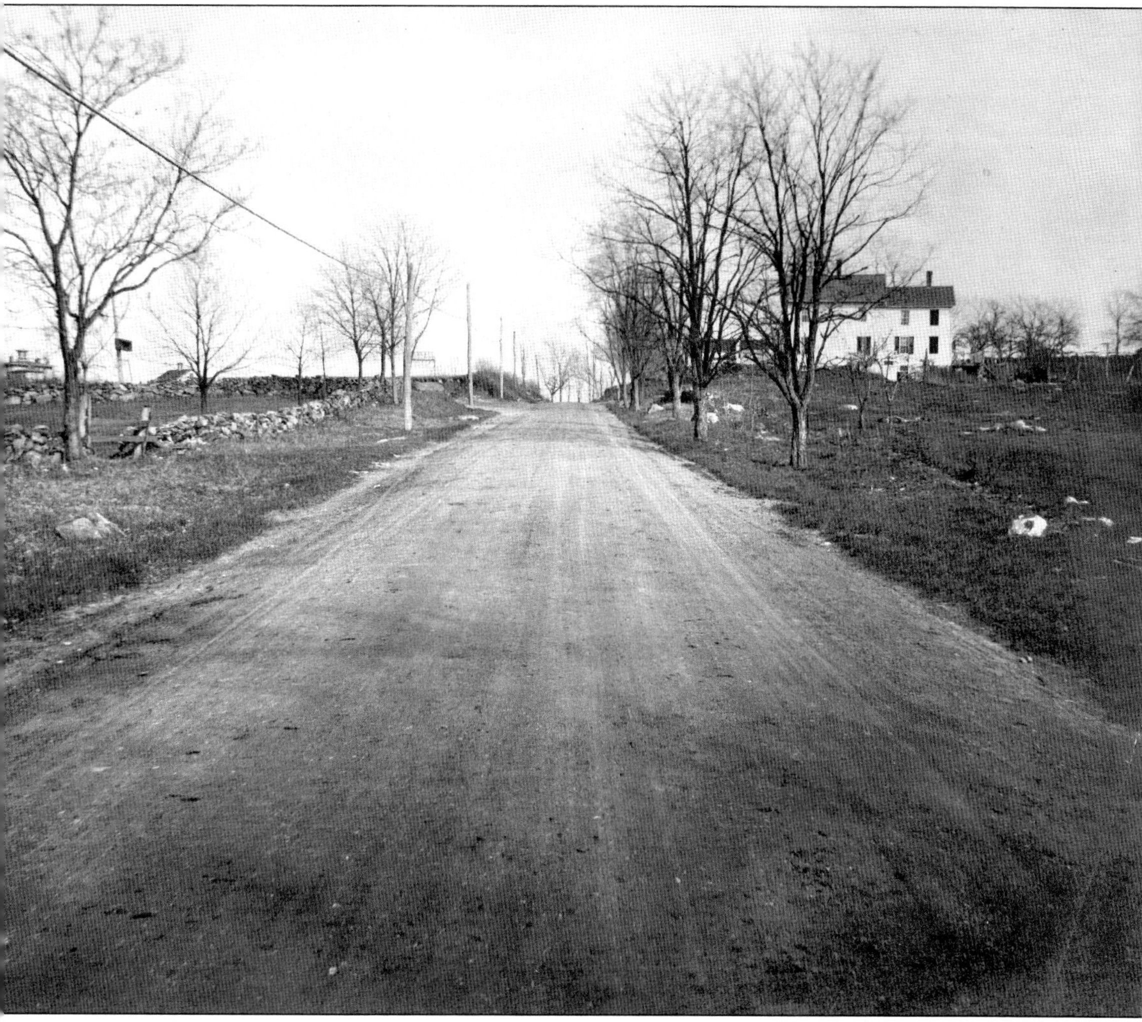

A VIEW OF MIDDLESEX TURNPIKE IN ESSEX, LOOKING SOUTH FROM PHELPS CORNER, 1913. Middlesex Turnpike became Route 9 and now is Route 154. It was completed as a toll road in 1801 and was the first main road between Saybrook Ferry and Wethersfield. Tolls were collected in every town along the way. Up the road is the Victorian home of Capt. Henry Hovey. Hovey was the son of the Reverend Aaron Hovey and Huldah Hayden Hovey. Huldah Hayden had previously been married to a son of Ebenezer Hayden and had four children by him, including the well-known Amelia Prudence Hayden Champlin. Hovey built a large home on South Main Street in 1855 and sold it for $10,000 in 1865, the largest sum up to that time for a house in Essex. It became the Lord Essex restaurant in the 1960s. Hovey was lost at sea in 1871 while in command of the *Ladona*. (Photograph courtesy of Connecticut River Museum.)

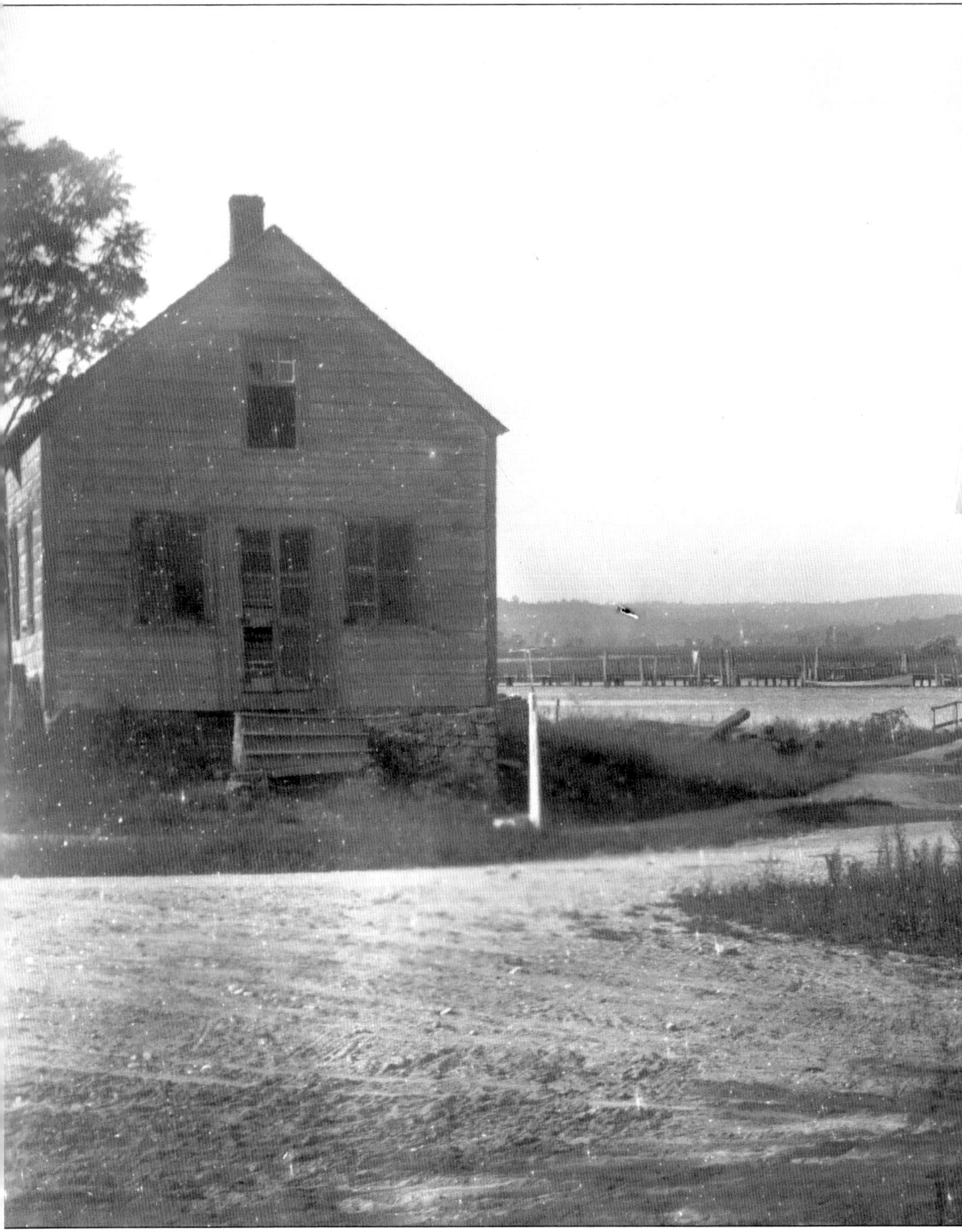

The Steamboat Dock, with Approaching Horse and Buggy. Phebe Hayden was one of the most important people in Essex village in the second half of the 19th century. She owned a great deal of property, including that upon which she built the Steamboat Dock in 1878. Her

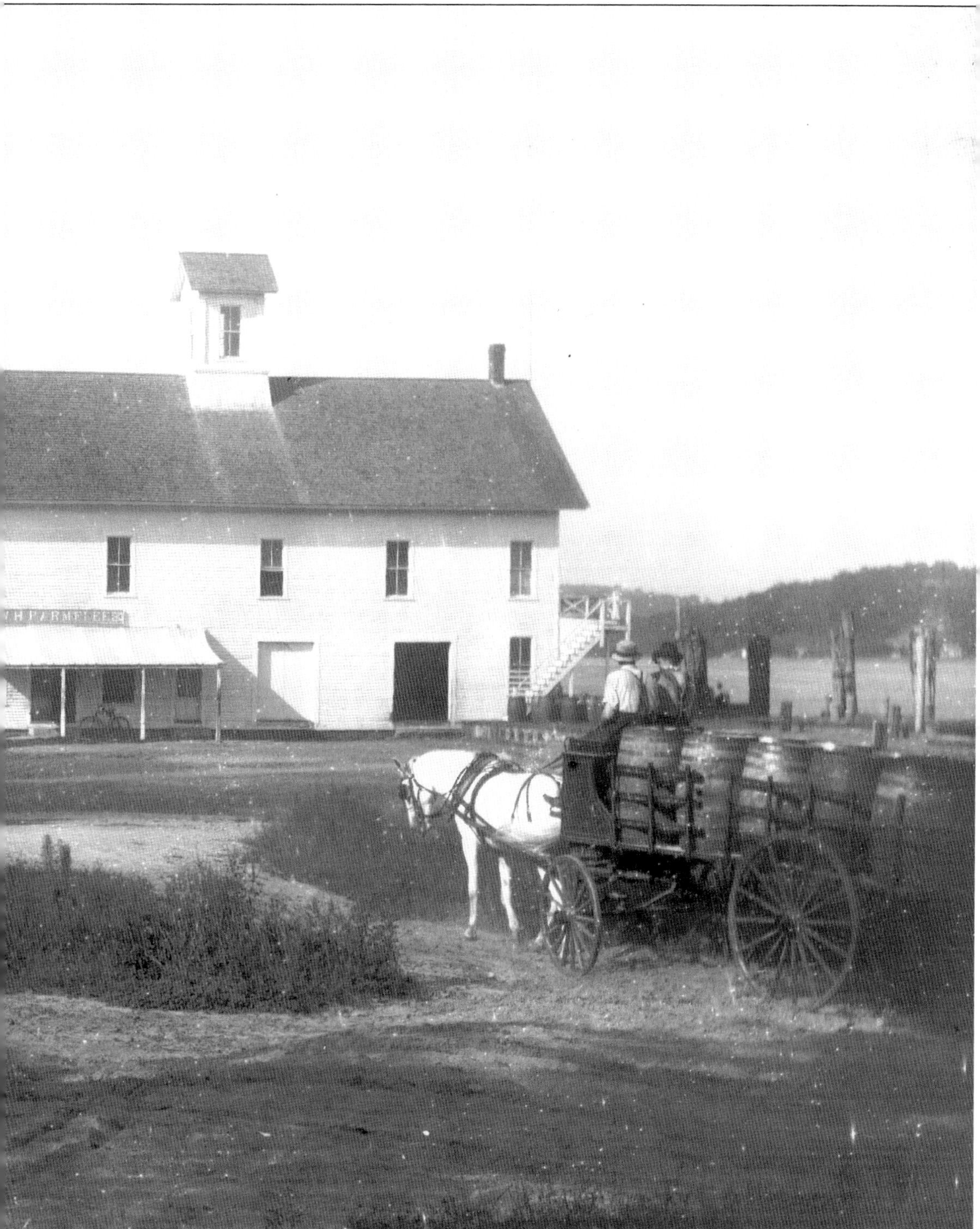

nephew, William S. Parmelee, operated a store there for many years and later became president of the Essex Savings Bank. The building on the left was once the shop of Ezra L'Hommideau, who invented the double-twist auger bit. (Photograph courtesy of Essex Historical Society.)

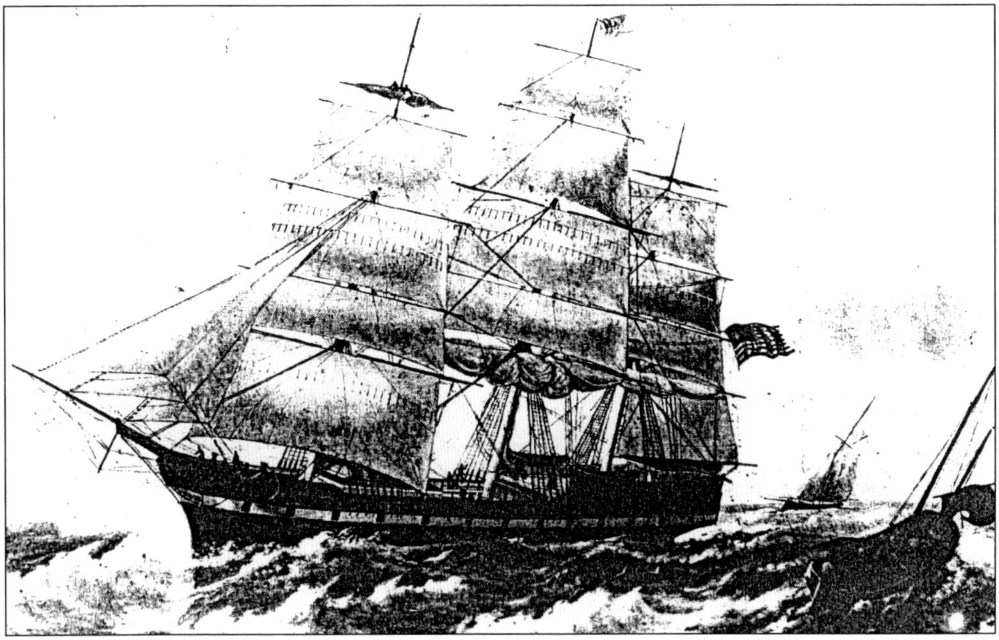

THE *JOHN H. ELLIOTT*. Joseph Hayden Tucker was a well-known ship captain who commanded the *John H. Elliott* and later became a philanthropist. Born Joseph Tooker in 1824, he married twice into the Hayden family, and used wealth from his second wife to help finance the building of St. John's Episcopal Church in 1895. In the same period, he helped finance the Essex Library. He died in 1896. (Photograph courtesy of Essex Historical Society.)

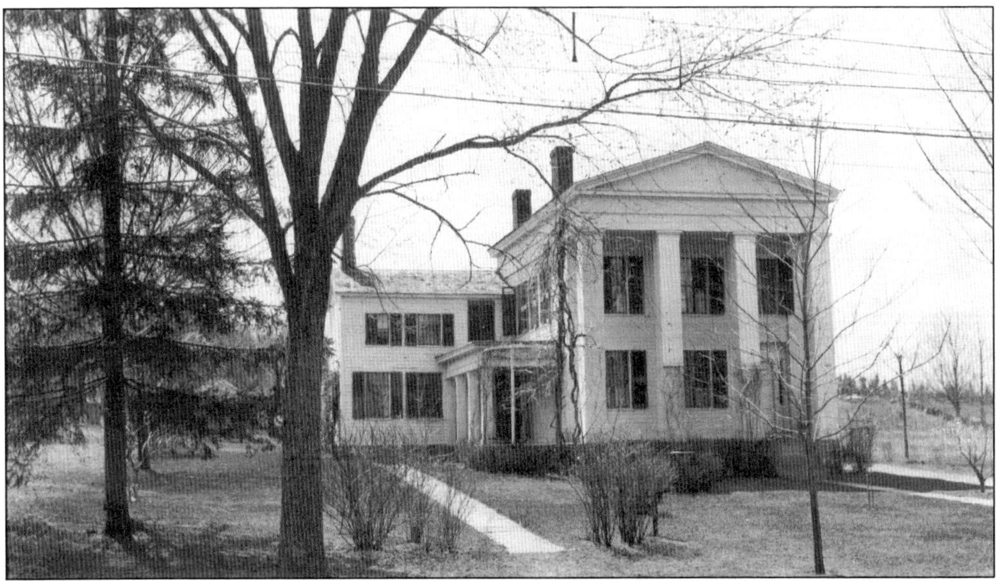

THE 1834 GREEK REVIVAL HOME OF FRANCIS WEST, PHOTOGRAPH 1922. This house is located on North Main Street at the head of Maple Avenue. It was built in 1834 by Francis West, who moved to Essex in 1825. Captain West was a prominent sea captain, shipbuilder, and ivory entrepreneur. West built 10 ships locally, most of them at the Williams Shipyard, not more than 300 yards from his house. This is one of very few Greek Revival houses in Essex. (Photograph courtesy of Don Malcarne.)

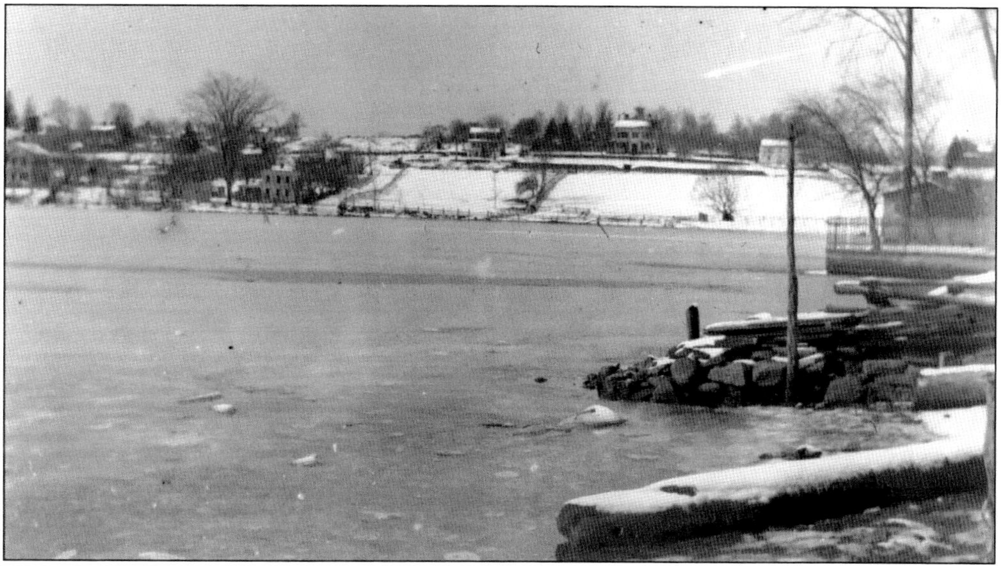

MIDDLE COVE, PHOTOGRAPH c. 1890. This photograph shows Middle Cove and the South Main Street area when Essex village was in a period of relative decline. Most of the houses seen here were a result of the shipbuilding era, but that golden period when men's "blood ran tar and their muscles were hempen rope" had passed. Although two banks were established in the middle of the 19th century in Essex, the major industrial activity had left the village. Few houses existed in the center of the village that were not tenements. At one time, the field shown in the center of this photograph was harvested for tobacco—a crop that never grew well in the lower valley. (Photograph courtesy of Essex Historical Society.)

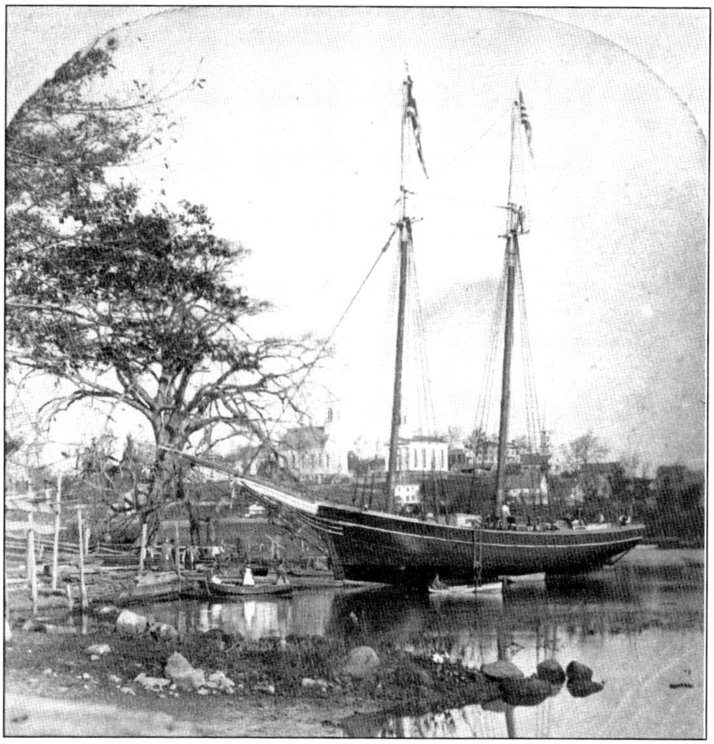

THE DAVID MACK SHIPYARD, PHOTOGRAPH 1870. Wooden shipbuilding was losing its vitality as early as 1840 and, by 1870, it was practically nonexistent. The one shipyard that continued to build ships, was the David Mack yard on what is now Middle Cove. David Mack was a shipbuilder and an entrepreneur who realized that economics were changing. In 1874, he invested in a Main Street store, which in the mid-1900s was known as Pratt's Store. (Photograph courtesy of Connecticut River Museum.)

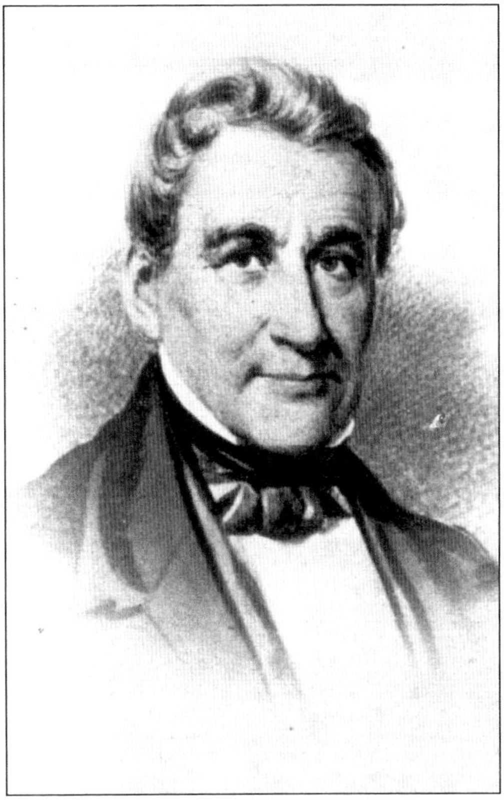

CHAMPLIN SQUARE. Henry Champlin (left) and Amelia Prudence Hayden were married in 1815. Champlin was a prosperous mariner, commanding the Black X Line for John Griswold of Old Lyme. Amelia Hayden's father, Uriah Hayden II, was the son of Ebenezer Hayden, and her mother was the daughter of Rev. Robert Ely, pastor of the Second Ecclesiastical Society. Amelia Hayden went to a private boarding school and inherited part of her grandfather's large fortune in 1818. She and Champlin built a beautiful home (below) on Champlin Square shortly after her grandfather's death. Champlin died in 1859, having accumulated a large fortune of his own. By 1879, when Amelia died, much of this wealth had disappeared. Among the few assets listed in her estate were her husband's gold watch and her portrait, which had been painted in France. In 1998, the Paul Foundation published a children's book by Beverly Page of East Lyme entitled *Portrait in Blue*, a fictionalized story of three Essex children who search for and locate the painting. Members of the Paul family currently occupy the Champlin house.

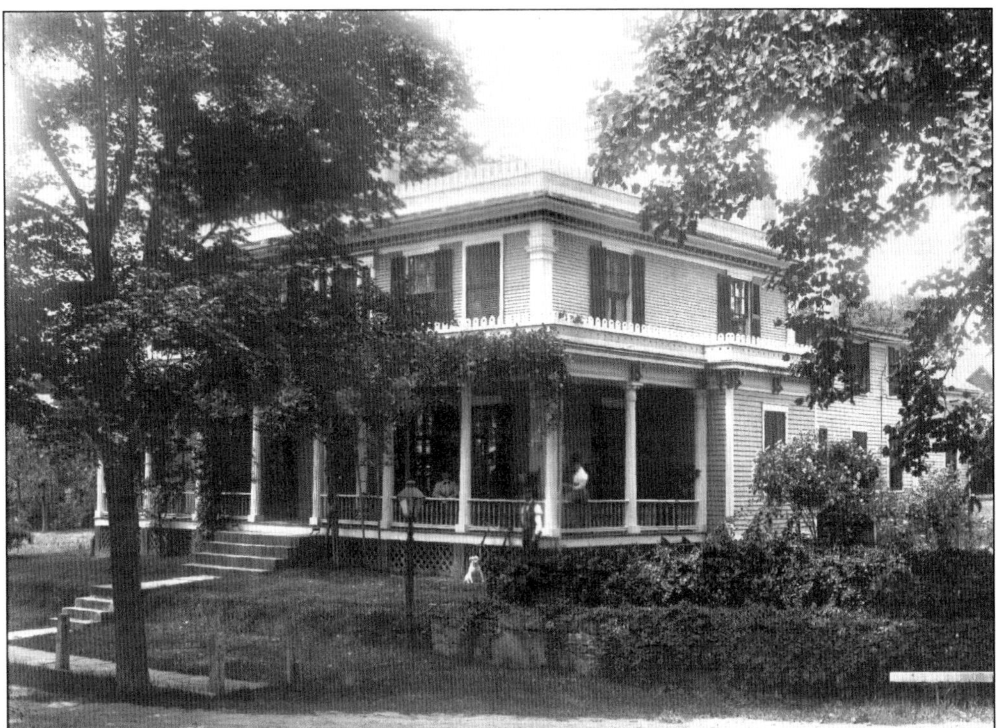

Three

THE BURNING OF THE SHIPS

The Privateer Navy was a vital addition to U.S. naval strategies in the War of 1812. Commissioned by the state of Connecticut, privateers received letters of marque allowing them to operate as warships. The ships and cargoes captured were divided among the state, boat owners, captains, and crew.

The federally imposed embargo and the subsequent blockade of the Connecticut River by the British navy frustrated the Potapoug shipbuilders. As a result, some of them turned to the building of privateers. Richard Hayden and his partners, Nathaniel and George Griswold, advertised their new "sharp model privateer schooner" ("sharp" referring to a very advanced design) in a New York newspaper. Pierced for 24 guns, the *Black Prince* would make an ideal privateer, according to the advertisement. The British, upon perusal of this ad in the paper, investigated Potapoug and saw the advertised ship on the stocks, along with 27 others in the yards, up to six of which were being fitted as privateers.

As a result, a British force of 136 marines and sailors, under the command of Capt. Robert Coote, rowed up the Connecticut River from Long Island Sound in six longboats on the night of April 7, 1814, and arrived at Potapoug Point (foot of Main Street in Essex) early on the morning of April 8, 1814. The group had departed from a small flotilla of British vessels led by the ships *Borer*, *La Hogue*, *Maidstone*, and *Endymion*, all anchored at the mouth of the Connecticut River. The troops had to row against a strong spring freshet that impeded their planned progress.

Potapoug residents were caught by surprise and offered no opposition when confronted by the British. The 1650 fort at Saybrook Point (rebuilt and reinforced during the Revolutionary War) was neither manned nor armed, indicating a lack of enthusiasm for the War of 1812. No one was injured in Potapoug, no prisoners were taken, and no personal property was destroyed other than some naval stores and rope.

Within six hours, the British departed, taking the famous schooner *Black Prince* (the advertised boat) with them, plus a brig being fitted as a privateer. During this disastrous, short period, the British burned 26 other vessels, including the *Osage* at the famous Samuel Williams shipyard in the Falls River Cove. The cost to the Americans was estimated at $200,000, a veritable fortune at that time. The newspapers called it the greatest sea loss of the war. The British sailors scuttled and burned the two ships as they retreated downriver. Militia from Lyme and Killingworth fired upon the sailors from both shores, killing two of them in this final skirmish.

The Americans suffered a humiliating defeat. There is no question the area had been well scouted and the British well guided. They knew the location of thc shipyards and carried out this act with efficiency.

In addition to the *Black Prince* and the 344-ton *Osage*, owned by Horatio Alden and Company of Hartford, other famous ships were burned: the 272-ton *Superior*, owned by Henry Champlin; the 230-ton brig *Felix*, owned by Justin and Elias Lyman of New York and Vermont;

the 150-ton schooner *Emblem;* and the small sloop *Mohalia*, owned by the Hayden and Starkey firm. Two pleasure boats owned by the Hayden and Scovell families were also destroyed. These were an indication of the wealth that shipbuilding had brought to the lower valley.

An unpopular war had come home to roost in Potapoug. The local entrepreneurs were now the victims of their own success. The very existence of the privateers in the harbor kindled this attack. A few questions remain unanswered concerning what happened on that fateful morning. First, did an American turncoat guide the British for a substantial amount of money? For example, the *Osage*, in the Williams yard, one-half mile up North Cove and not readily visible from the Point, was efficiently destroyed. This lends credence to the notion that the British had local assistance. There has always been suspicion as to the identity of this person, but concrete evidence does not exist. Second, was the original ropewalk (a rope manufactory) in Potapoug destroyed by the British? It was an open shed 15 feet wide and 900 feet long running from Essex Square to the river. Although in operation during March 1814, it was out of business in April.

To officially honor the ships that were burned, Essex commemorates this British attack with an annual Loser's Parade the first weekend in May. April is usually too cold for a good parade.

—Don Malcarne

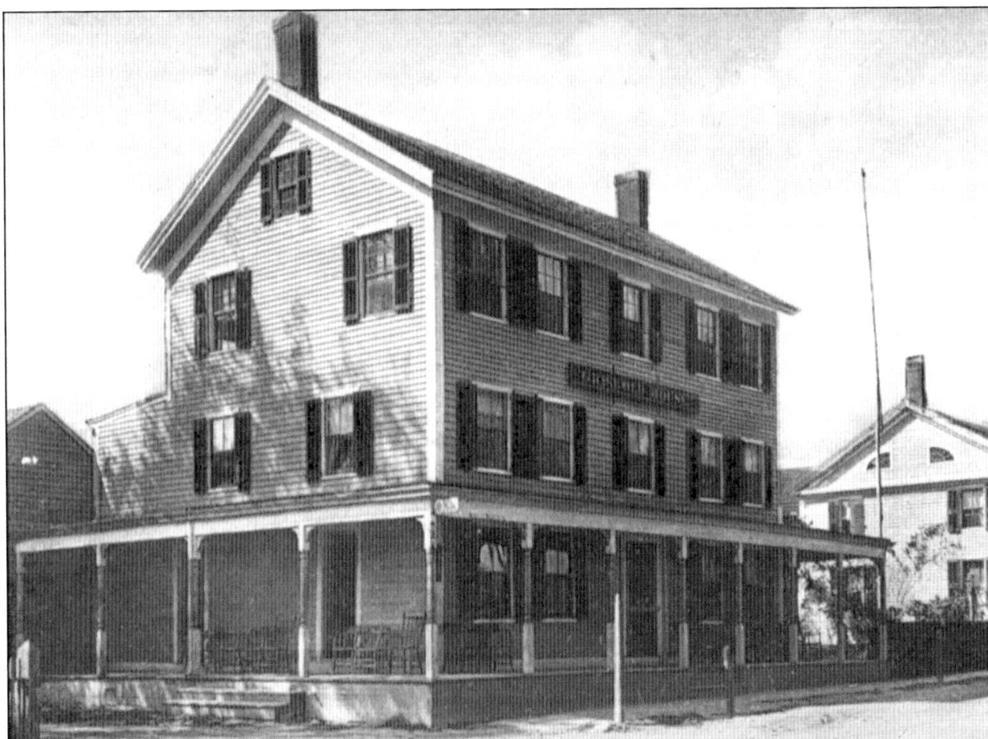

THE GRISWOLD HOUSE, PHOTOGRAPH 1920. The building that was known as Ethan Bushnell's Tavern when the British attacked is now known as the Griswold Inn. From 1801 to 1807, it was the home of Richard Hayden. Older brother John G. Hayden lived in a smaller gambrel-roofed house to the left (not shown.) John was a master figurehead carver. *Sea Lady*, a children's book written by Julie Forsyth Batchelor in 1956, tells a story of a young boy on the night of the British attack who slips out of the house to save the figurehead his grandfather had recently carved. (Photograph courtesy of Essex Library Association.)

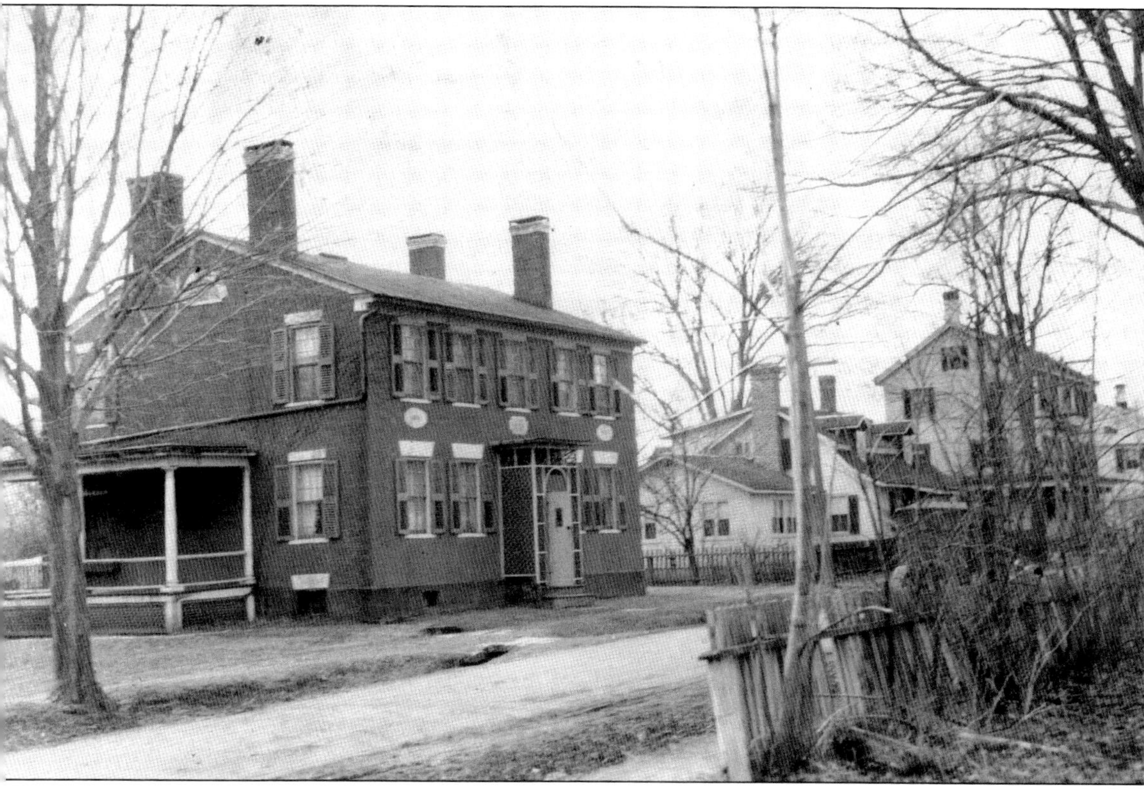

THE 1806 RICHARD HAYDEN HOUSE (ST. JOHN'S RECTORY), PHOTOGRAPH 1922. Richard Hayden's new house (left) was the first brick house built in Potapoug. Richard Hayden was the nephew of Uriah Hayden, builder of the *Oliver Cromwell,* and became head of the famous Hayden shipyard. In 1813, he built the 300-ton schooner *Black Prince* for himself and Nathaniel and George Griswold of New York City. Fitted for 24 guns, it was over 100 feet long and it had been advertised as a possible privateer. The ship's value was $13,000. This, along with the presence of other privateers being built in Potapoug, is what led to the British attack. The British attempted to tow the *Black Prince* away, but shore batteries south of Nott Island prevented this, so they set the boat on fire. The April 8, 1814 attack underscored the prominence of Potapoug as a strategic target and dealt a temporary blow to local shipbuilders. The Hayden family suffered nearly half of the financial loss from the British attack. In 1981, the Essex Historical Society published an account of the attack, written by Albert Dock and Russell Anderson. (Photograph courtesy of Don Malcarne.)

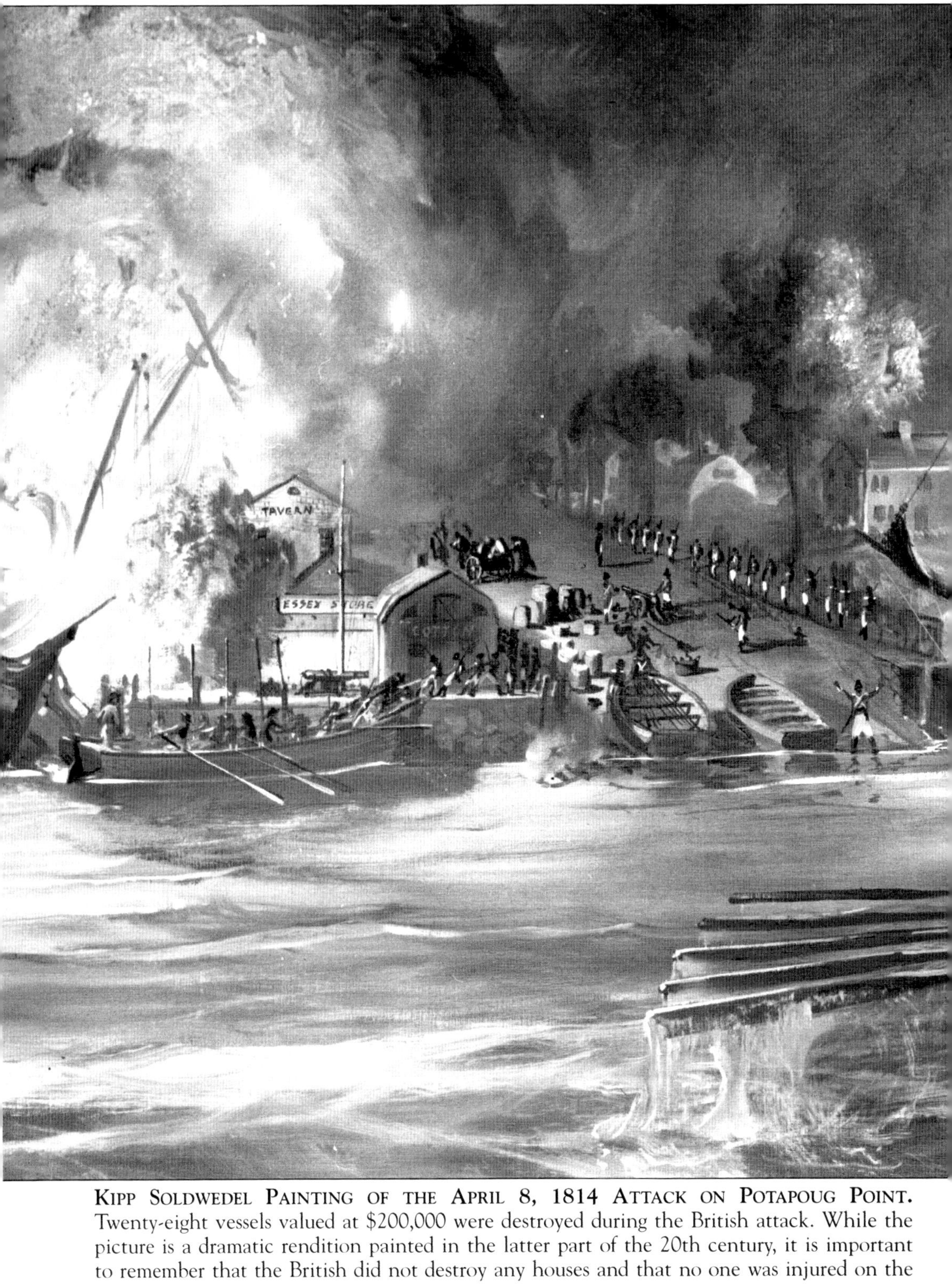

KIPP SOLDWEDEL PAINTING OF THE APRIL 8, 1814 ATTACK ON POTAPOUG POINT. Twenty-eight vessels valued at $200,000 were destroyed during the British attack. While the picture is a dramatic rendition painted in the latter part of the 20th century, it is important to remember that the British did not destroy any houses and that no one was injured on the

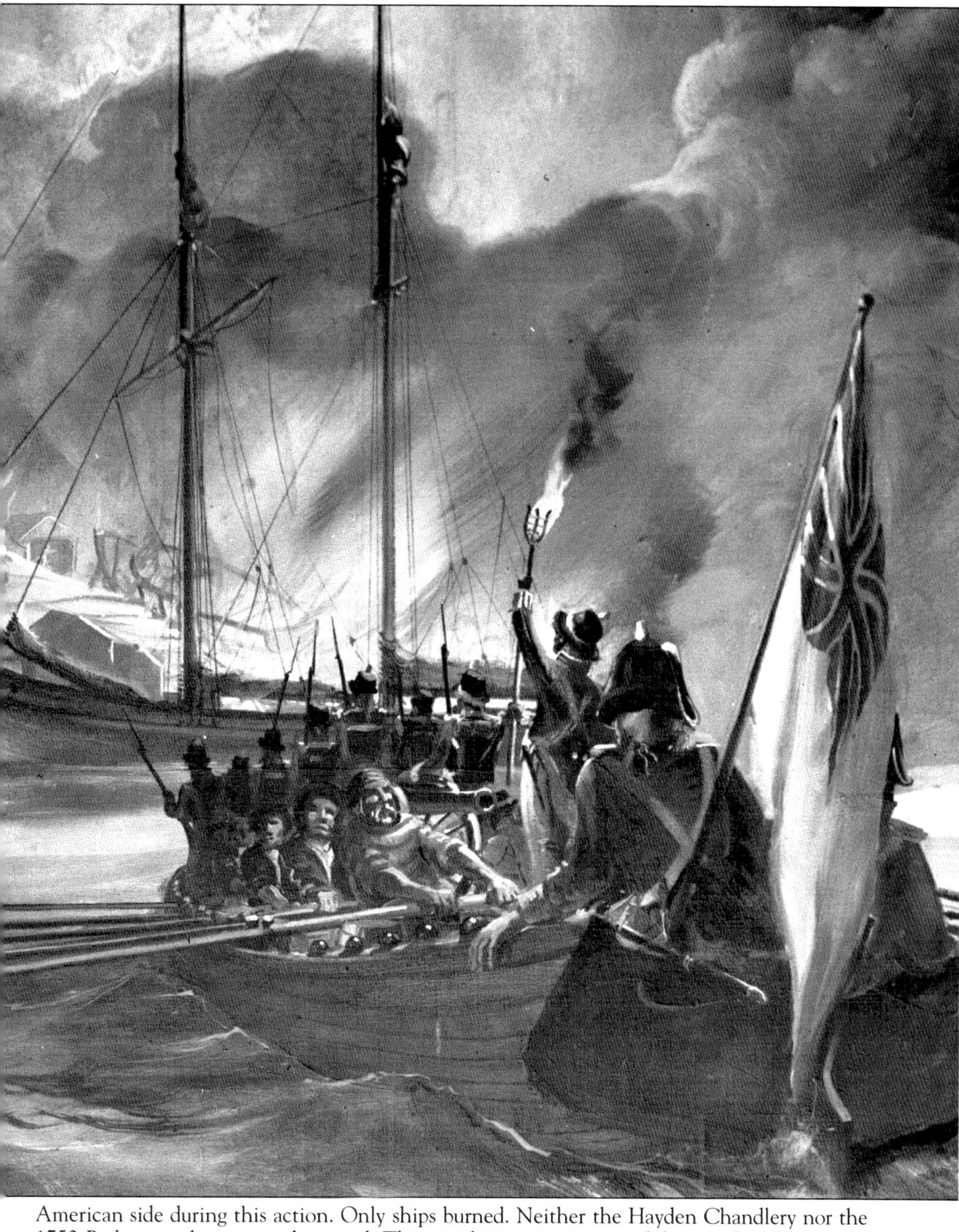

American side during this action. Only ships burned. Neither the Hayden Chandlery nor the 1753 Parker warehouse was destroyed. This is a fascinating aspect of the attack. (Photograph courtesy of Connecticut River Museum.)

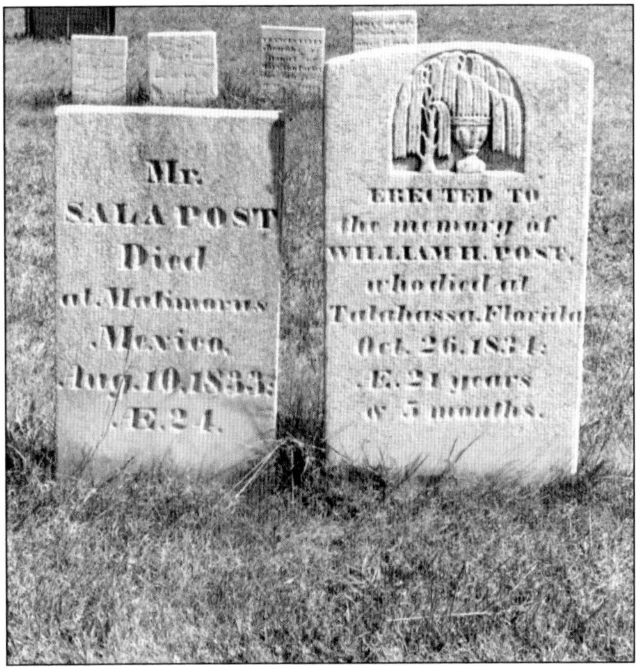

THE GRAVES OF SALA AND WILLIAM POST, PHOTOGRAPH C. 1910. The Post brothers were the sons of shipbuilder Sala Post, who was instrumental in bringing the Baptist church to Potapoug and who was an owner of the original ropewalk constructed in 1797. The ropewalk was located in Potapoug between what today is Pratt Street and Main Street. Its destruction in 1814 led to a change in the direction of Main Street. Did the British set fire to this ropewalk? A second ropewalk was started shortly after the British attack on April 8, 1814. (Photograph courtesy of Connecticut River Museum.)

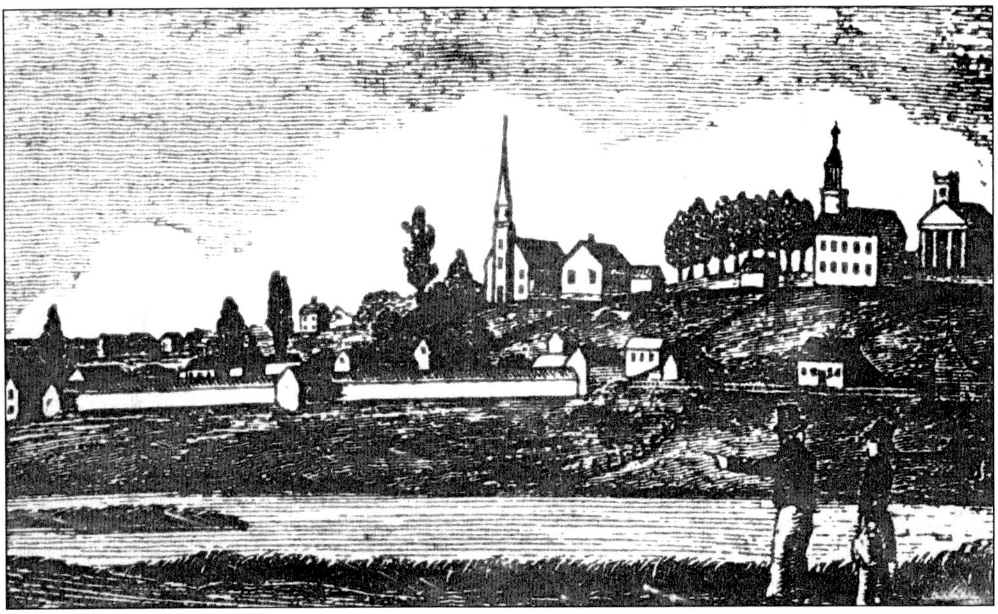

A BARBER LITHOGRAPH OF ESSEX, 1836. The building in the front is the second ropewalk—1,200 feet long—replacing the earlier ropewalk destroyed in 1814. Ropewalks were critical to the shipbuilding industry. Middletown was the only other town in the county that had a ropewalk. Tar, housed in the building adjacent to the ropewalk, was used to hold the hemp together. Sailors were known as "tars" because their hands became coated with tar as they used the ropes. The buildings in the background, from left to right, are the Episcopal church (later the Catholic church), the original Methodist church (now an apartment house), the old brick Baptist church (replaced in 1846 by the new Baptist church), and Hills Academy. (Photograph courtesy of Essex Historical Society.)

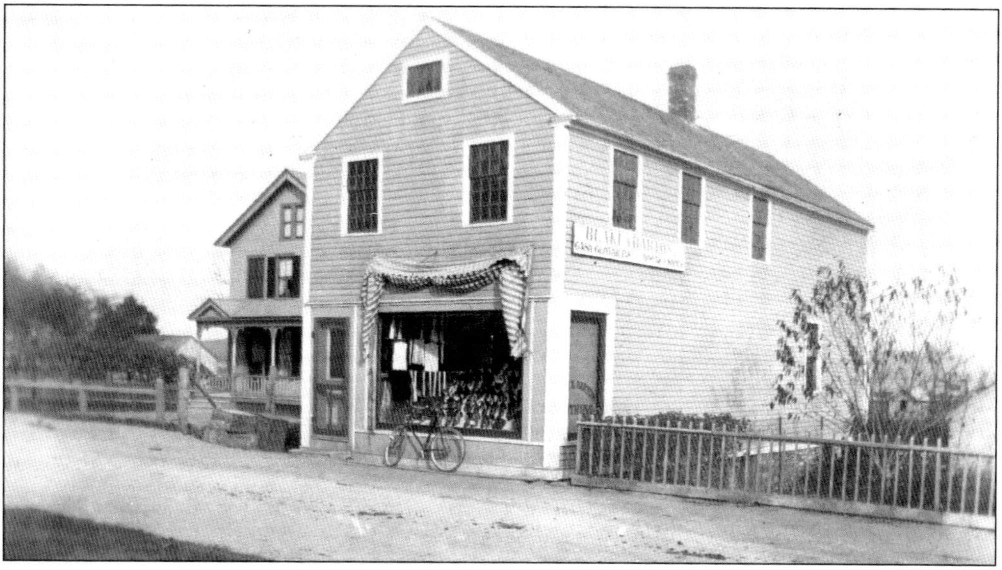

A NORTH MAIN STREET BUSINESS BUILDING, PHOTOGRAPH C. 1900. During the golden years of shipbuilding, the second ropewalk extended from what is now North Main Street to North Cove. After the ropewalk was destroyed by fire in 1893, the above structure was moved to the foundation of the ropewalk's former office. The building has housed several businesses in the 20th century, including a clothing store, a shoemaker, and a flower shop. (Photograph courtesy of Essex Historical Society.)

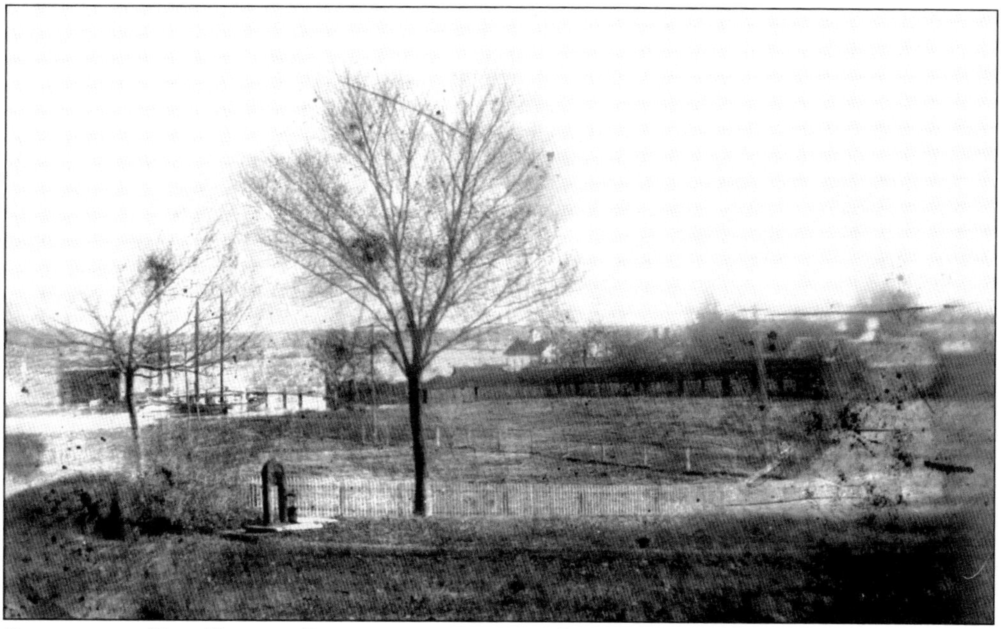

ONE OF THE FEW KNOWN PHOTOGRAPHS OF THE ROPEWALK. Through most of the 1800s, the ropewalk stretched between North Main Street and the river. Shown in the center of the photograph, it runs parallel to the picket fence and stretches from the right side of the photograph to the tree in the center. The ropewalk was run with horsepower. A horse was tied to the front treadmill and walked continuously in a circle. (Photograph courtesy of Connecticut River Museum.)

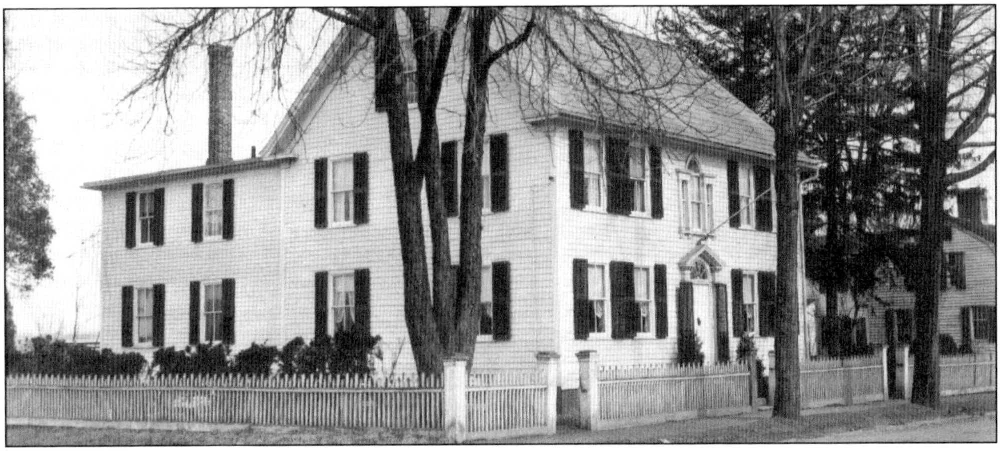

The 1800 Timothy Starkey Jr. House, Main Street, Photograph 1922. Timothy Starkey's marriage to his first cousin Mary Ann Hayden, daughter of Uriah Hayden, gave him wealth and influence. In 1800, he leased land on the corner of Main and what is now Ferry Street from Samuel Lay to build the above house. Since the middle of the 17th century, the Lays had owned all the land from the north side of Main Street to the present Riverview cemetery, land which they leased rather than sold. Starkey eventually bought the entire lower Main and Pratt Street area, including the Lay homestead and the entire wharf complex for $8,000 with his new son-in-law, William S. Hayden. Besides Starkey's successful business ventures, he commanded several ships and contracted more than 25 to be built. With his brothers-in-law, Samuel and Ebenezer Hayden II, he owned the waterfront Hayden-Starkey Store, which the British ransacked and stole cordage from in 1814. (Photograph courtesy of Don Malcarne.)

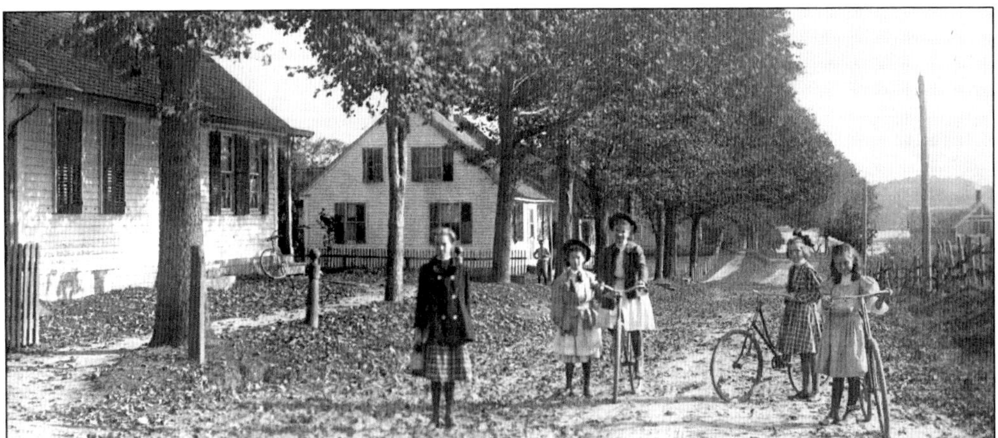

New City Street, Photograph c. 1899. Ebenezer Hayden developed an area in Essex c. 1800 that was meant to be a new city. The street through this development was known as the road to the shipyard, which was owned by Hayden and Samuel Williams. This shipyard was on North Cove at the end of what would become New City Street. Hayden suffered a great loss with the British attack in 1814, since he had financed some of the burned vessels. Some thought the attack might have brought on his death, since it occurred only four years later. The British spared two vessels moored near this shipyard. Judea Pratt, a member of the Masonic order, asked the British commander, Capt. Richard Coote, also apparently a Mason, not to burn his vessels. This Masonic connection may have been the reason the British left Pratt's two vessels unharmed. (Photograph courtesy of Don Malcarne.)

THE OSAGE. On the mantle in the Essex Corinthian Yacht Club (formerly the Essex Yacht Club) above the fireplace is a piece of oak from the *Osage*, donated by Charles Tiley in 1936. The *Osage* of 344 tons was under construction in 1814 at the Williams Shipyard. It had been neither launched, rigged, nor registered at the customs house when the British raided. In an effort to save the *Osage*, it was launched just after the British had set it on fire. It finally sank in the cove and remained there for more than 100 years until rediscovered. Valued at $8,500, it was the largest vessel burned by the British and the largest ever built in Essex prior to 1815. This drawing is representative of what the *Osage* would have looked like. It was taken from a Pratt High School yearbook, which was named *Osage*.

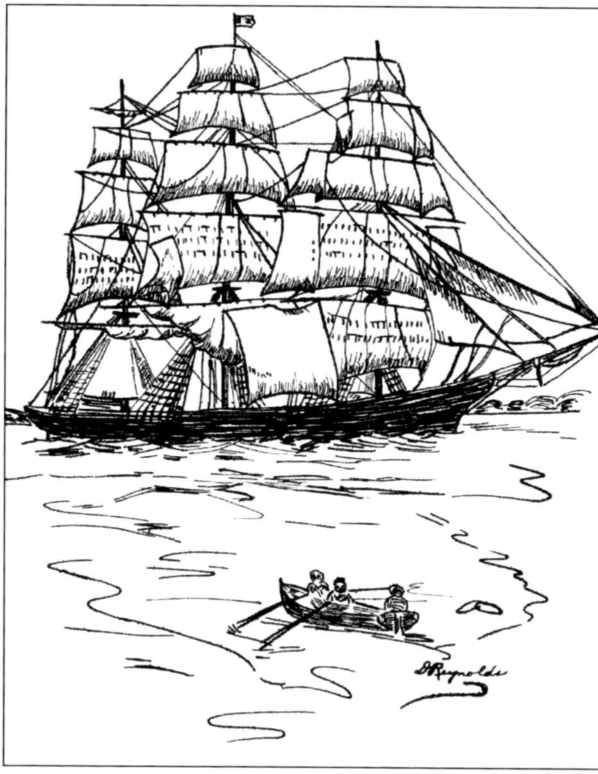

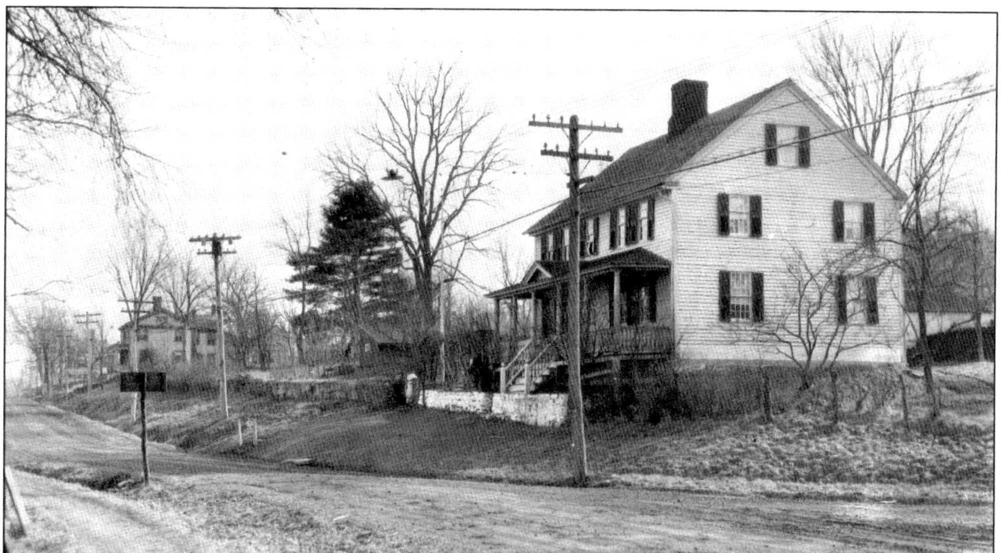

THE C. 1781 NOAH STARKEY HOUSE, PHOTOGRAPH 1922. Noah Starkey was the first and probably most famous of the shipbuilding Starkeys. He built many vessels in the South Cove area and was a sea captain as well. The importance of his house is revealed in many deed descriptions of South Main Street. Homes located on South Main were often referred to as being located "on the road from Ebenezer Hayden's store to the home of Noah Starkey." Hayden's store was located on Champlin Square, which was the business center of Essex village until 1815. (Photograph courtesy of Don Malcarne.)

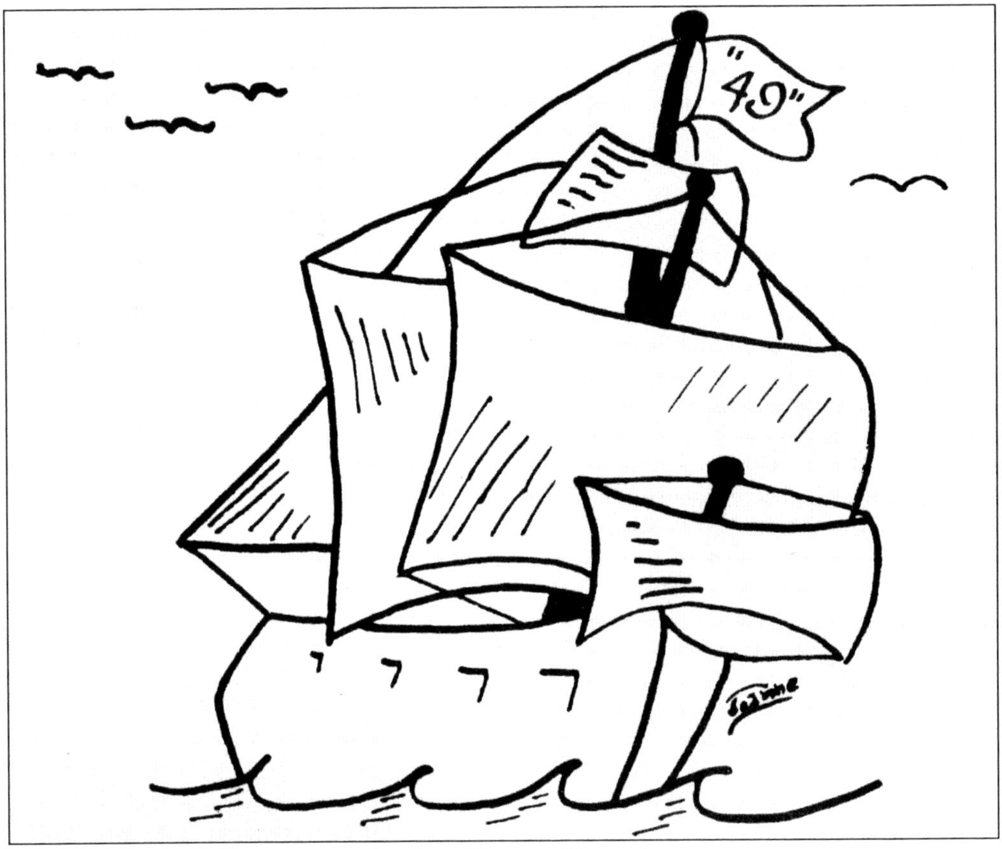

THE OLD WRECK (*OSAGE*)
A RELIC OF THE WAR OF 1812

Resting below the grist-mill old,
   Mid eddying foam flakes from its wheel,
It shows when drained the tide at ebb
   A few black ribs along a keel.

There has it stood for eighty years
   And marked the busy seasons go
From the bloom of shad-bush on the shore
   To the hazel's pale and dying glow.

But few remember when 'twas laid,
   Or heard the mallet's echoing rhyme;
Or saw its rib uprise—a frame—
   As some monster of the olden time.

Yet did it never part the tide,
   Its sail to bend 'neath favoring breeze,
And ride by Ceylon's perfumed isle
   Or harbor in far distant seas.

Its hulk shall be a funeral pyre—
   The calm Connecticut be its grave;
And the charred form of many a ship
   Shall thy gently rippling waters lave.

Unknown the British sailed the stream
   When darkness brooded over all;
Besieged the shores, the vessels burned
   And held the town in terrors thrall.

Still 'mong the annals old and quaint
   The story is still handed down,
And the old wreck is pointed proof
   Of when the British came to town.

—Samuel Morley Comstock

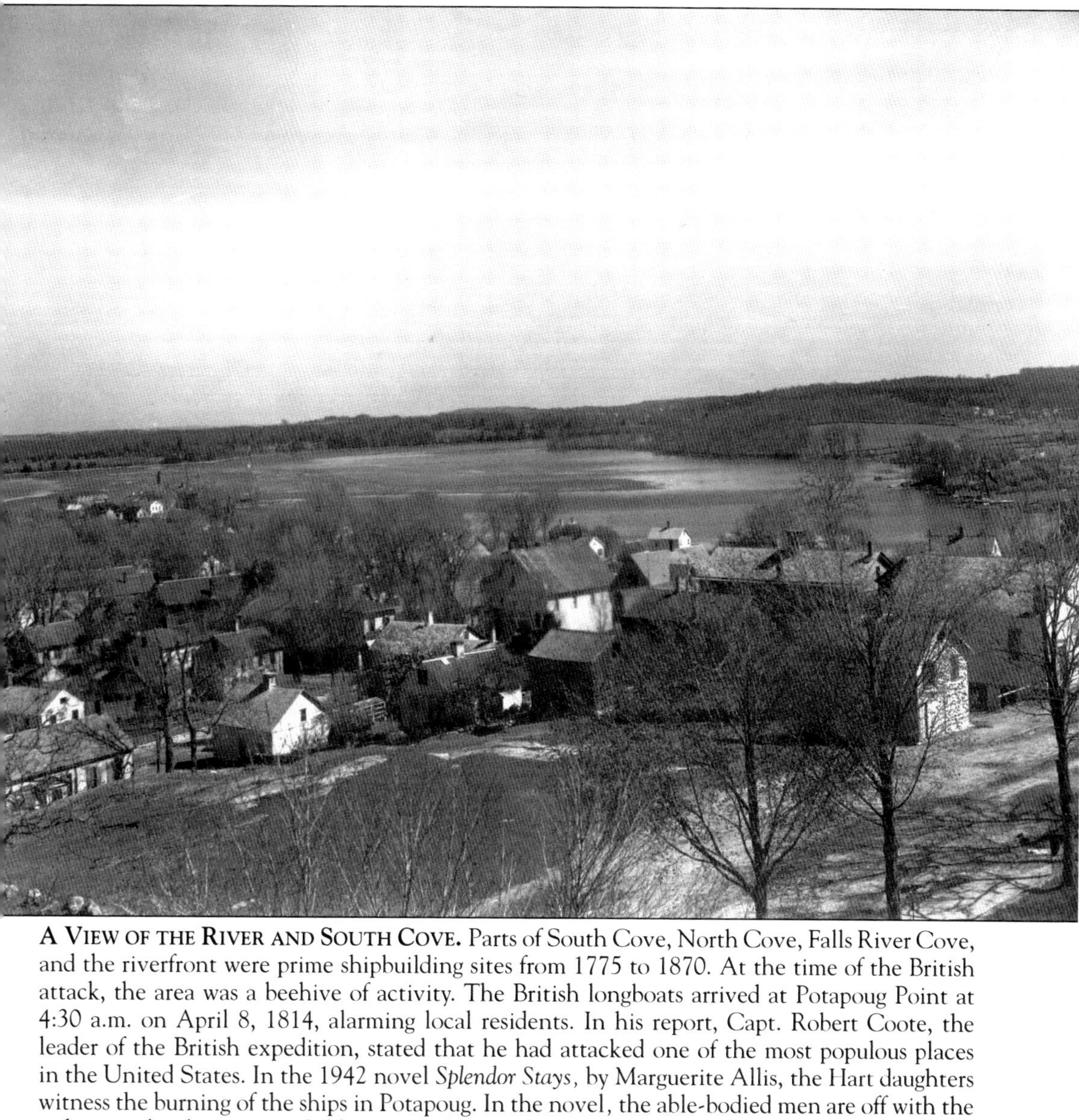

A View of the River and South Cove. Parts of South Cove, North Cove, Falls River Cove, and the riverfront were prime shipbuilding sites from 1775 to 1870. At the time of the British attack, the area was a beehive of activity. The British longboats arrived at Potapoug Point at 4:30 a.m. on April 8, 1814, alarming local residents. In his report, Capt. Robert Coote, the leader of the British expedition, stated that he had attacked one of the most populous places in the United States. In the 1942 novel *Splendor Stays,* by Marguerite Allis, the Hart daughters witness the burning of the ships in Potapoug. In the novel, the able-bodied men are off with the militia, and only women, children, and old men, held back by the bayonets of British marines, witness the early morning conflagration. The *Hector* became a "glowing furnace" while the *Guardian* "blazed high as a giant's torch." "[A]nother vessel branched into a tree of flame with red leaves dancing along each outstretched limb until the whole became a fiery cross against the black night sky." In the novel, three ships, the *Osage,* the *Felix,* and the *Black Prince,* spared from the fire, were taken away and floated downstream. Actually, the British took two ships, and not the *Osage,* which was burned in its stocks.

VESSELS AT ESSEX BURNED BY THE BRITISH, APRIL 8, 1814.

Name	Tons	Value	Owners
Guardian	316	$15,000	Ebenezer Hayden II, Timothy Starkey, Richard Powers
New Schooner	140	$4,000	Hayden and Starkey Company, Hull & Griswold Company, Richard Powers
Sloop *Mohala*	49	$1,500	Hayden, Starkey, Richard Powers, Phillip Tucker Jr., Noah Tucker
Superior	272	$13,000	Asahel Pratt, Judea Pratt, William Hull, John Griswold Jr., H. L. Champlin
Atlanta	270	$8,500	Ebenezer and Horace Hayden, Johnson and Ezra Pratt, Richard Hayden
New Schooner	160	$7,500	Horace Hayden, Richard Hayden II
Schooner *Black Prince*	301	$13,300	Richard Hayden, Nathaniel L. and George Griswold
Sloop *Comet*	22	$1,200	Richard Hayden, William Marvin, Richard Hayden II
Brig *Felix*	230	$11,000	Justin and Elias Lyman
Sloop *Thetis*	75	$2,600	Hezekiah Pratt, Asahel Pratt, Ebenezer Hayden, Luther Belden
Brig *Cleopatra*	169	$7,500	Richard Ely, L. Chapman, Noah Starkey
Schooner *Emblem*	150	$6,200	Joseph Hill, Jessie Murray, G. Conklin, Gilbert Avery, L. Belden, G. Stannard heirs, G. W. Pratt
New Sloop	75	$2,000	Ebenezer Hayden, Jessie Hurd, Richard Hayden, Augustus Jones Jr.
Sloop *Emerald*	52	$2,500	John Platts Jr., Ambrose Pratt, Ebenezer Pratt Jr. heirs
Ship *Osage*	344	$8,500	H. Alden & Company
Brig *Amazon*	137	$5,000	William Hall
Brig *Hector*	340	$15,000	William C. Hall, Dodd & Robbins, Ansel Treat
Sloop *Mars*	49	—	William Scovel, John Williams II
Sloop *Sally Ann*	62	—	Isaac Bacon, Samuel Wetmore, Ashley Gibbs, Sylvester Adams
Sloop *Roxann*	50	—	S. Peck
Sloop *Washington*	58	$5,000	Justin, Elias, and Gains Lyman, David Strong, Jacob Robertson
Sloop *William*	70	—	Tryon
Sloop	60	—	—
Pleasure boat	—	—	Noah Scovel
Pleasure boat	—	—	Ebenezer II and Samuel Hayden
Brig	—	—	—
Schooner	—	—	—
Schooner	—	—	—

Four

THE VILLAGE THAT ELEPHANTS BUILT

Samuel Merritt Comstock, a pioneer with a sterling vision and an inventive mind, was born in what is now the village of Ivoryton on August 14, 1809, the ninth of 10 children. His father, also Samuel, was reputed to be a sea captain plying the West Indies trade.

In 1847, he set up a business directly across the street from his boyhood home on the Falls River, taking advantage of existing water privileges on the stream. This became the firm of S.M. Comstock Company, a manufacturer of combs and toothpicks. In 1850, Ivoryton had only 26 buildings. By contrast, the village of Essex had a population of close to 800 and more than 100 homes by 1820.

The Comstock firm expanded and, in 1851, Comstock sold the home he had built 13 years earlier and built a new one close to the new factory. This new home established the center of Ivoryton. The gate on this property was the fulcrum for new building lots established along Main Street.

In the year he built his first home, Comstock married Harriet Hovey, granddaughter of Rev. Aaron Hovey of the Centrebrook Congregational Church and, more importantly, related to the wealthy Hayden family. The marriage established somewhat of a link between the Haydens and the Comstocks.

George Arthur Cheney was born on August 25, 1828, in New Salem, New Hampshire, and married Sarah, daughter of ivory magnate Rufus Greene, who set him up in the ivory trade. Cheney and his wife spent much of their time in Zanzibar, an island off the coast of East Africa, buying ivory from hunters and traders. Interestingly, one of their sons was the first white child born in Zanzibar.

In 1860, Cheney purchased part of the S.M. Comstock Company. Charles Rose and William C. Comstock also purchased a small portion of the company. The new organization became Comstock, Cheney & Company.

Cheney's role in the factory became most influential after Comstock's death. In 1868, Cheney purchased a home on Champlin Square in Essex village and lived there until his death at the beginning of the 20th century. He was the only executive to live outside of Ivoryton at the time.

Between 1867 and 1900, Ivoryton became what is known as a company town. Comstock sold land to the executives of the new company, resulting in a long line of Gothic homes in a planned, orderly development along Main Street.

The construction of the large upper factory, which started in 1873, was a signal to expand the workforce. The original lower shop was the ivory manufacturing and handling area, and the new factory produced piano keyboards and actions. Establishment of a company store, meeting hall, and boardinghouses, along with a men-only Wheel Club with bowling alleys, a ladies' social club, a cornet band, and a baseball team, kept employees wedded to the company. In addition, Comstock, Cheney & Company partially financed the grammar school, the Ivoryton Library, and the Swedish and Congregational churches, both in Ivoryton.

By the beginning of the 20th century, Comstock, Cheney & Company's growth was astounding. Between 1891 and 1903, it processed almost a million pounds of soft ivory and a quarter of a million pounds of hard ivory. Until *c.* 1900, the tusks were brought by boat up the Connecticut River. The company then bought six acres next to the train station in Centerbrook and used the railroad to bring the ivory to the factory, where it was used to make billiard balls, dominoes, combs, spatulas, letter openers, and a host of ornamental goods typical of the Victorian era. Most important, by far, were ivory piano keys. The finished goods were shipped out by railroad.

R.H. Comstock became president of the company after Cheney died. The Comstock family stayed involved with the operation of the company after its merger with and renaming as Pratt Read & Company in 1936.

The Great Depression, which started in 1929, had taken its toll on both firms. As a result, the new company decided to sell all nonfactory real estate owned by the former Comstock, Cheney & Company. The Ivoryton Realty Corporation was formed to carry out this process.

It was Samuel Merritt Comstock who essentially created the village of Ivoryton, but it was not until after his death that the village was named. With his inventive spirit and mechanical ability, Comstock strove for success and built the first modern factory system in the lower valley. The familiar whistle of that factory no longer blows, the common sight of trucks delivering lumber has disappeared, and law now protects the elephants that brought fame and fortune to Ivoryton. Although these strange and exotic threads that tied this community to the plains of Africa have long been broken, the landscape, homes, and much of the architecture built from 1840 to 1940 stand in testimony to the grandeur of what the ivory industry once was.

—Don Malcarne

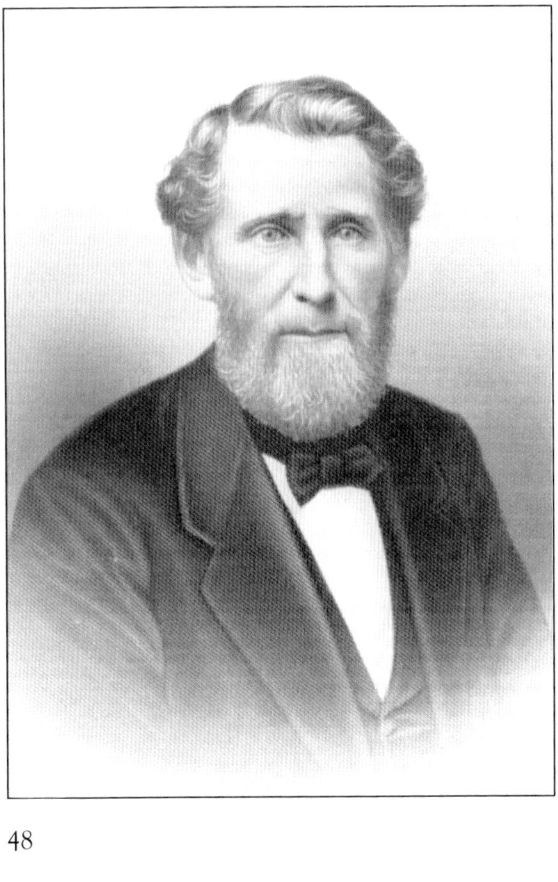

A Portrait of Samuel Merritt Comstock (1809–1878). When the manufacture of screwdrivers proved unprofitable in 1834, Samuel Merritt Comstock and his partner, Edwin Griswold, began producing combs as the firm of Comstock and Griswold. In 1847, Comstock started his own firm, the S.M. Comstock Company. Comstock became one of the leading industrialists in the lower Connecticut River Valley. An artisan and planner, he formed a perfect partnership with George A. Cheney, with the formation of Comstock, Cheney & Company. With extraordinary vision, Comstock created the village of Ivoryton to meet the needs of his workers, keep them happy and, through his generosity, educate them. He was elected to the state legislature in 1869, serving one term.

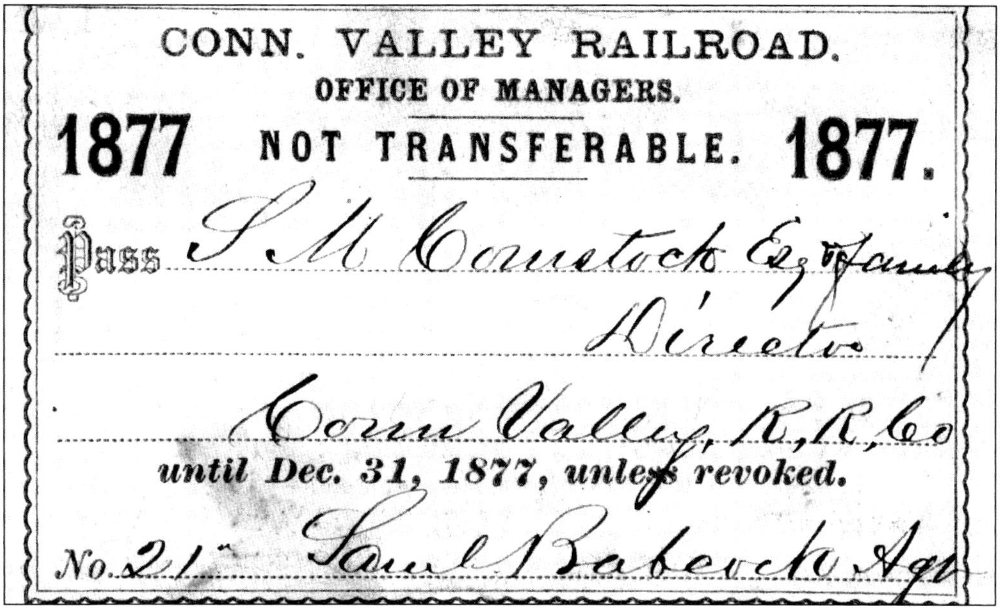
CONN. VALLEY RAILROAD.
OFFICE OF MANAGERS.
1877 NOT TRANSFERABLE. 1877.
Pass S. M. Comstock Esq. & family
Director
Conn Valley R. R. Co
until Dec. 31, 1877, unless revoked.
No. 21 Saml Babcock Agt

A Connecticut Valley Railroad Pass. Serving as director of the Connecticut Valley Railroad for nine years from 1870 until he died on January 17, 1878, Samuel Merritt Comstock was given this pass to ride the train without charge. He died in Wilmington, North Carolina, probably while on vacation. (Photograph courtesy of Charlotte T. Comstock.)

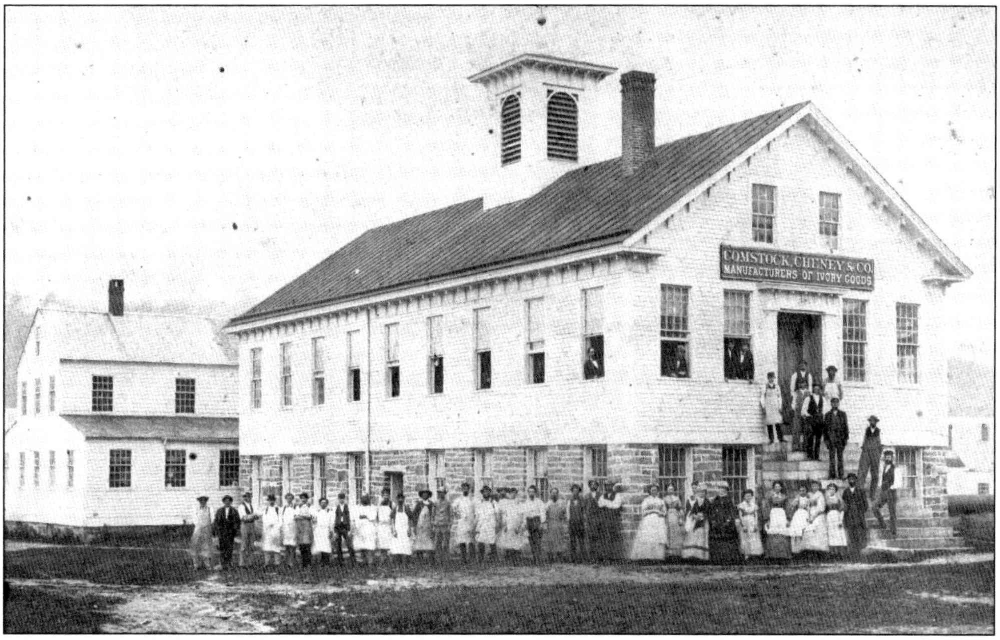

The Original Comstock, Cheney & Company Factory, c. 1870. Owners Samuel Merritt Comstock and George A. Cheney, are pictured in the windows of their factory. The number of employees at the factory varied. Work was generally six days per week, 10 to 12 hours a day. Women were employed to sort and match the bleached ivory into keyboard units. The building in the background is the original 1848 S.M. Comstock Company shop. (Photograph courtesy of Connecticut River Museum.)

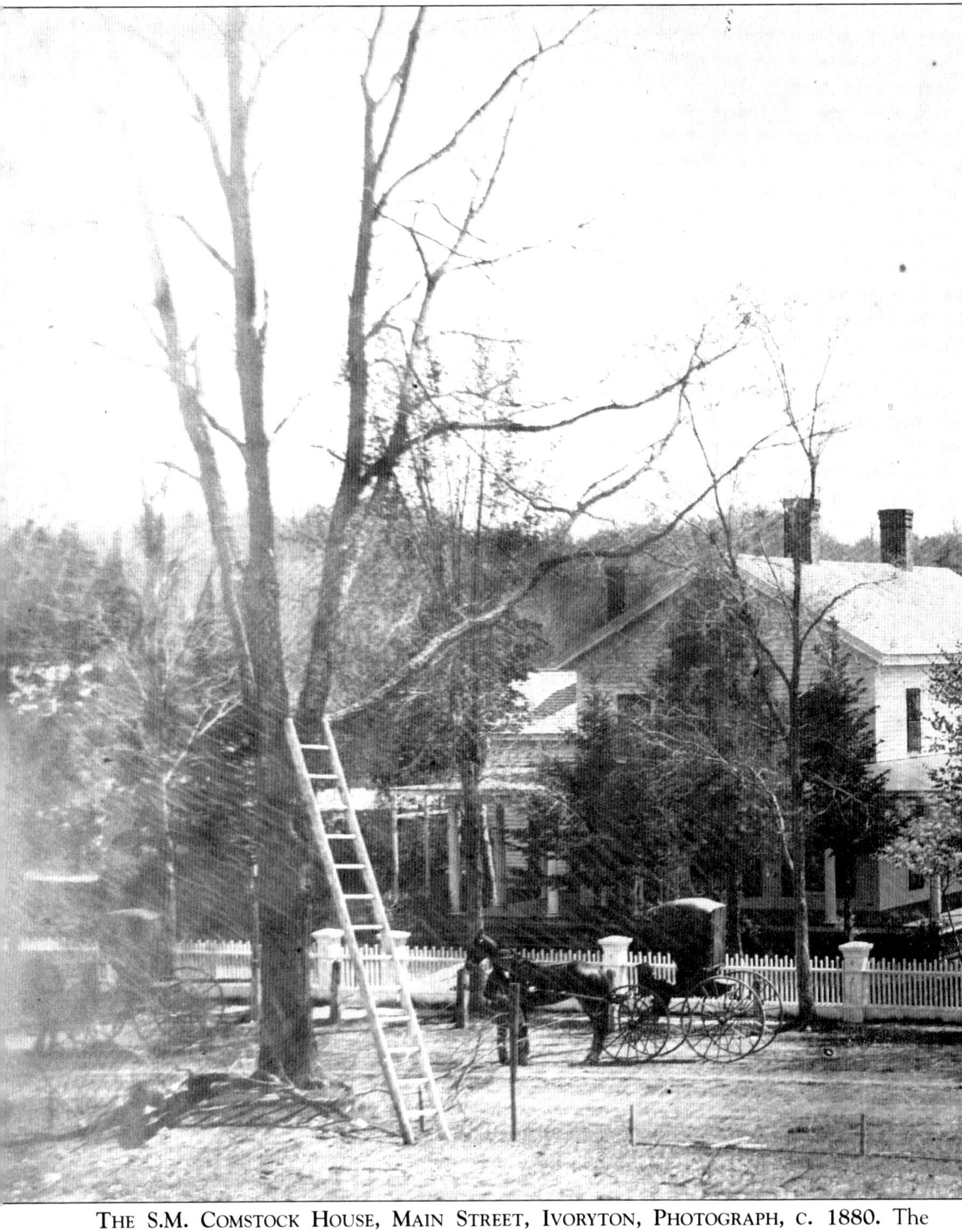

THE S.M. COMSTOCK HOUSE, MAIN STREET, IVORYTON, PHOTOGRAPH, C. 1880. The second house built by Harriet and Samuel Comstock was located east of the present-day post office. The new house was constructed as a result of Comstock's moving the factory west from the location of the Comstock and Griswold Company. It had a large rear ell that was removed

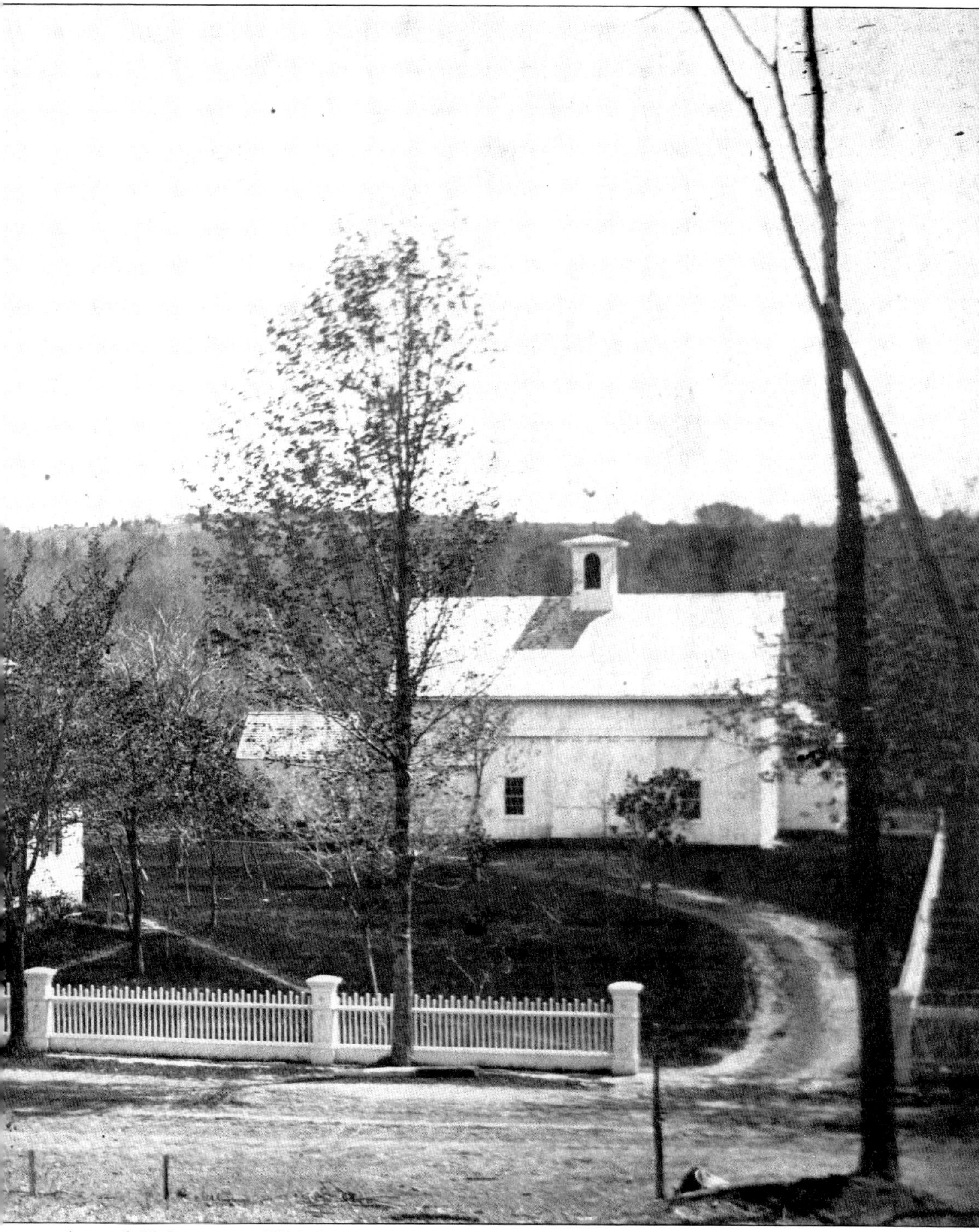

in the mid-20th century. With living quarters at a premium in Ivoryton, the ell may have been used to house workers. East Main Street, shown in front of the house, was once known as the Pettipaug Guilford Turnpike. (Photograph courtesy of Harwood Comstock.)

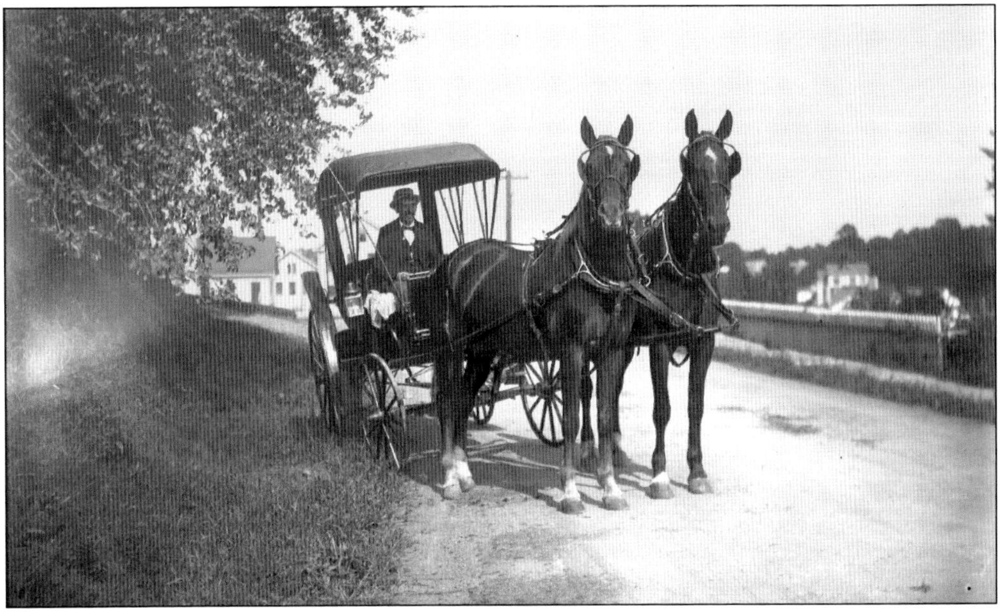

WILL DOANE AND TEAM, EAST MAIN STREET. The Comstock, Cheney & Company saw to it that the banks along the streams were mowed and the sidewalks were kept neat and clean. In the winter Will Doane plowed the wooden sidewalks early in the morning after a snowfall, so that workers would not have to trudge through the snow. Roads were rolled and not plowed in the village until after World War I. (Photograph courtesy of Essex Historical Society.)

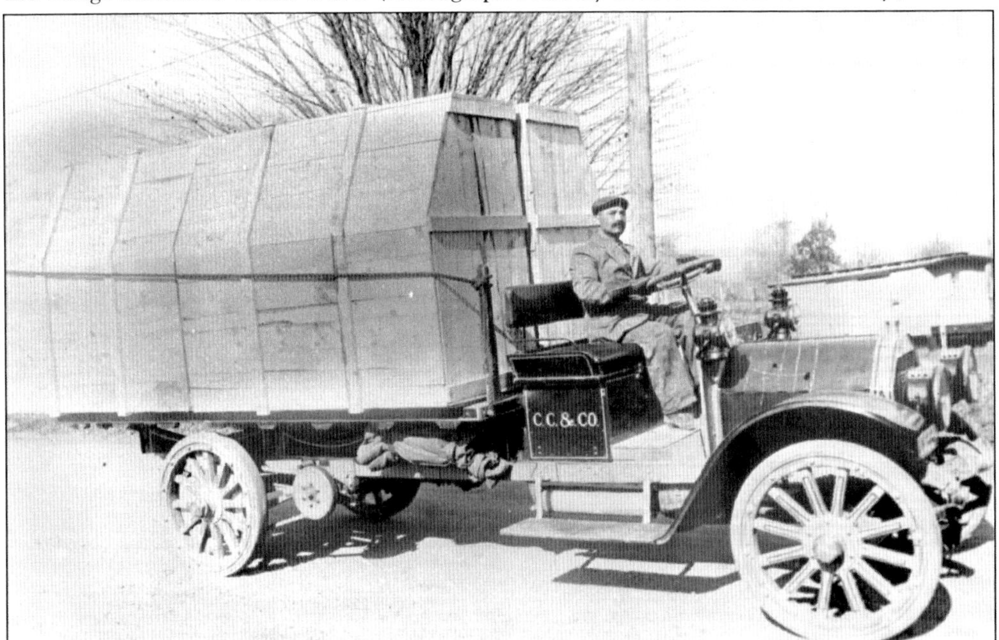

A COMPANY TRUCK TRANSPORTING PIANO ACTIONS AND KEYS TO THE DEPOT, 1913. Frank Santi is seen delivering four crates of piano actions and keys to the Connecticut Valley Railroad station in Essex. He is driving Comstock, Cheney & Company's one-and-one-half-ton chain-drive Federal truck. (Photograph courtesy of Max Miller.)

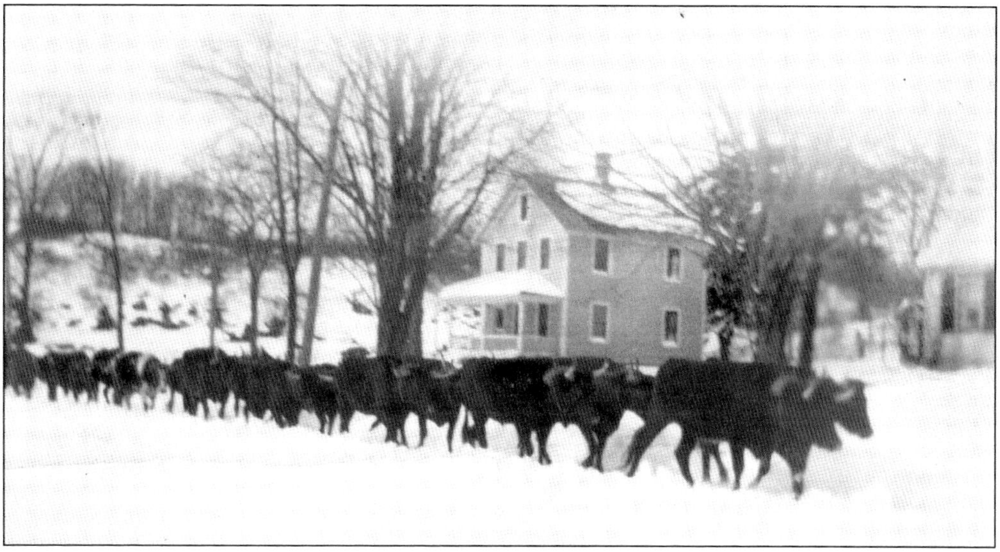

TEAMS OF OXEN PULLING THE SNOW ROLLER. Before snow was cleared from roads with plows, the roads were rolled. This was accomplished with teams of oxen pulling a large wooden roller. No attempt was made to remove the snow. With the advent of automobiles, a more efficient way of handling the snow was required and contemporary snowplows were put into use. (Photograph courtesy of Essex Historical Society.)

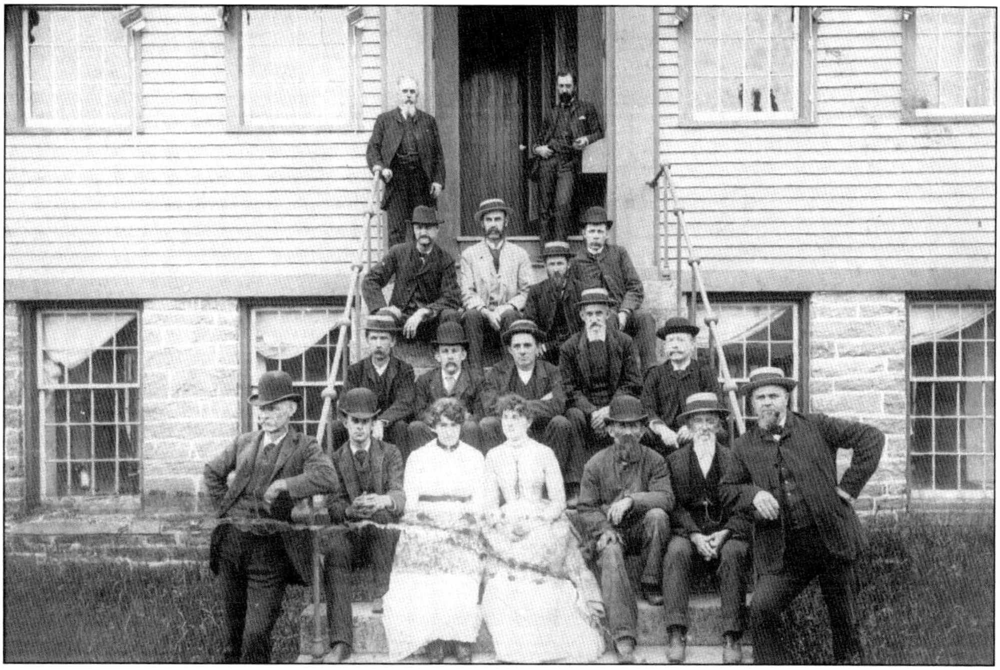

EMPLOYEES POSING ON THE FRONT STEPS OF THE FACTORY. Comstock, Cheney & Company co-owner George A. Cheney (top left) was born in Salem, New Hampshire. He married Sarah Green and spent years engaged in East African ivory trade as a cargo agent. He was 20 years younger than his partner, Samuel M. Comstock. From Comstock's death in 1878 to c. 1900, Cheney ran the company, and during this time it became one of the largest producers of piano actions and keyboards in the world. (Photograph courtesy of Deep River Historical Society.)

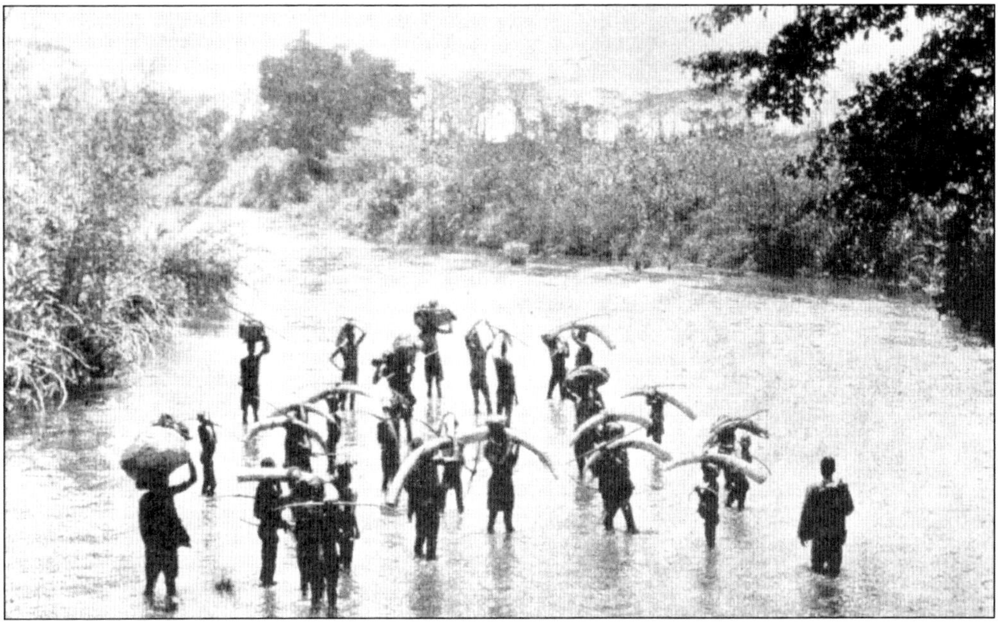

CARRYING THE TUSKS OUT OF AFRICA. Each tusk was carried from central Africa to Zanzibar on the East African coast and then shipped to the United States and Europe. It is estimated that five natives either died or were sold into slavery for every tusk that came out of Africa. If Comstock, Cheney & Company used 100,000 tusks over a 60-year period (they probably used that many at least), over half a million people died or were sold into slavery to bring the raw material to Ivoryton. (Photograph courtesy of Richard Conniff.)

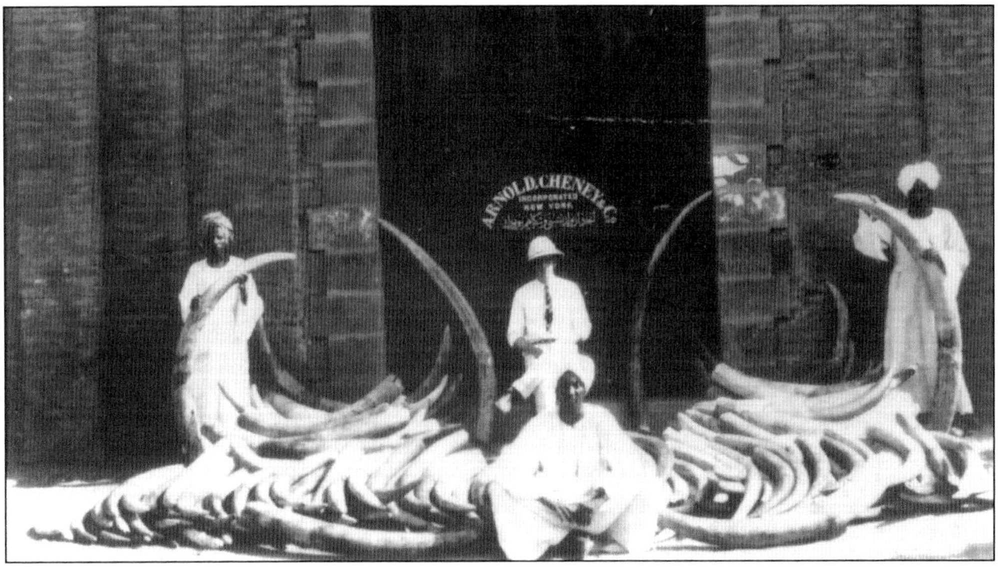

THE IVORY BUYER. Ernest D. Moore (1888–1932), pictured in the back center, served as the ivory buyer for Comstock, Cheney & Company and its neighboring Pratt Read factory from 1907 to 1911. He purchased tons of elephant tusks from Arab traders and traveled into the interior of Africa himself to meet with Kaffir chiefs. In 1931, Moore wrote *Ivory: Scourge of Africa*, which details the slave trade connected with the slaughter of elephants. (Photograph courtesy of Deep River Historical Society.)

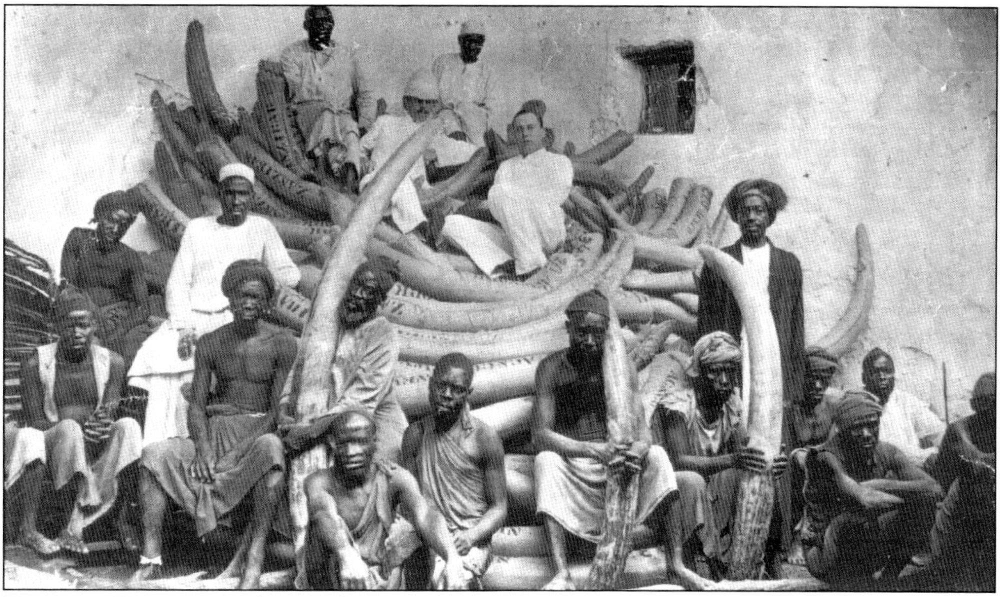

TUSKS IN ZANZIBAR. These tusks were carried to Zanzibar from the interior by natives. Kaffir chiefs usually organized the hunt and slaughter of elephants. Natives coming upon a group of elephants would herd them together and slaughter them with javelins. The tusks would be removed after a few days. Roughly half the male elephants in the herd would prove to be tuskers. (Photograph courtesy of Hugo Nickse.)

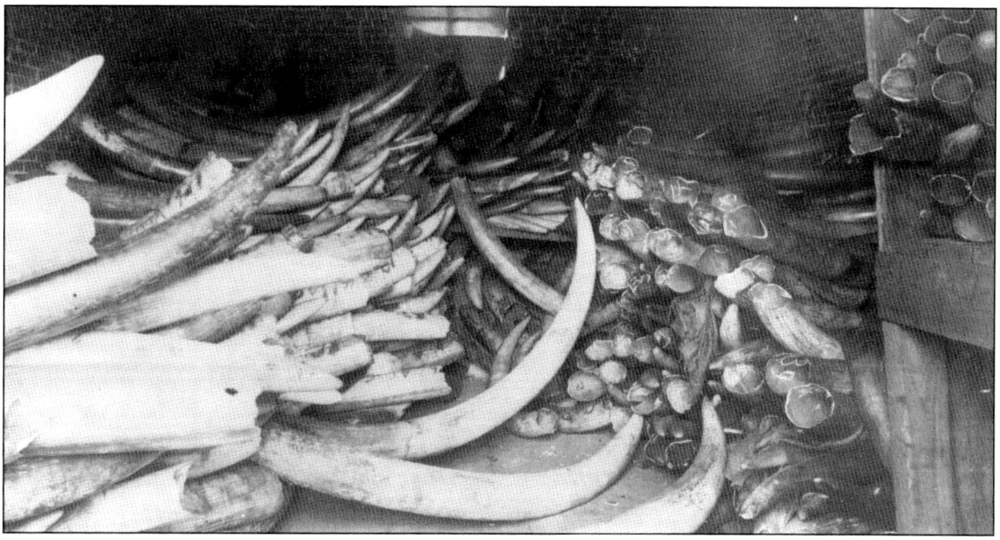

TUSKS IN AN IVORY VAULT, C. 1890. Until they were ready to be worked, tusks were stored in a vault, a small separate building where thick walls and no windows maintained the temperature and humidity. The average tusk was 90 pounds. Soft ivory from the elephants of East Africa was preferred for piano veneers. The tusk was taken from the vault to the junker operator, who used a converter band saw to cut the tusk into four-inch sections. The sections were marked to achieve the best grain and maximum quantity and then cut into uniform sizes and shapes. A blocking saw was used to cut the ivory into head blocks (the wide forward end of the piano key) or tail blocks (the longer narrow key). Running water into the saw bed cooled the ivory saws. (Photograph courtesy of Connecticut River Museum.)

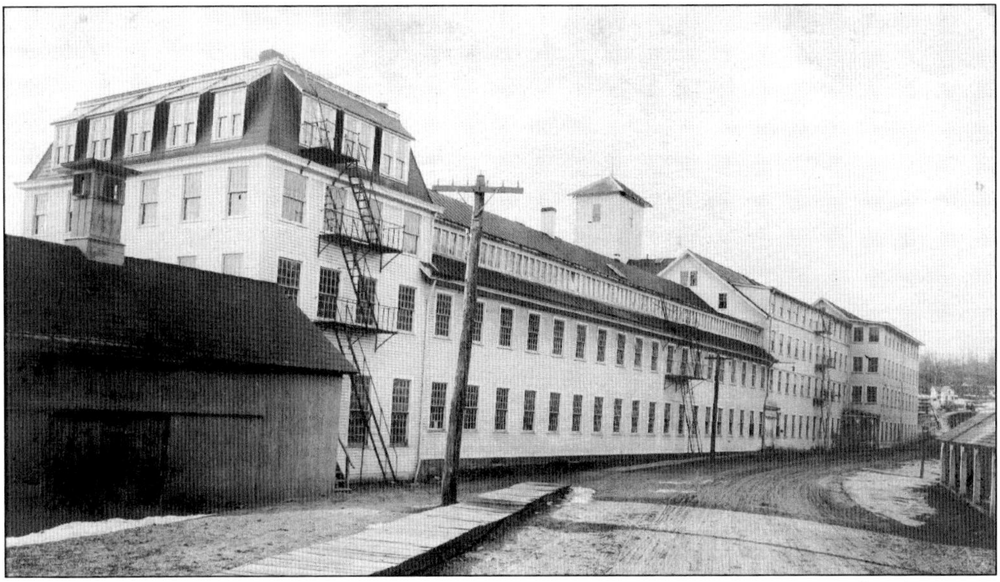

THE COMSTOCK, CHENEY & COMPANY, PHOTOGRAPH 1900. By 1900, Comstock, Cheney & Company was the largest factory ever built in Middlesex County, employing up to 700 workers. The first section of the factory was built in 1873; the second section was added in 1875; the third section was built in 1890; the fourth section was added in 1892; a new smokestack was built in 1900. The company began building homes for its workers in 1871 and, by 1925, had constructed 135 houses. These were small homes for what was fast becoming a workforce dominated by immigrants. (Photograph courtesy of Essex Historical Society.)

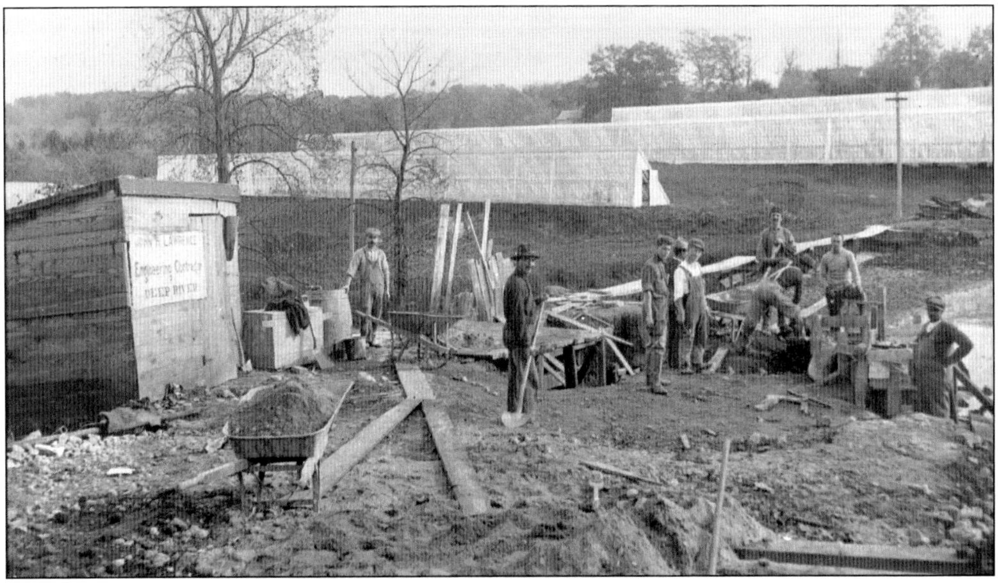

REPAIRING THE DAM, 1915. This dam was located behind the ivory shop opposite the Ivoryton Inn. The ivory-cutting industry required a highly trained workforce, bleach houses, and consistent waterpower to run the precision saws and lathes. Bleach houses can be seen on the hill in the background. The wealth of Ivoryton was partially a result of immigrant labor, primarily Polish and Italian, from 1890 to World War I. This dam was destroyed in the flood of 1982. (Photograph courtesy of Deep River Historical Society.)

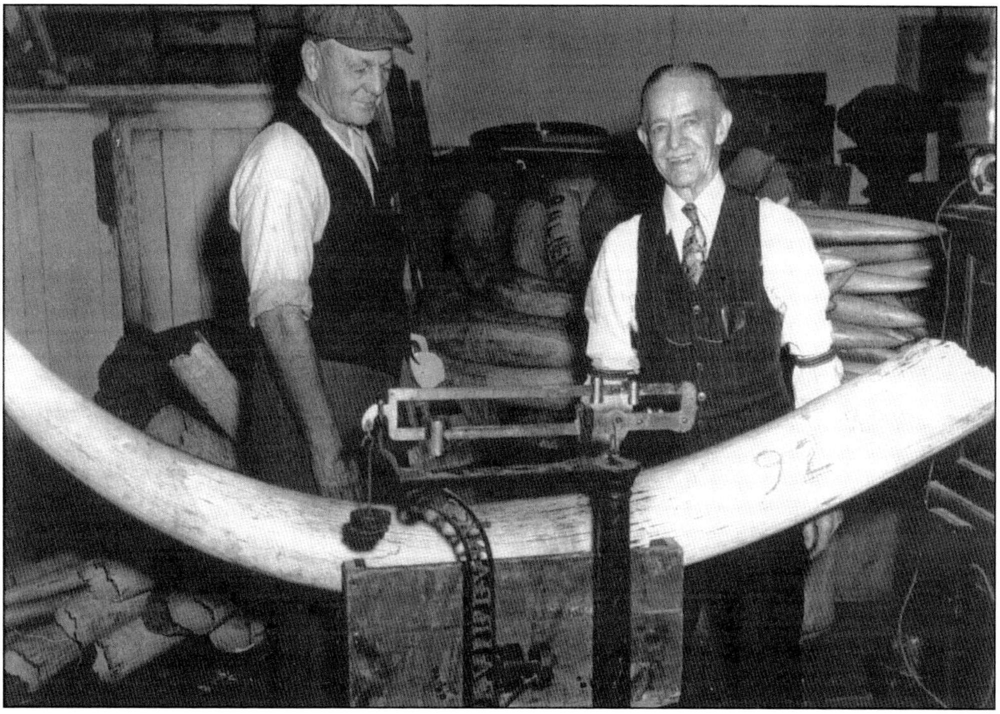

WEIGHING A TUSK, C. 1955. Oscar Lynn (left) and Louie E. Pratt, an ivory selector and grader, set up, weigh, and grade a tusk. The 92-pound tusk was then cut, depending on the type of ivory it was and the use to which it was to be put. Certain tusks were used for billiard balls, toothpicks, combs, and piano keys. (Photograph courtesy of Deep River Historical Society.)

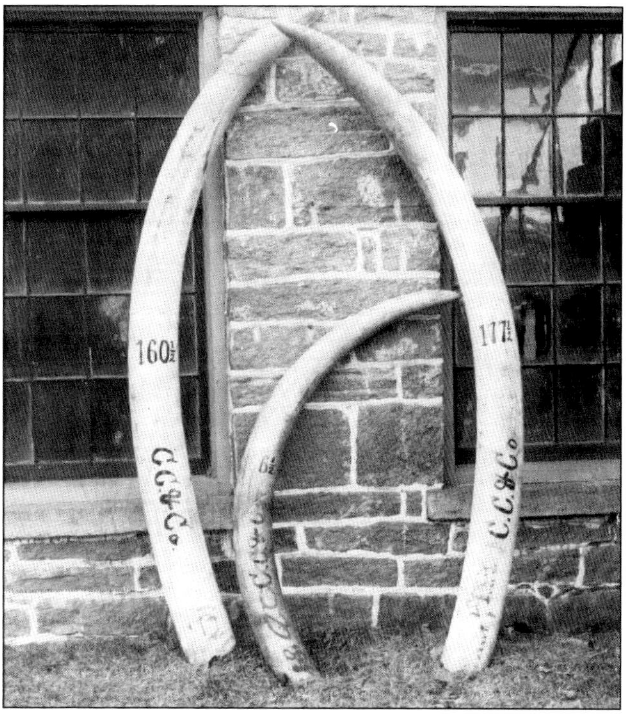

HUGE TUSKS, PHOTOGRAPH C. 1900. Outside the Comstock Cheney ivory vault are two huge tusks, each weighing over 160 pounds, and a smaller one, all marked CC&C. Originally, tusks arrived via steamboat from New York City. Later, the raw materials were shipped into Ivoryton on the railroads. Mature elephants, having the larger tusks, were the first to be killed, leaving behind a population of immature elephants with only a 50 percent chance of survival. In the 21st century, the African elephant has become a most endangered species. The elephant population has plummeted dramatically. (Photograph courtesy of Connecticut River Museum.)

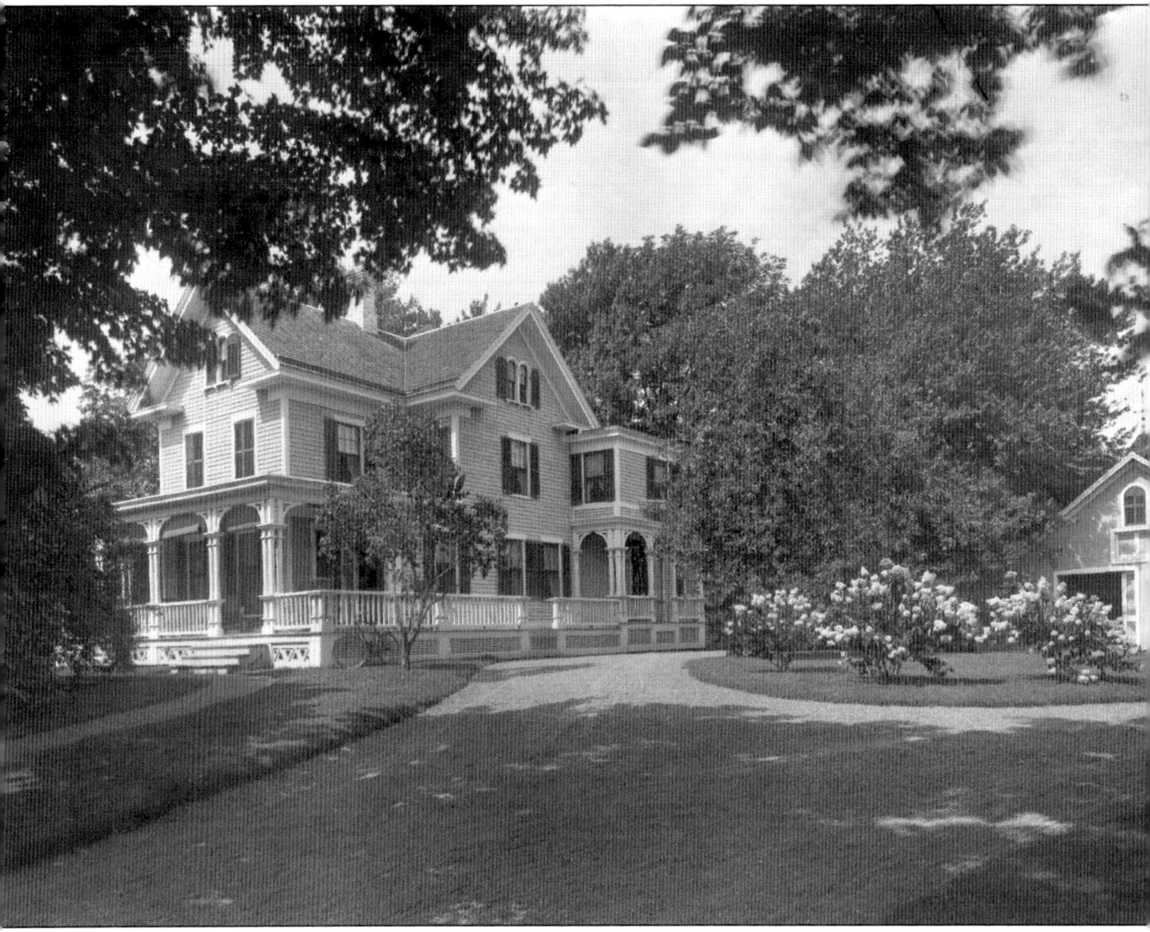

THE ROBERT H. COMSTOCK HOUSE, MAIN STREET, PHOTOGRAPH EARLY 1900S. The original house on this site was built in 1868 by the uncle of Robert H. Comstock, William A. Comstock. Robert Comstock rebuilt the house in 1888, a decade before he became president of Comstock, Cheney & Company. The rear, or main, entrance pictured here testifies to the grandeur of this dwelling. Comstock, his wife, daughter Ethel, and sister-in-law Isabel Kelsey spent six months traveling in Africa. Although George Cheney had spent years in Africa, Robert was the first Comstock to go there. It took three weeks for the family to reach Cape Town, where, they said they were overwhelmed by the acres of calla lilies growing in profusion. They then traveled 823 miles on steamer, stopping at East London, where they were lowered over the side into small boats in a basket carrying a dozen passengers each load. This was for a journey into Zululand, where they mused about the natives' "lack of costumes." They traveled by railroad to Transvaal to tour what they referred to as the theater of the Boer War and then by auto to Cape Colony, spending three days visiting the diamond mines where Comstock descended 700 feet to view a mine manned by Kaffirs. From there they continued their journey to Victoria Falls. Comstock described the spray of the falls surging upward as "wreathing the falls with a crown of glory." Without succumbing to heat or sickness (they brought their own water for the entire trip), they traveled another 1,000 miles to Zanzibar to get their first sight of untamed Africa. This was the shipping point for getting ivory out of the country. Next they traveled to the Uganda game preserve. For the trip, Comstock dressed in white: white-lined trousers, white shoes and stockings, white linen coat buttoned under the chin, and a white helmet. (Photograph courtesy of Essex Historical Society.)

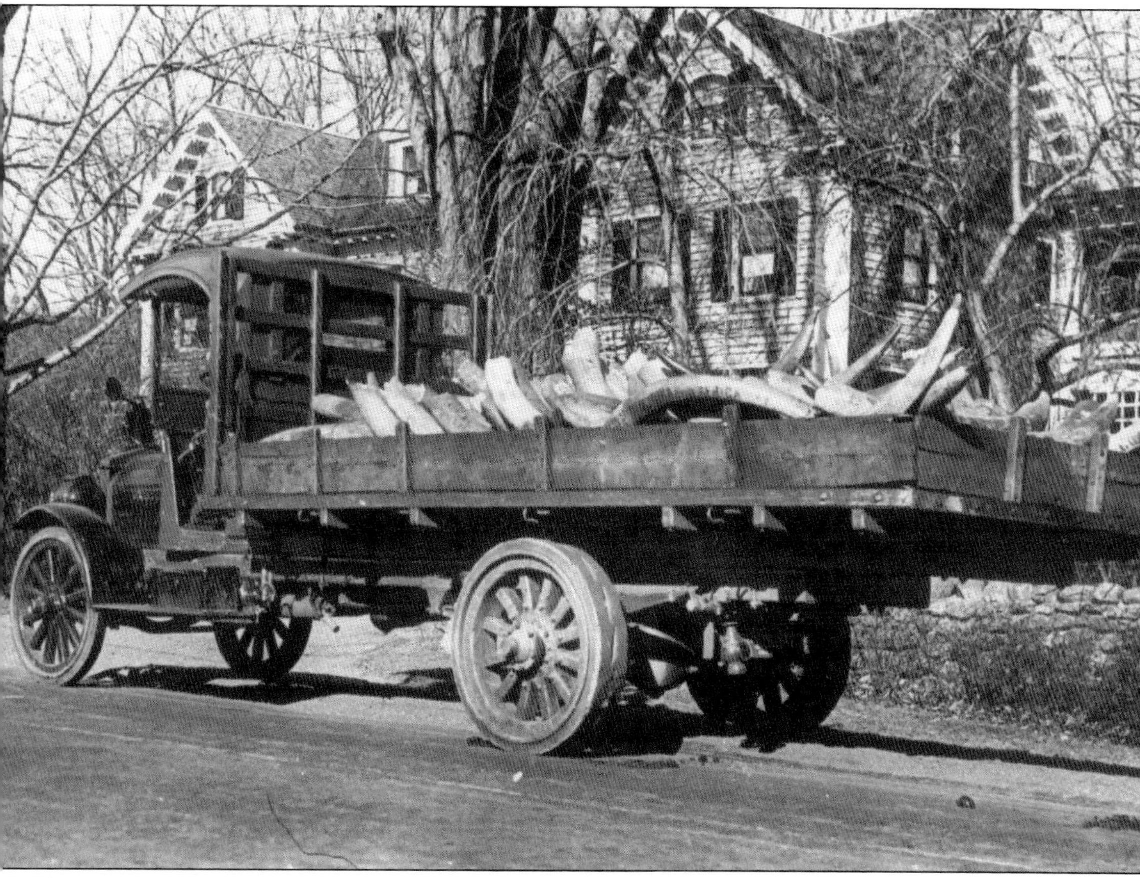

A IVORY-LADEN TRUCK IN FRONT OF THE COMSTOCK HOME, 1924. The ivory came by both steamboat and rail. In this photograph, the Comstock, Cheney & Company truck, hauling a load of tusks to the vault at the ivory shop, has parked in front of the home of Robert H. Comstock, the company president. Behrens & Bushnell, a local garage and bicycle shop, converted this Ford truck to transport tusks. In an earlier day, a horse and wagon went down to meet the boat at the Steamboat Dock. Robert Comstock succeeded George A. Cheney as head of the company. He served as president until his death in the 1930s. (Photograph courtesy of Connecticut River Museum.)

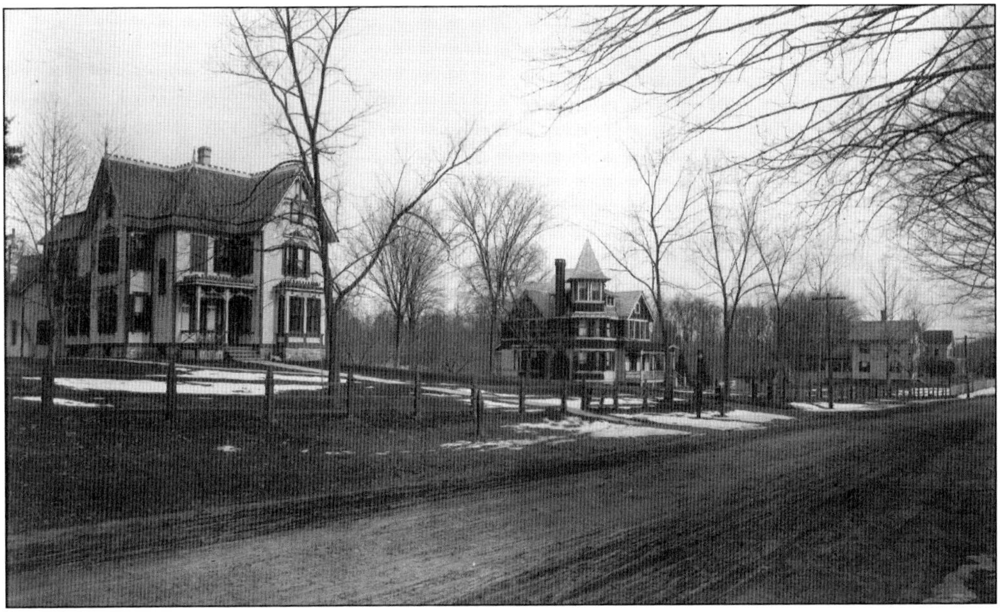

EXECUTIVE HOUSES, MAIN STREET, PHOTOGRAPH C. 1900. These four houses on the north side of Main Street still stand. They were built for and lived in by executives of Comstock, Cheney & Company. In the late 19th century, Main Street in Ivoryton was the most fashionable address in town. The house on the left was that of Lorenzo Dow Webber, the superintendent of the factory. The Victorian home in the center was built for Wooster Webber, an executive of the company and the son of L.D. Webber. (Photograph courtesy of Connecticut River Museum.)

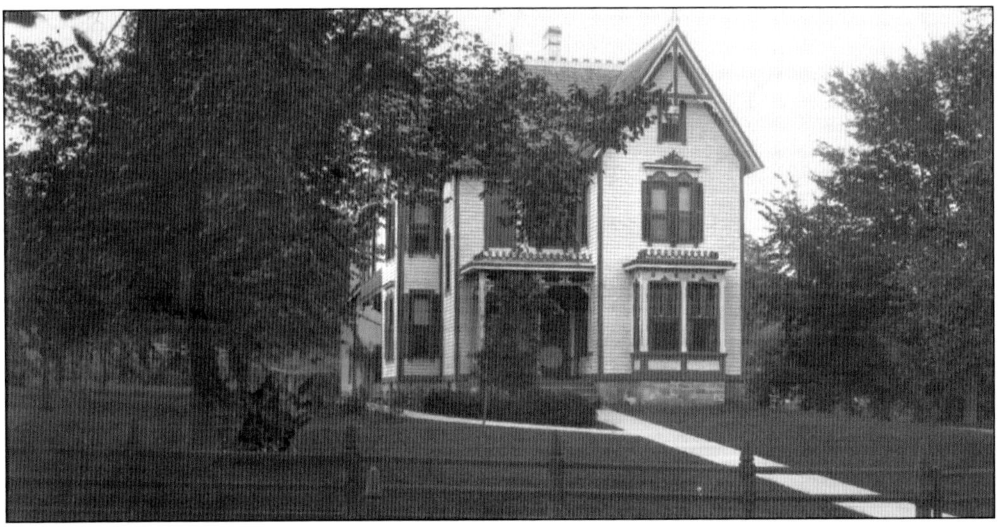

THE HOME OF LORENZO DOW WEBBER. This house was built in 1874 on land originally owned by Samuel Comstock. Lorenzo Dow Webber, was the superintendent of the upper factory for over 30 years, until 1908. In 1890, Deep River's Pratt Read & Company attempted to lure Webber away from Comstock, Cheney & Company. Pratt Read offered him a salary of $3,500, with a $10,000 cash bonus and 200 shares of stock. Webber declined, saying the distance was too far, and he stayed with Comstock, Cheney & Company until his death at age 71. (Photograph courtesy of Essex Historical Society.)

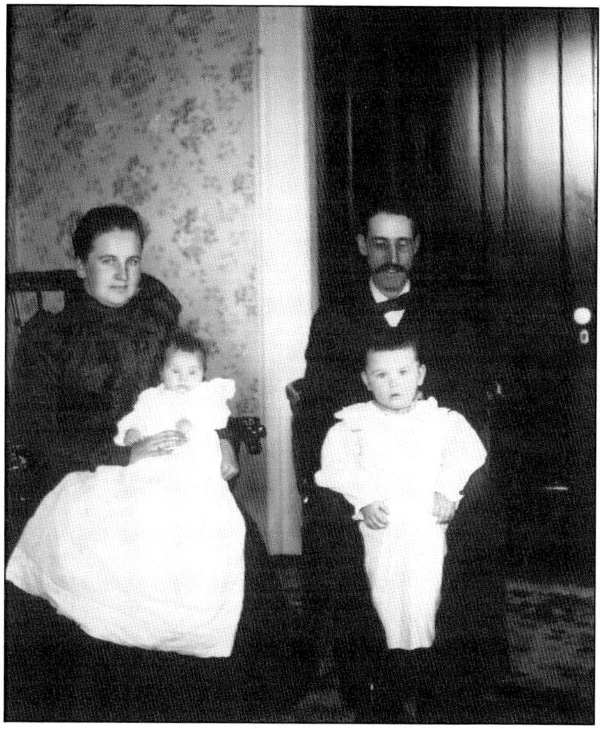

BESSIE AND WOOSTER WEBBER AND FAMILY. In 1893, Wooster Webber married Bessie Wright, daughter of Sen. Alfred M. Wright of Centerbrook. Webber was an executive with Comstock, Cheney & Company and gained the reputation of being one of the best-informed men in the country in the field of piano manufacturing. Webber moved his family to Hartford because of the fine reputation of the schools there. He lived in Ivoryton during the week and in Hartford on weekends. The Webbers spent summers at their cottage at West Beach in Westbrook. Webber helped plan the site and design of the Ivoryton Playhouse. (Photograph courtesy of Essex Historical Society.)

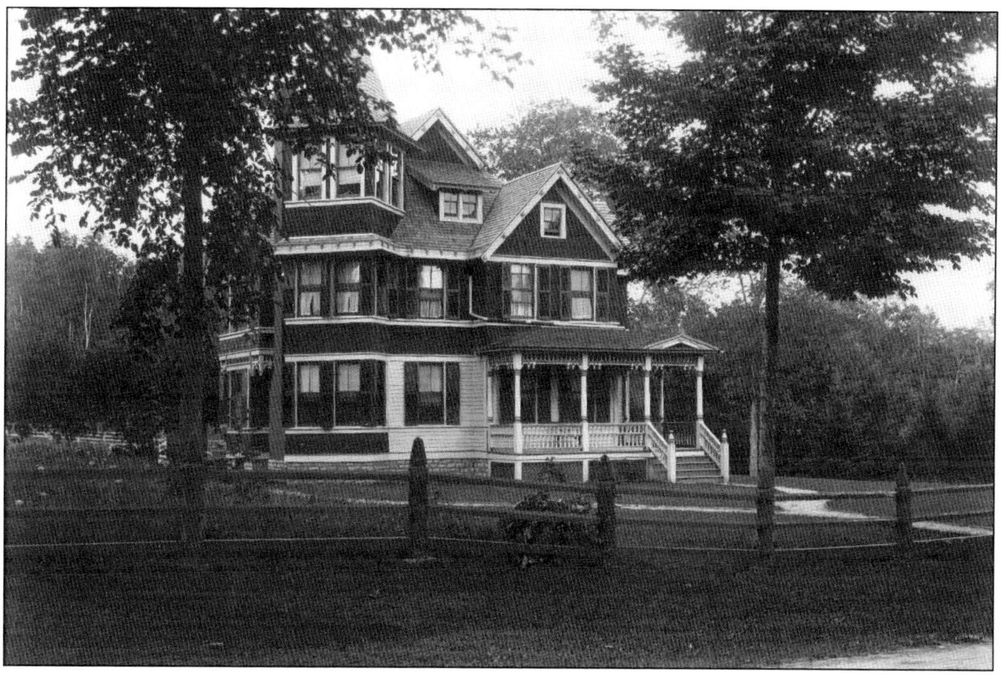

THE HENRY WOOSTER WEBBER HOMESTEAD. Henry Wooster Webber built this house in 1896 on land owned by his parents. This is one of the most striking Victorian houses along Victorian Row, a name that can be truthfully applied to East Main Street, Ivoryton. Webber was an executive of the Comstock, Cheney & Company. (Photograph courtesy of Essex Historical Society.)

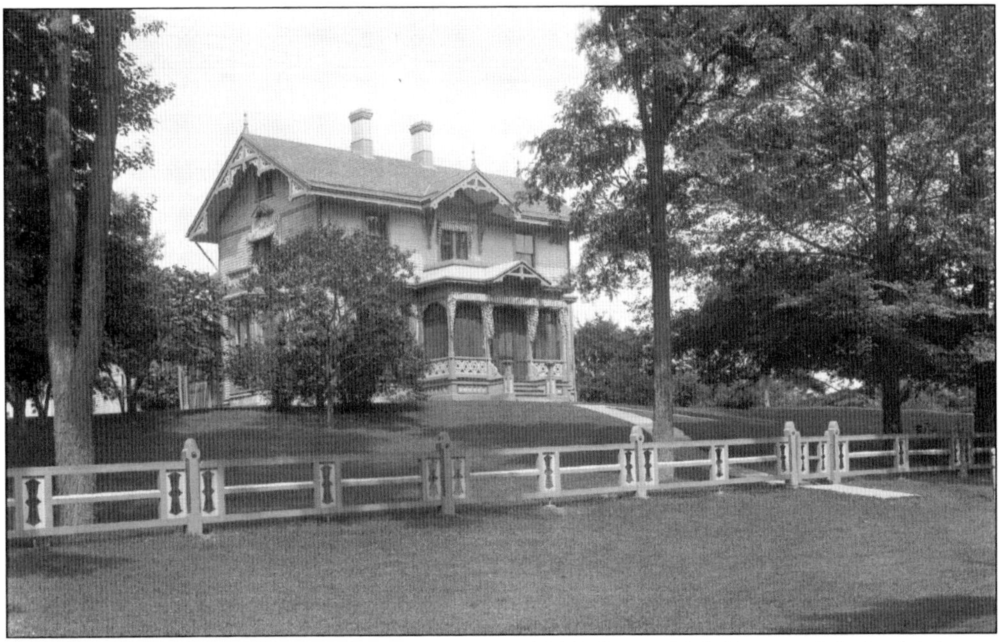

THE JOHN NORTHROP HOUSE, PHOTOGRAPH C. 1900. Samuel M. Comstock built this house for his daughter Elizabeth Comstock and her husband, John Northrop, in 1870. Northrop was treasurer of Comstock, Cheney & Company. This house, located directly across from the Ivoryton Store, was "de-Victorianized" in the 20th century. (Photograph courtesy of Essex Historical Society.)

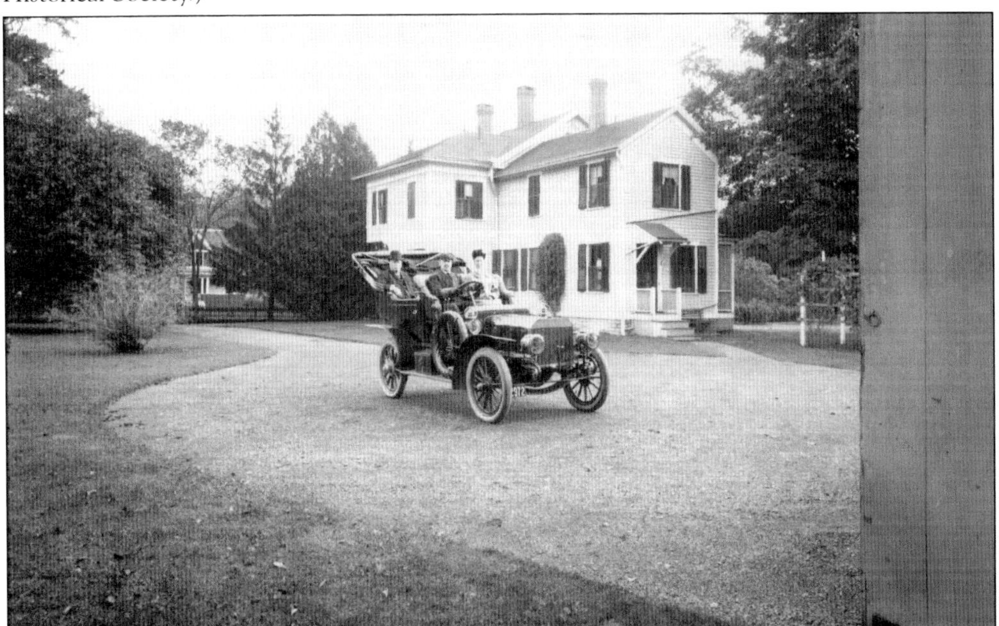

THE CHARLES ROSE HOUSE, MAIN STREET, IVORYTON. Samuel M. Comstock sold slightly over one acre of land to Charles Rose in 1868 for a home. Rose was a businessman closely involved with Samuel Comstock and operated Rose Brothers', the store owned by Comstock. (Photograph courtesy of Essex Historical Society.)

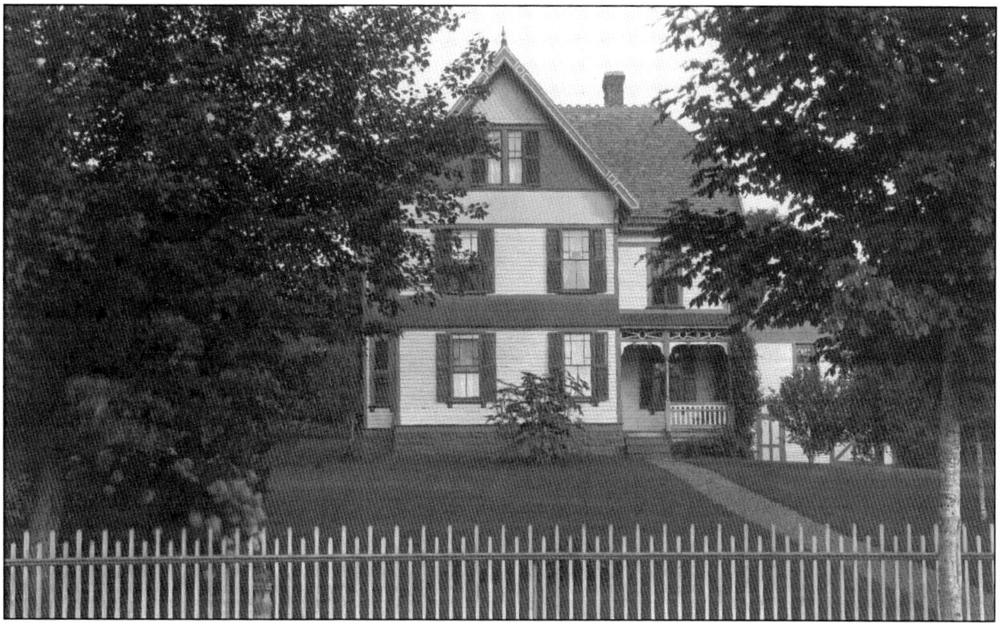

THE THEODORE ROSE HOUSE. This Victorian-style house was built on Comstock Avenue in Ivoryton in 1888 by Theodore Rose. After his death, it was sold by his son, Reginald Rose, in 1913 for use as a parsonage. In the 1940s, the church sold the house, which then once again became a private residence. (Photograph courtesy of Essex Historical Society.)

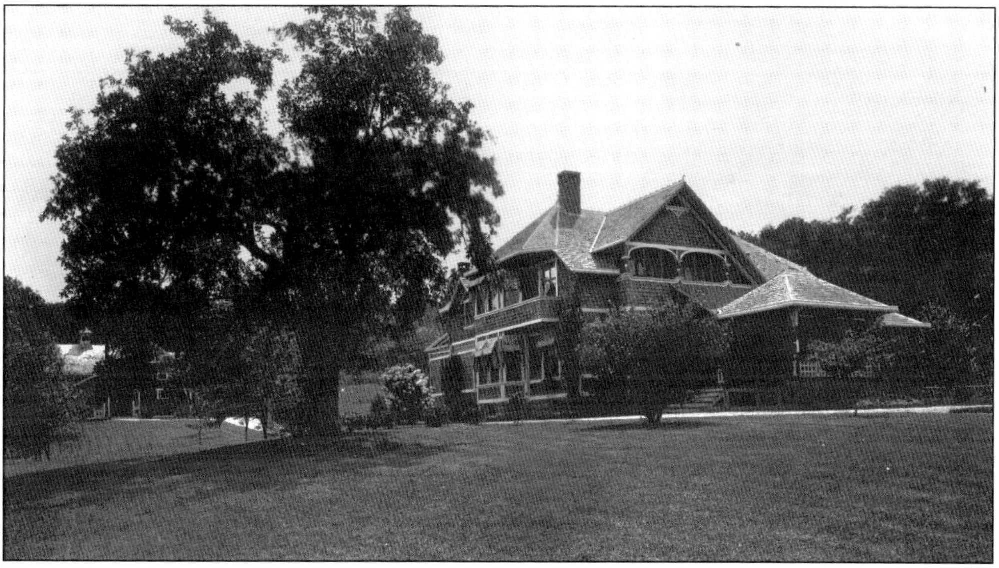

THE ARCHIBALD W. COMSTOCK HOUSE, PHOTOGRAPH EARLY 1900S. Archibald W. Comstock, son of S.M. Comstock, built this home (now the Copper Beech Inn) in 1890. He became president of the company after the death of his brother, Robert H. Comstock. He later headed Ivoryton Realty Corporation, set up at the time of the 1936 Pratt Read & Company merger to sell off nonfactory assets, such as the factory houses and the playhouse originally owned by Comstock, Cheney & Company. He was the first man to drive a car up Mount Washington nonstop, possibly in a 1903 Winton. (Photograph courtesy of Essex Historical Society.)

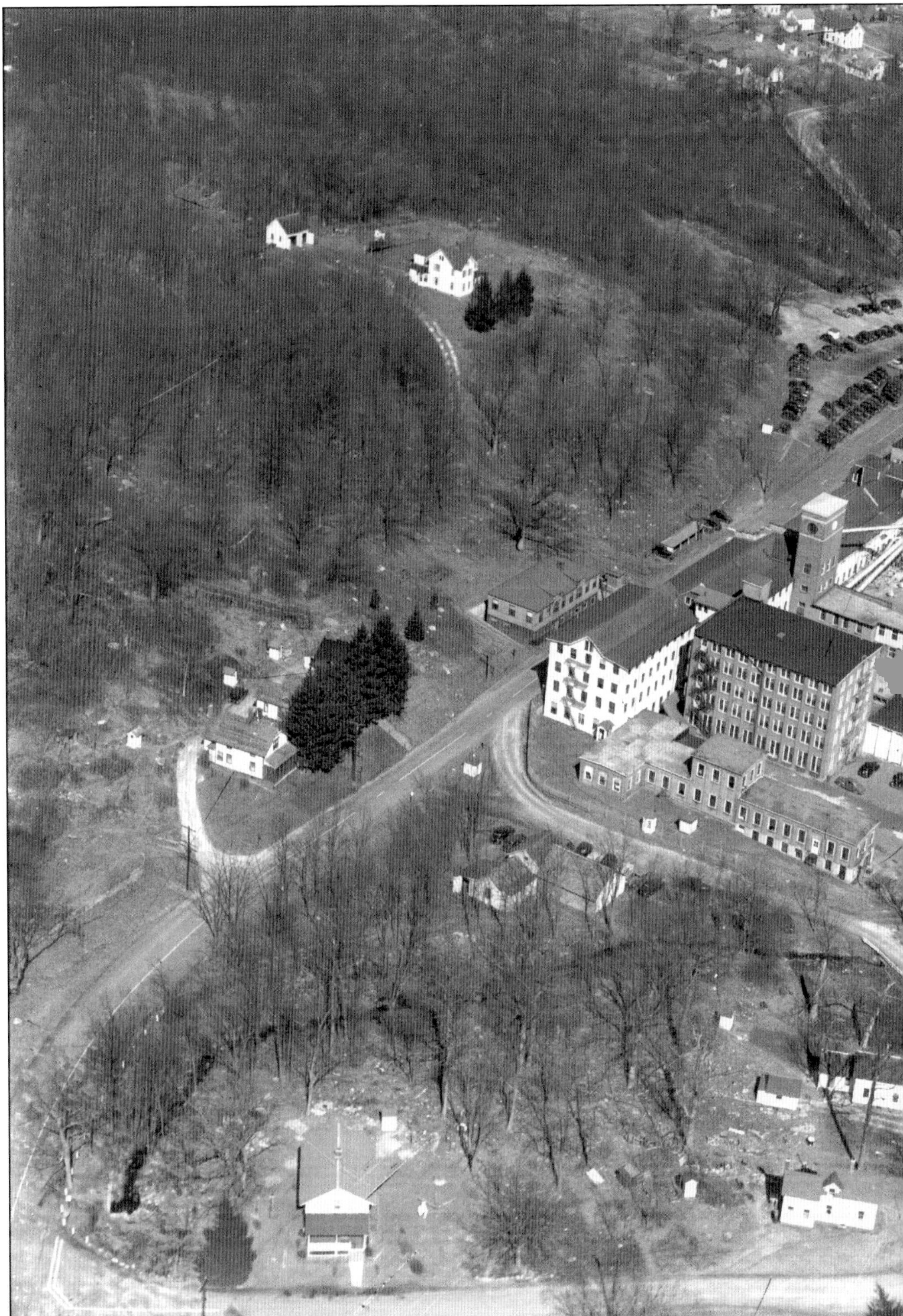

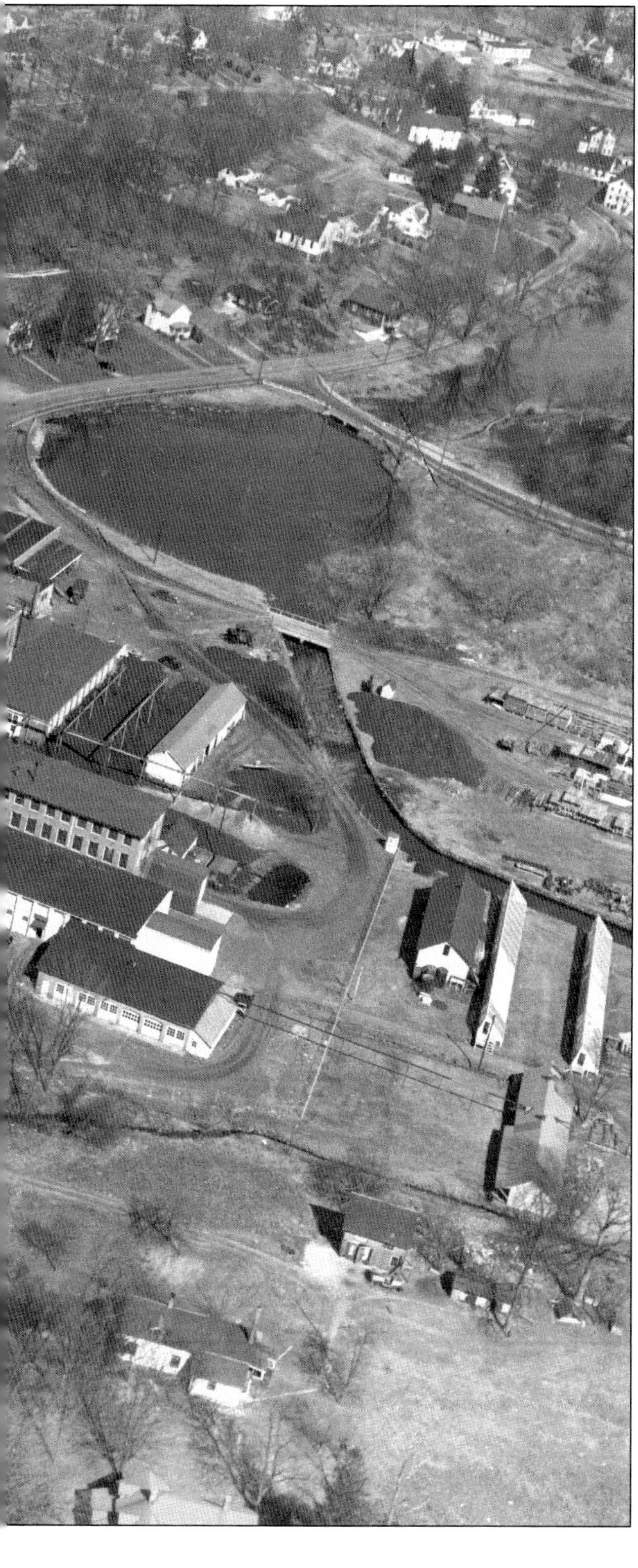

PRATT READ & COMPANY, AERIAL PHOTOGRAPH BEFORE 1959. Comstock, Cheney & Company combined with its competitor, Pratt Read & Company of Deep River in 1936. The company took the Pratt Read name even though it was located in the old Comstock, Cheney & Company buildings and offices, shown in this photograph. The Falls River, which runs through the complex, originally provided part of the power to run the machines in the factory. The automobile has replaced the bicycle as the worker's main form of transportation. The ivory shop is visible in the upper right corner with its dam backing up Lily Pond. (Photograph courtesy of Mary Bowers.)

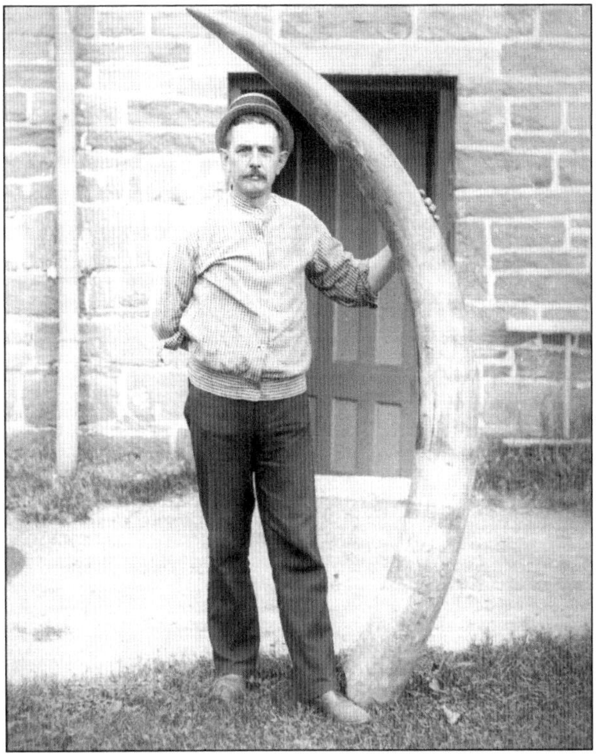

WILL SHAILER, POSING WITH A TUSK, C. 1890. This photograph, taken in front of a factory vault, was used by the company for promotional purposes. It gives a good indication of the size of an elephant tusk. The valuable material was stored in the vault for security and preservation. (Photograph courtesy of Connecticut River Museum.)

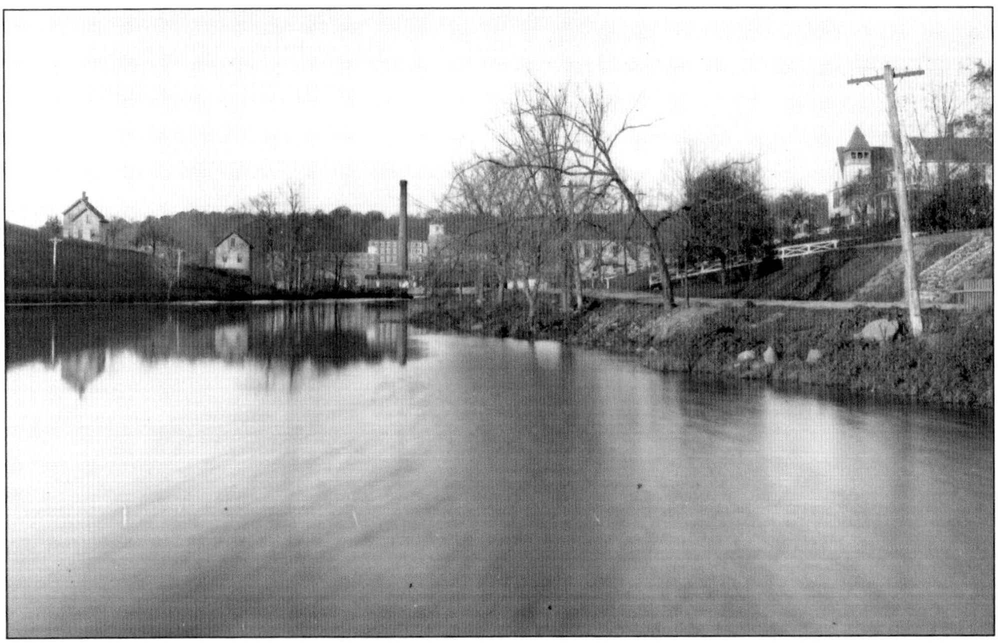

THE POND BELOW COMSTOCK, CHENEY & COMPANY. Shown, from left to right, are houses on Walnut Street, the Comstock, Cheney & Company keyboard shop, Champlin's Store, the Swedish church, and the Chapman house. Champlin's, which later became Bob's Restaurant, was just a step away from the factory at the foot of Walnut Street. (Photograph courtesy of Essex Historical Society.)

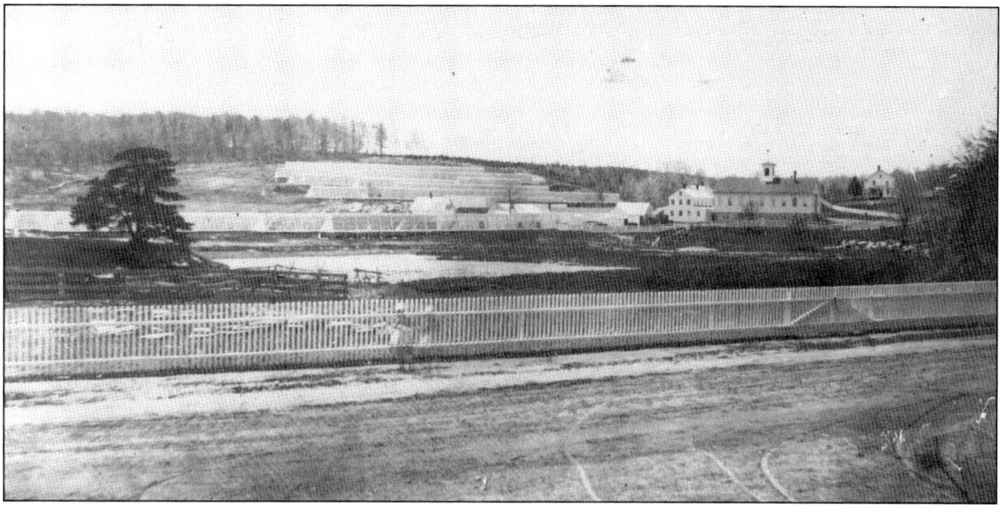

THE COMSTOCK, CHENEY & COMPANY FACTORY AND BLEACH HOUSES, PHOTOGRAPH BEFORE 1880. If anything characterized Ivoryton over the years, it was the rows of bleach houses that lined the slope behind the factory and stood across the brook from the bracket shop. Built similar to greenhouses, bleach houses used the sun to bleach the ivory heads and tails that had been bathed in peroxide. The cut pieces were put against the glass on the south side and had to stay there for seven days. Rainy days had to be made up. Racks in each bleach house held up to 400 heads and tails. Bleach houses were up to 300 feet long, costing as much as $4,000 in 1880. This photograph was taken looking toward Ivoryton Heights, now Comstock Avenue. (Photograph courtesy of Connecticut River Museum.)

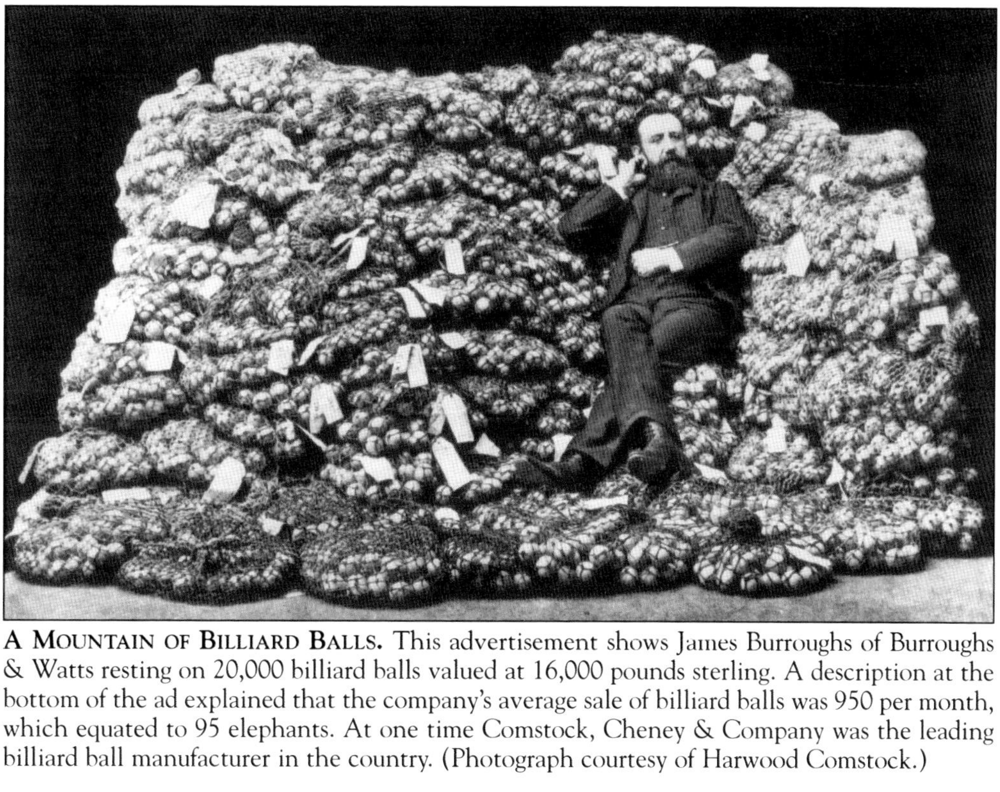

A MOUNTAIN OF BILLIARD BALLS. This advertisement shows James Burroughs of Burroughs & Watts resting on 20,000 billiard balls valued at 16,000 pounds sterling. A description at the bottom of the ad explained that the company's average sale of billiard balls was 950 per month, which equated to 95 elephants. At one time Comstock, Cheney & Company was the leading billiard ball manufacturer in the country. (Photograph courtesy of Harwood Comstock.)

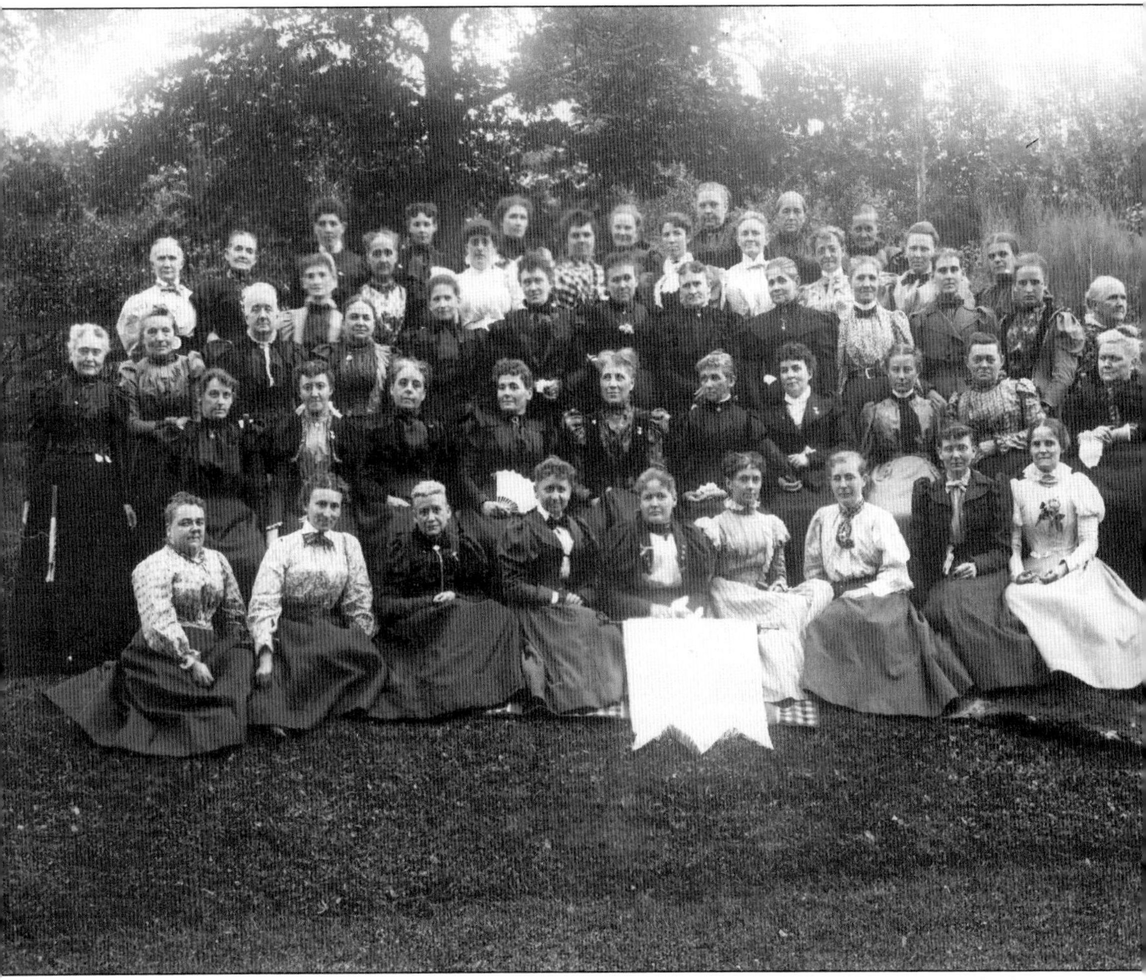

The Resolute Circle King's Daughters, 1889. The King's Daughters Society had its own hall on North Main Street and provided harvest suppers and entertainment for the community. Members included Laurel Behrens, Lydia French, Phoebe Reed, and Emeline Norris. Dues were 2¢ a month. The motto of the society was "Be ye kind one to another, tender hearted, forgiving one another, even as God for Christ's sake has forgiven you." The group set up an endowment of a free bed for the use of the King's Daughters in the New York Infirmary for Women and Children. Aid was given to the Christian Herald Fresh Air Fund for an outing for children in the slums. The Essex branch of the King's Daughters was housed in the current Essex Art Association building. This organization had purchased the building from the town, it having been the Point School from 1845 to 1911. (Photograph courtesy of Essex Historical Society.)

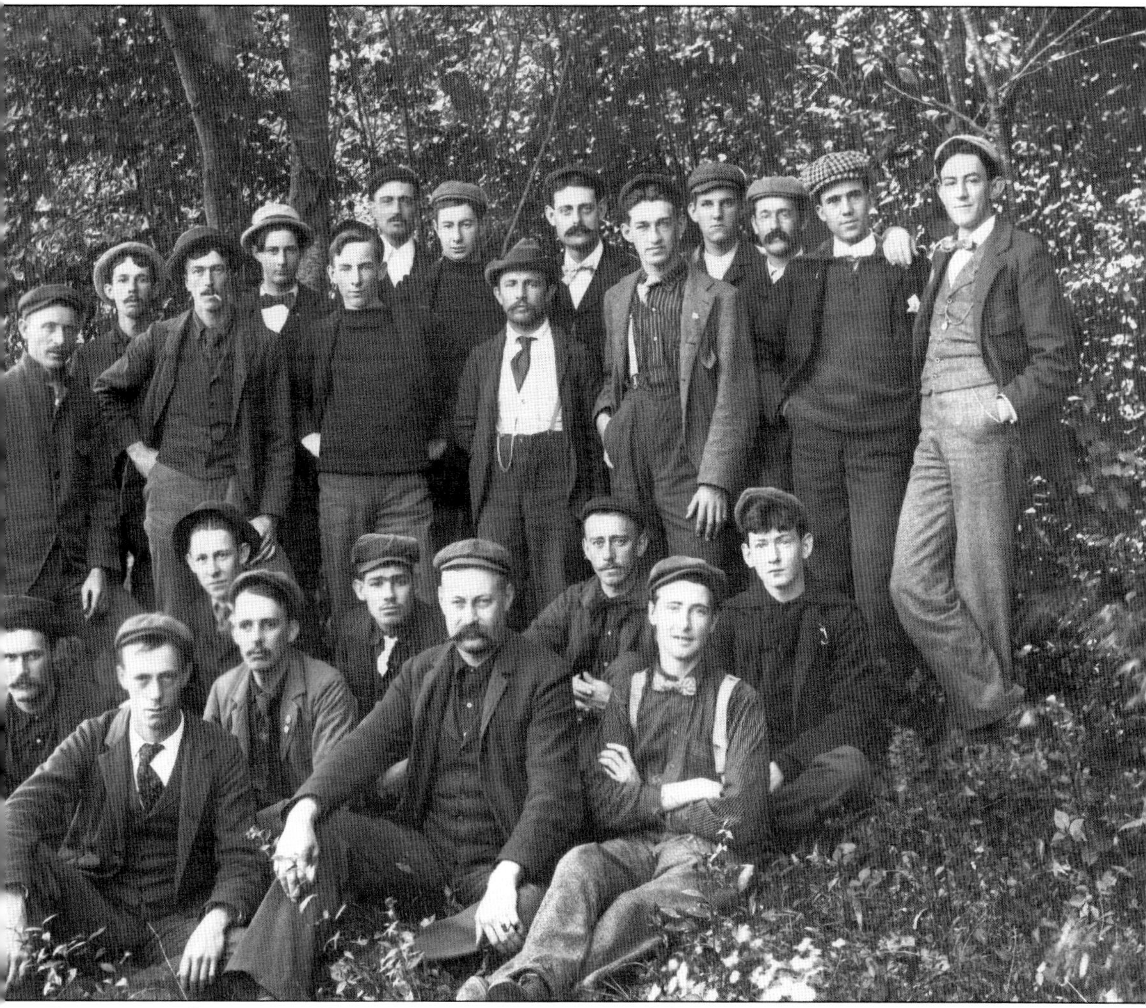

COMSTOCK, CHENEY & COMPANY WORKERS. Many of the 23 people in this picture were immigrants. Beginning in 1870, European immigrants from Sweden, Germany, Italy, and Poland began to take their places alongside the native Yankees. Between 1880 and 1924, some 135 houses were built to accommodate new workers. The houses had small lots, from one-half to two acres. The rent was reasonable ($9 to $12 per month during the 1930s), and employees could cut wood for fuel on company land at $1 per cord. (Photograph courtesy of Connecticut River Museum.)

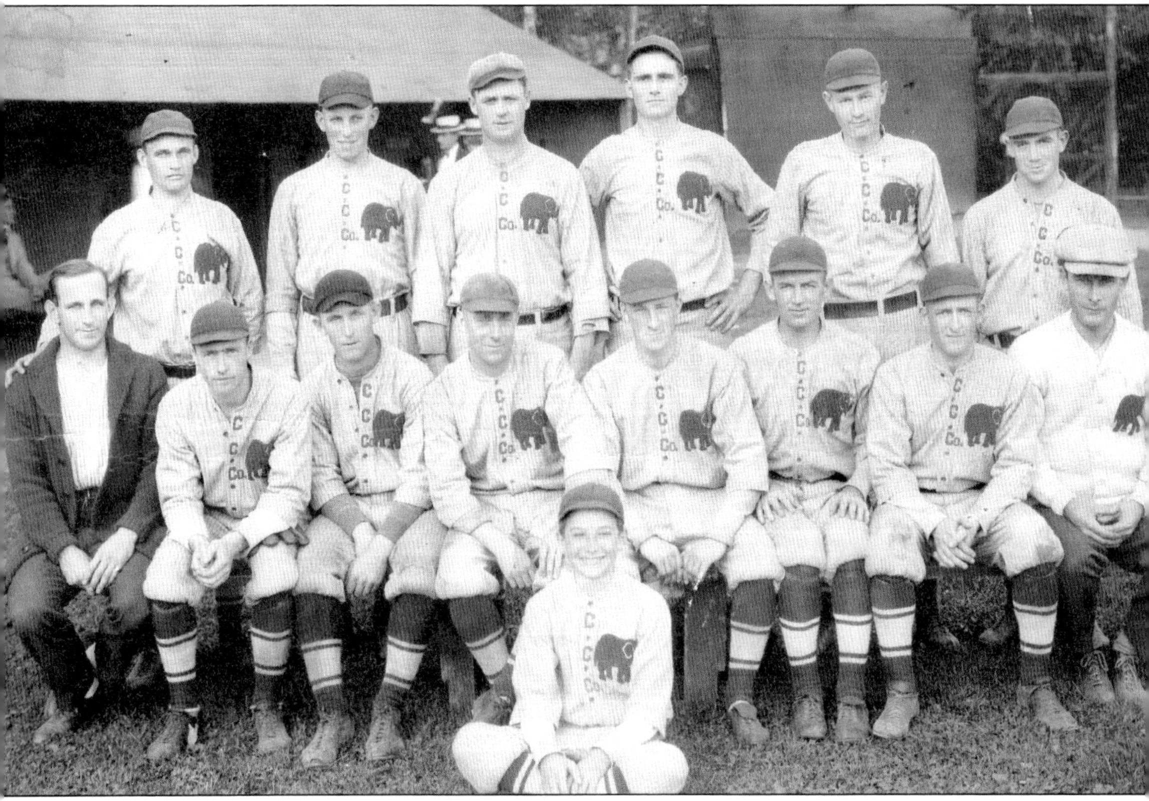

THE COMSTOCK, CHENEY & COMPANY BASEBALL TEAM. During the years when Comstock, Cheney & Company dominated Essex and owned most of the village of Ivoryton, the officers of the company wished to do something more to raise the morale of its employees and promote a spirit of pride in their work and their town. Edward M. Hilley, an employee of the company, advanced the idea of making a baseball diamond in the woods south of the company. Work on the field began in 1913. The park was carved out of Mares Hill, the brook was moved back 30 feet, and drains were laid under the entire field. When completed, the field was considered one of the best in the state. Hilley was turned loose with a checkbook to get together the best ball players that could be found. The men were given jobs in the factory, but it was clear their tenure depended on what they did on the field. It took three years for Hilley to build a team. The opening game was played in July 1916 and was a doubleheader with the West Ends of New Haven. Oscar Lynn (page 57) played first base. The Comstock nine, under the management of Hilley, took the state title in 1917, and often as many as 1,500 fans would come to see the games. The field was later given to the town, and Little League is played there today. (Photograph courtesy of Ivoryton Library.)

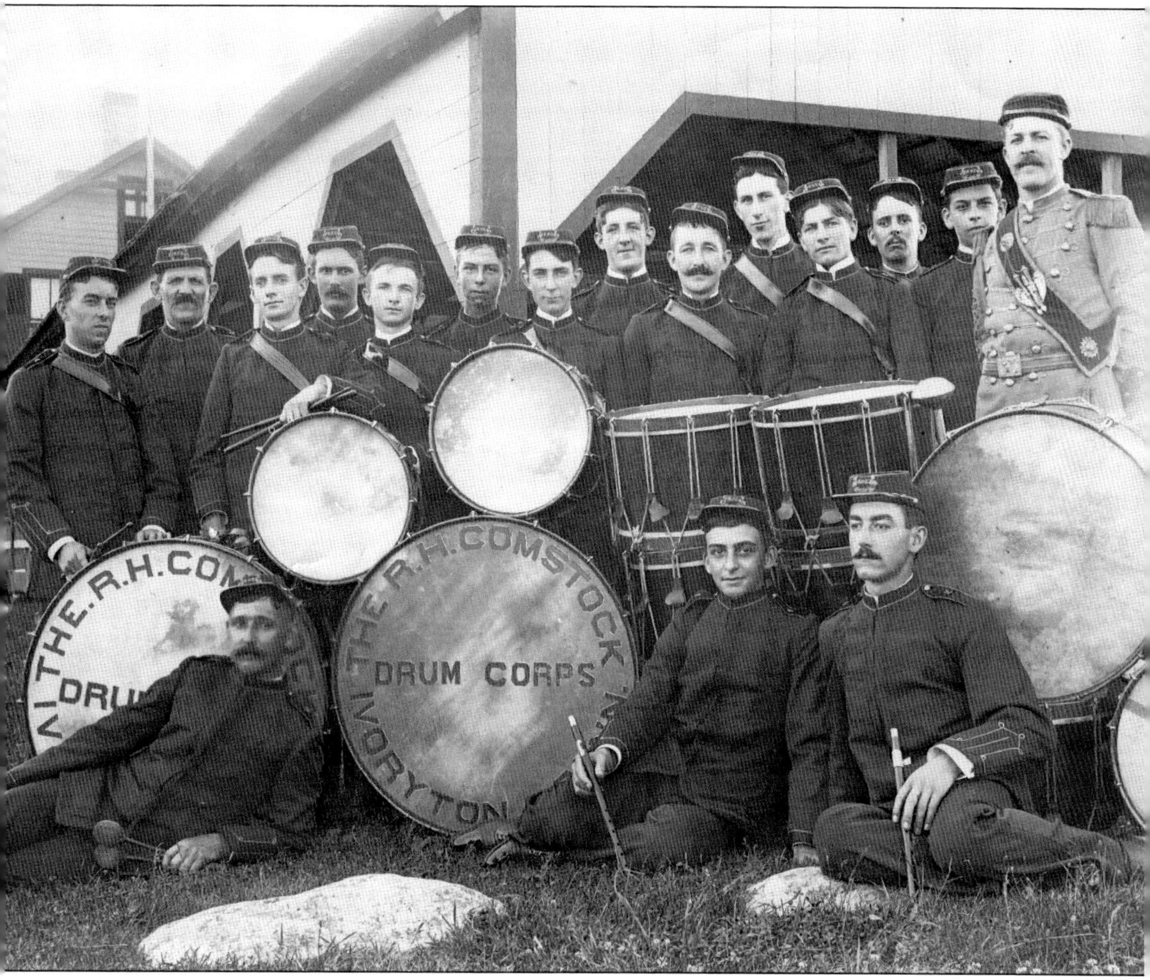

THE R.H. COMSTOCK DRUM CORPS. Founded by R.H. Comstock in 1888, the drum corps was nicknamed "Little Thunder" because, although it had few members, it had a mighty volume. A committee of five men, H.W. Webber, Joseph B. Clapp, H.N. Booma, Ezra Spencer, and John A. Wright, were appointed to choose a name and were given five minutes in which to do so. At the end of that time, they asked for an extension, proposing the name R.H. Comstock Drum Corps at the next meeting. The corps was so competitive that new members had to learn 23 musical pieces in order to join. The corps had an enviable reputation and was invited to take part in nearly all events of the neighboring towns. R.H. Comstock erected a small building called the Drum Corps House, which stood in the woods on what is now Falls River Drive so that practice sessions would not disturb village residents. There was a bandstand for concerts on the land that is now the Congregational church parking lot. (Photograph courtesy of Essex Historical Society.)

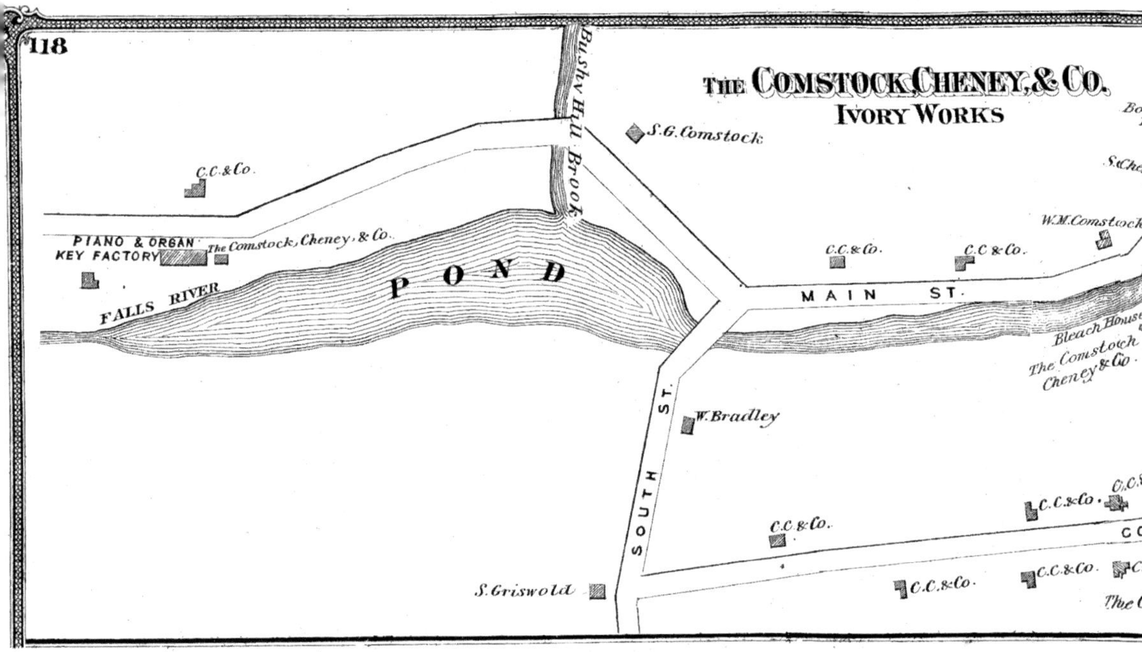

AN 1874 MAP OF WEST CENTRE BROOK. This map clearly shows how Comstock, Cheney & Company owned most of the property here. The skating pond was located behind the library

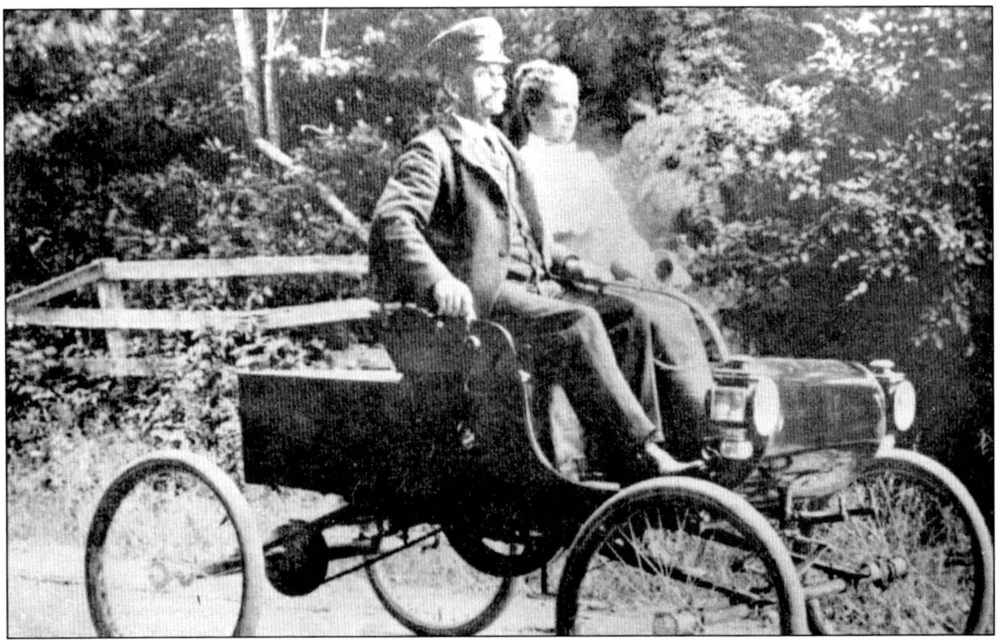

N.D. MILLER IN HIS NEW CAR, PHOTOGRAPH C. 1901. Nathaniel D. Miller is shown in his 1901 Oldsmobile, purchased from Behrens & Bushnell Company of Ivoryton. Miller, an executive of Comstock, Cheney & Company, lived immediately west of S.M. Comstock on executive row. This was the first automobile sold by Behrens & Bushnell. (Photograph courtesy of Ivoryton Library.)

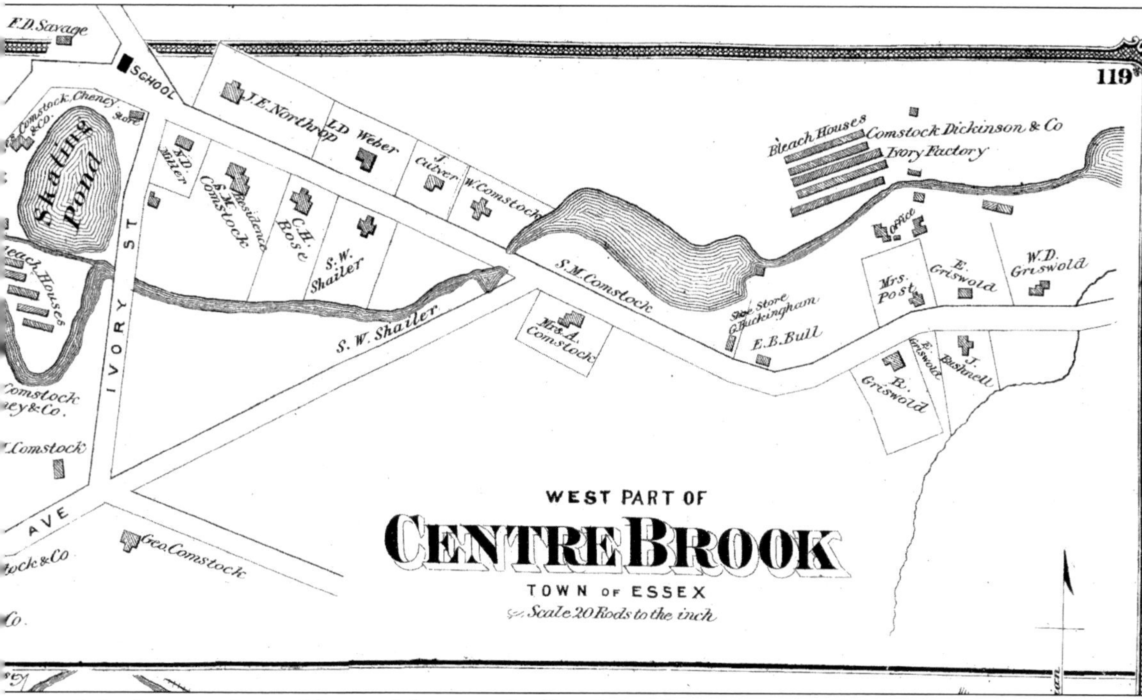

and the Ivoryton Store. The road that is today East Main Street was executive row, where the Northrop, Webber, Culver, Miller, Comstock, Rose, and Shailer houses stood.

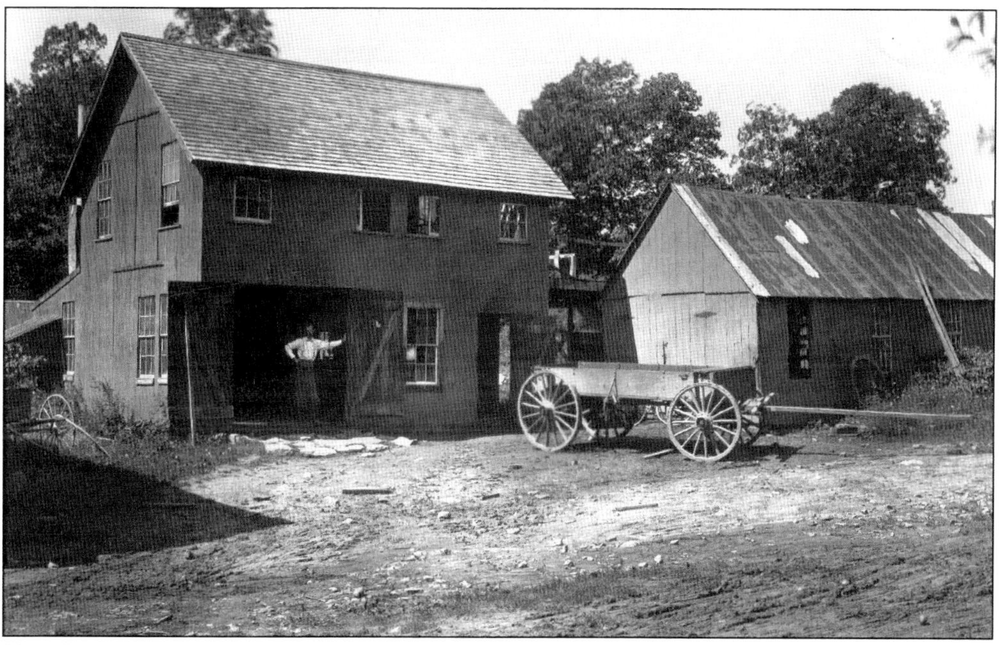

THE CHAPMAN BROTHERS BLACKSMITH SHOP, SUMMIT STREET. By the time this photograph was taken, retail business in the three villages was growing. The Chapman brothers shoed horses and repaired wagons. Soon, the old-fashioned blacksmith was replaced by the automobile mechanic. Today, the firehouse is located here. (Photograph courtesy of Essex Historical Society.)

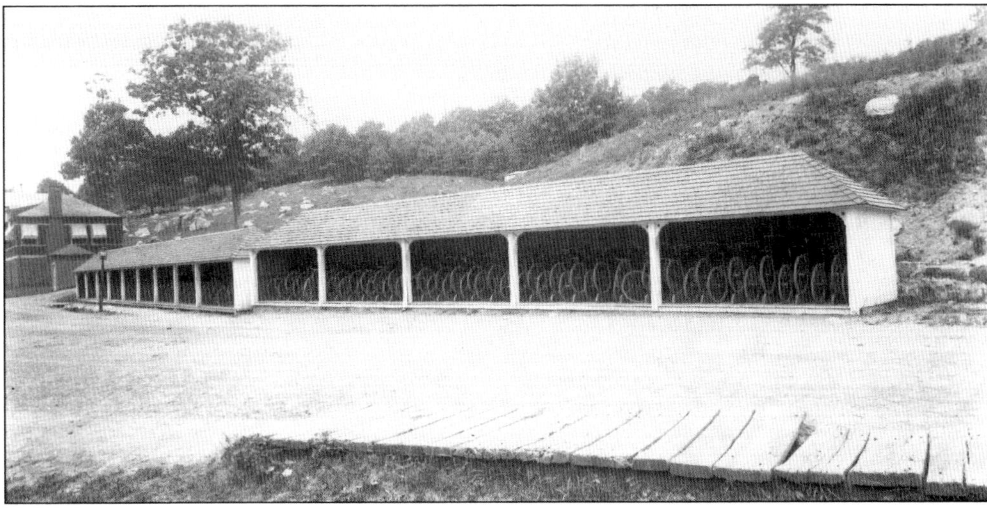

TWO BICYCLE SHEDS AND THE COMPANY OFFICE. Bicycles were the main form of transportation to work, other than walking. The large number of bicycles in the two sheds and the wooden sidewalk in front of it are indicative of these two modes of transportation. On the left is the office of Comstock, Cheney & Company. It contained a fireproof vault, which held all the records of the company. Peter H. Comstock, great grandson of S.M. Comstock and president of the company for 25 years, began the task of collecting photographs and machinery for a company museum in the early 1950s. It was completed in 1977 and was open until 1988 when, lacking a new home for the collection, all records and many materials were turned over to the Smithsonian Museum. (Photograph courtesy of Essex Historical Society.)

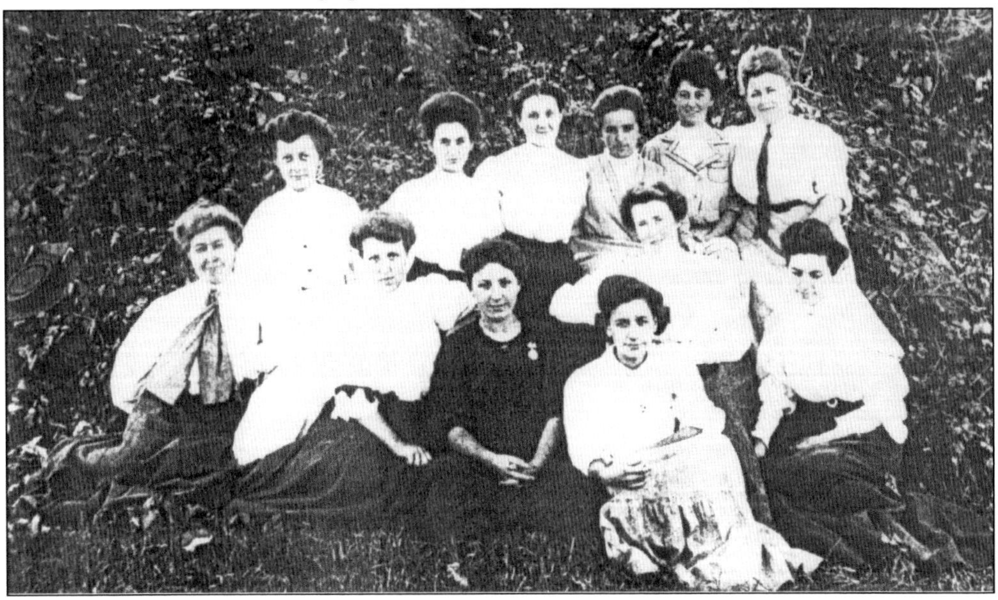

COMSTOCK, CHENEY & COMPANY MATCHING DEPARTMENT EMPLOYEES, PHOTOGRAPH C. 1905. This photograph shows the women employed at Comstock, Cheney & Company to inspect, sort, and match the "heads and tails." They are, from left to right, as follows: (front row) Elizabeth Dahlstrom, Freda Sweibel, Emma Sweibel, Tessa Canassa, Lottie Peck, and Beda Dahlstrom; (back row) Alfreda Palm, Kata Canessa, Mrs. Ray Readon, Sara Haskell, Margaret Cavanaugh, and Beda Anderson. (Photograph courtesy of Connecticut River Museum.)

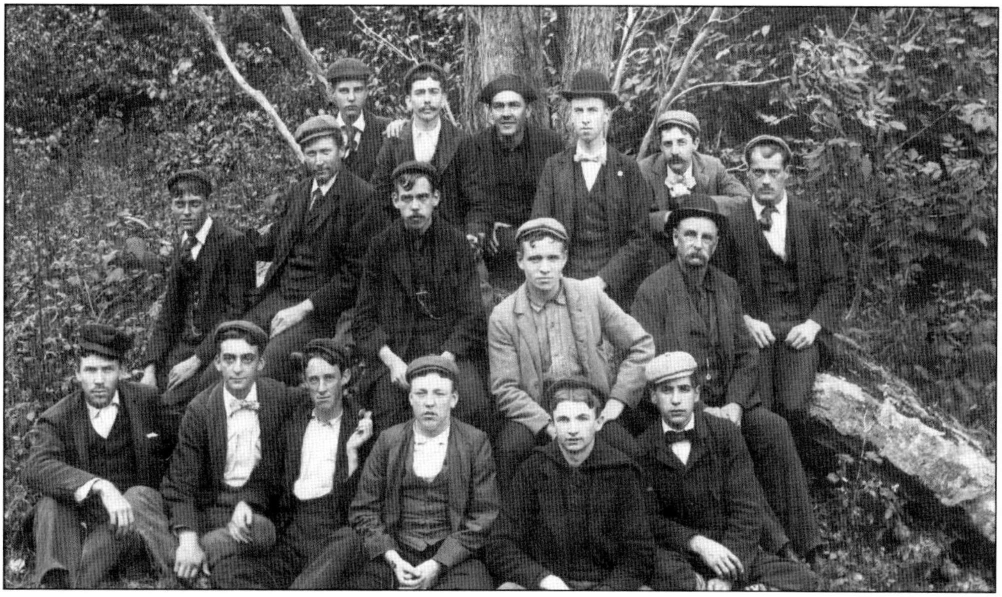

COMSTOCK, CHENEY & COMPANY WORKERS. Charlie Sizer, shown in the center of this early 1900s photograph, was the foreman of a group of men at the ivory factory. Many pictures were taken of groups of workers around the beginning of the 20th century. This may have been an attempt by the factory to maintain company spirit. (Photograph courtesy of Essex Historical Society.)

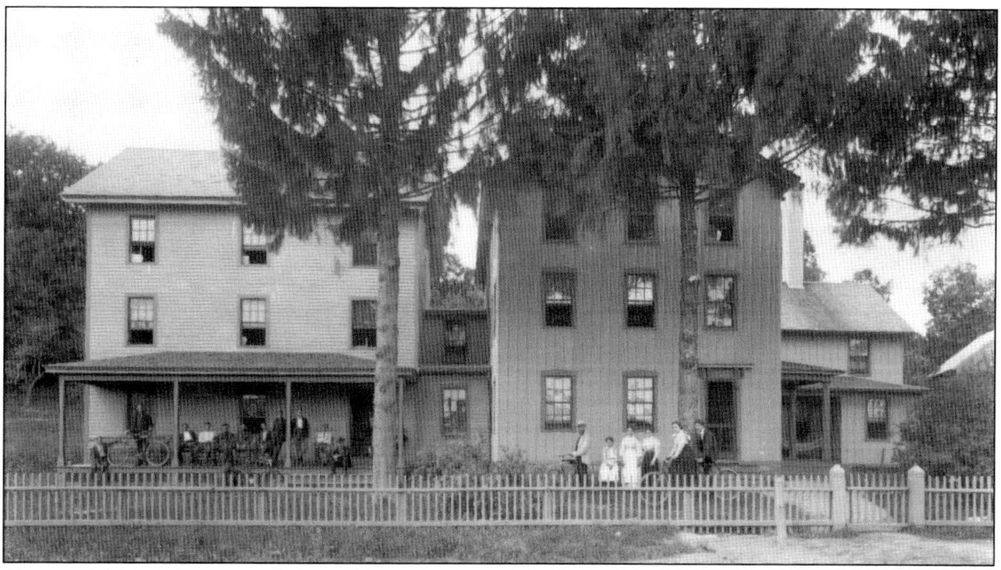

THE C. 1890S HOTEL DE IVORY BOARDINGHOUSE, MAIN STREET. The need to attract workers prompted the building of boardinghouses, tenement houses, and single-family houses. This boardinghouse was built across the street from the Ivory Shop and housed male workers and traveling salesmen. At the beginning of the 20th century, the cost of a room was $3.50 per week for company workers. The larger part of the building was moved to Ivoryton from Winthrop when the Denison Ladies Institute closed. Later the Ivoryton Inn, it now has 30 guest rooms and a ballroom, which can accommodate 120, a reminder of its more glorious days. (Photograph courtesy of Essex Historical Society.)

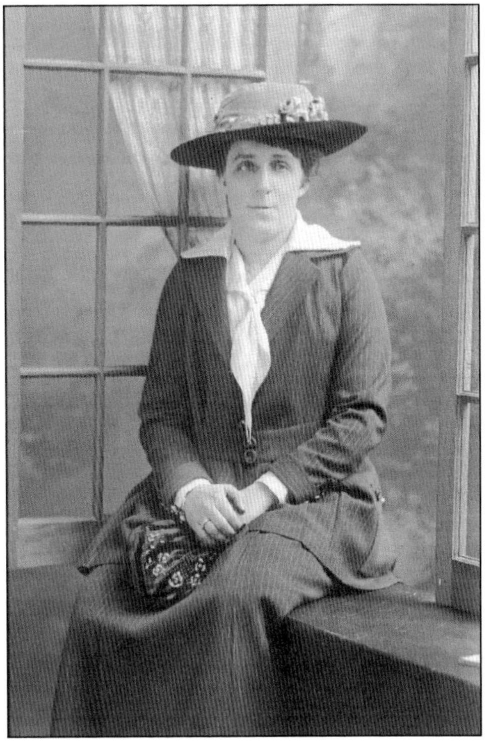

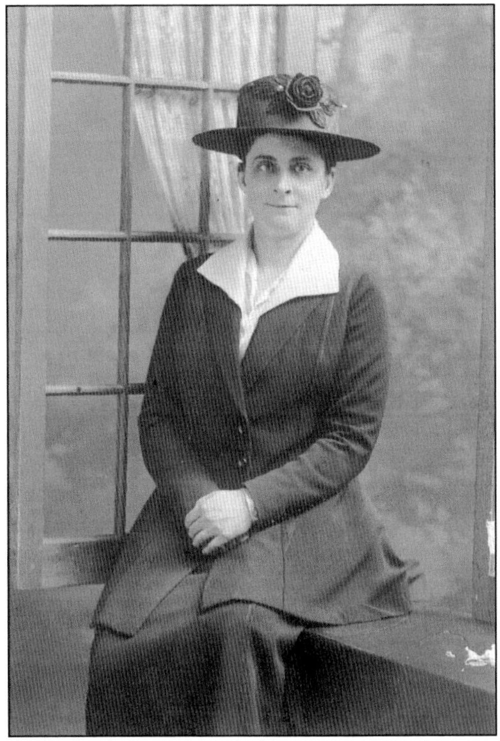

THE COMSTOCK GRANDDAUGHTERS AND THEIR HOME. Bessie Comstock (left) and Laura Comstock were granddaughters of Samuel Merritt Comstock, who built the Comstock house (below) for his son, who was their father, George Hovey Comstock. They lived in the house together all their lives. From the mid-1920s until the late 1950s, Bessie and Laura Comstock served as officers—president and treasurer, respectively—of the Ivoryton Library Association, built partly with Comstock, Cheney & Company funds. They are fondly remembered as the "heart" of the library. Their photographs, taken on the boardwalk in Atlantic City, New Jersey, were a gift to the library from Peter H. Comstock. (Photograph courtesy of the Robin family.)

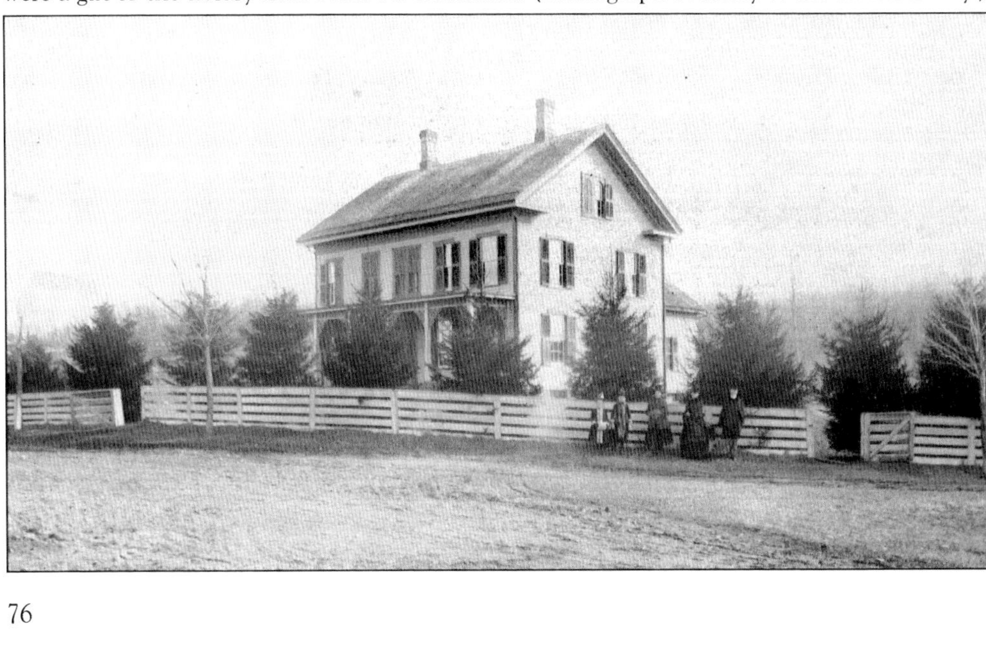

Five

A Theater for All Seasons

In their desire to provide for the needs of their employees, Comstock, Cheney & Company built Comstock Cheney Hall in 1910–1911. Dances, whist parties, local school graduations, and performances by touring vaudeville acts were brought to the hall to enrich the lives of the workers and their families. Beginning in 1915, silent movies were shown.

In 1930, Milton Stiefel, an actor and director looking for a place to escape the heat of the summer in New York City, came upon Comstock Cheney Hall. Stiefel fell back on a group of his thespian friends who helped him explore the novelty of summer theater. He rented the hall from Comstock, Cheney & Company and put together a summer season beginning with the play *Broken Dishes*, which had just launched Bette Davis's career.

By the end of the first summer, Stiefel broke even financially and decided to pursue the summer theater idea. Efforts to put Ivoryton on the map and draw audiences were successful and, in 1938, Stiefel bought the hall from Comstock, Cheney & Company and renamed it the Ivoryton Playhouse, home to his New York Players. Comstock, Cheney & Company limited what could be sold by Stiefel in the Ivoryton Playhouse. For 10 years, Stiefel could sell nothing that the Ivoryton Store sold, nor set up either a dry goods store or a barbershop. This was a tactic to prevent competition with Comstock, Cheney & Company holdings. The company was very gradually giving up control of the town. By 1942, the Ivoryton Playhouse had gained such prestige that invitations to actors to work there were highly prized.

World War II closed the Ivoryton Playhouse temporarily. When it reopened, the theater's productions changed from self-produced by a resident company to summer stock packages that toured the nation with stars as headliners. A star would tour with summer stock in a show that traveled throughout the Middle Atlantic and New England states during the summer vacation season. Ethel Waters, Ruby Keeler, Julie Harris, Marlon Brando, Michael Rennie, and Ginger Rogers were among the stars who performed in Ivoryton. Stiefel ran the Ivoryton Playhouse successfully until his retirement in 1976, at which time he sold the theater.

Running a summer theater in the 1970s proved to be a precarious business; thus, the Ivoryton Playhouse went dark again. Residents, concerned about the continued existence of what was considered a community treasure, raised the money to establish the Ivoryton Playhouse Foundation in 1978. The foundation bought the building in 1979. Audiences are again entertained in the summer by a resident company, the River Rep, and enjoy a wide variety of cultural programming year-round.

Among the stars that launched their careers at the Ivoryton Playhouse are Katharine Hepburn, Penny Singleton, Celeste Holm, Cornell Wilde, Cliff Robertson, and Buddy Ebsen. Young stars today, such as Gretchen Moll and Todd Ellison can claim the Ivoryton Playhouse as their point of departure.

—Ann Thompson

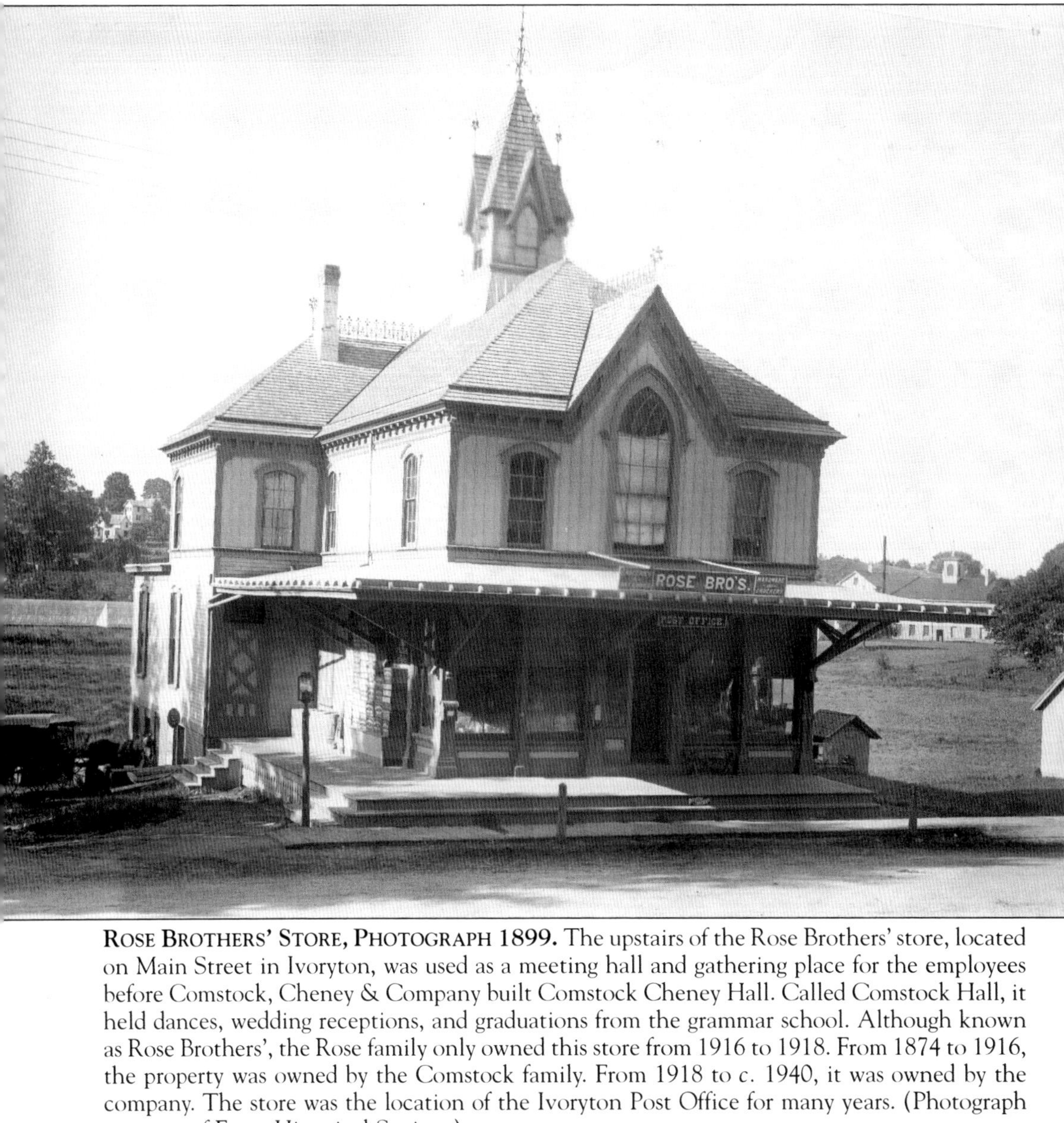

ROSE BROTHERS' STORE, PHOTOGRAPH 1899. The upstairs of the Rose Brothers' store, located on Main Street in Ivoryton, was used as a meeting hall and gathering place for the employees before Comstock, Cheney & Company built Comstock Cheney Hall. Called Comstock Hall, it held dances, wedding receptions, and graduations from the grammar school. Although known as Rose Brothers', the Rose family only owned this store from 1916 to 1918. From 1874 to 1916, the property was owned by the Comstock family. From 1918 to c. 1940, it was owned by the company. The store was the location of the Ivoryton Post Office for many years. (Photograph courtesy of Essex Historical Society.)

THE FIRST MASQUERADE RECEPTION, 1905. This event was held on December 4, 1905, in Comstock Hall, above Rose Brothers' store. (Photograph courtesy of Merritt M. Comstock.)

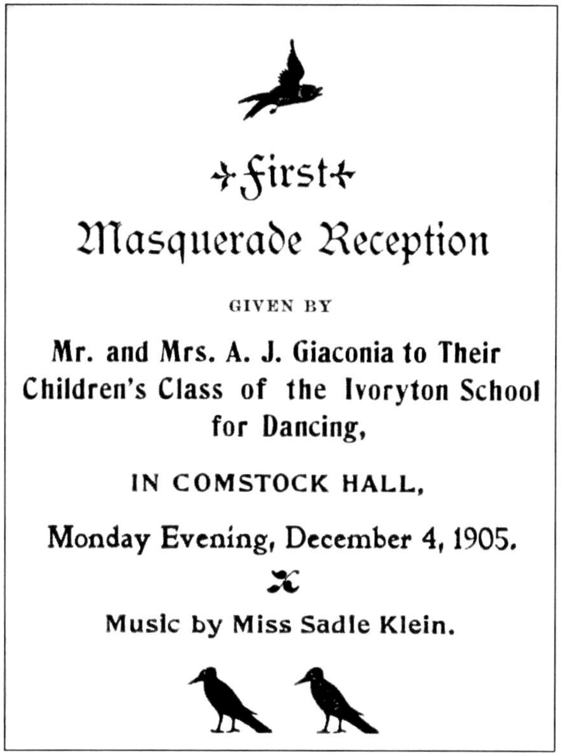
First

Masquerade Reception

GIVEN BY

Mr. and Mrs. A. J. Giaconia to Their Children's Class of the Ivoryton School for Dancing,

IN COMSTOCK HALL,

Monday Evening, December 4, 1905.

Music by Miss Sadie Klein.

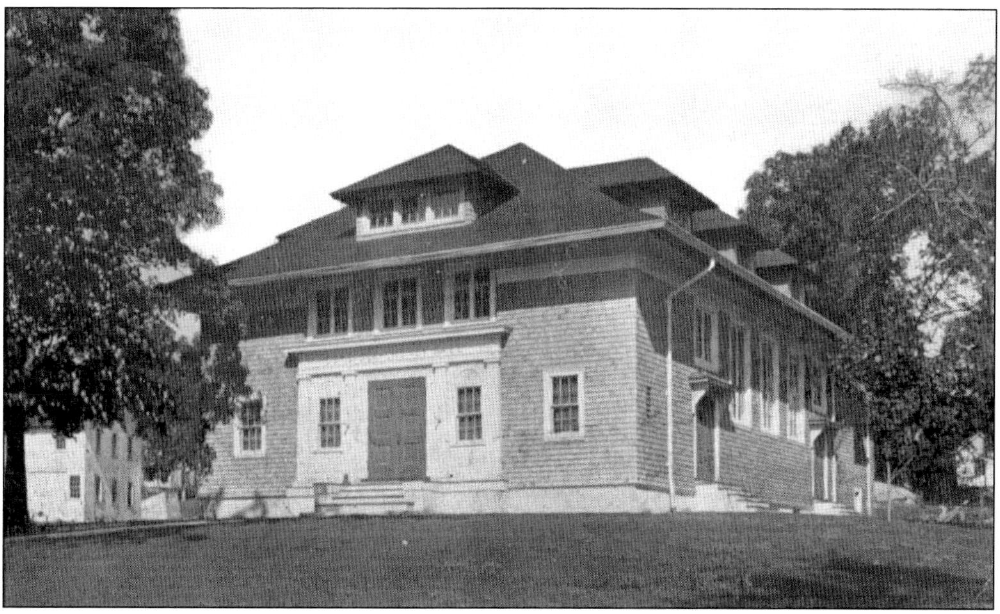

THE COMSTOCK CHENEY HALL. This building was designed to serve the employees of Comstock, Cheney & Company and did so for 20 years. Later, it became the Ivoryton Playhouse and subsequently was named a national historic site. The committee that chose the site and design for the Ivoryton Playhouse included R.H. Comstock, his brother A.W. Comstock, and Wooster Webber, the treasurer of the company. (Photograph courtesy of Ivoryton Library.)

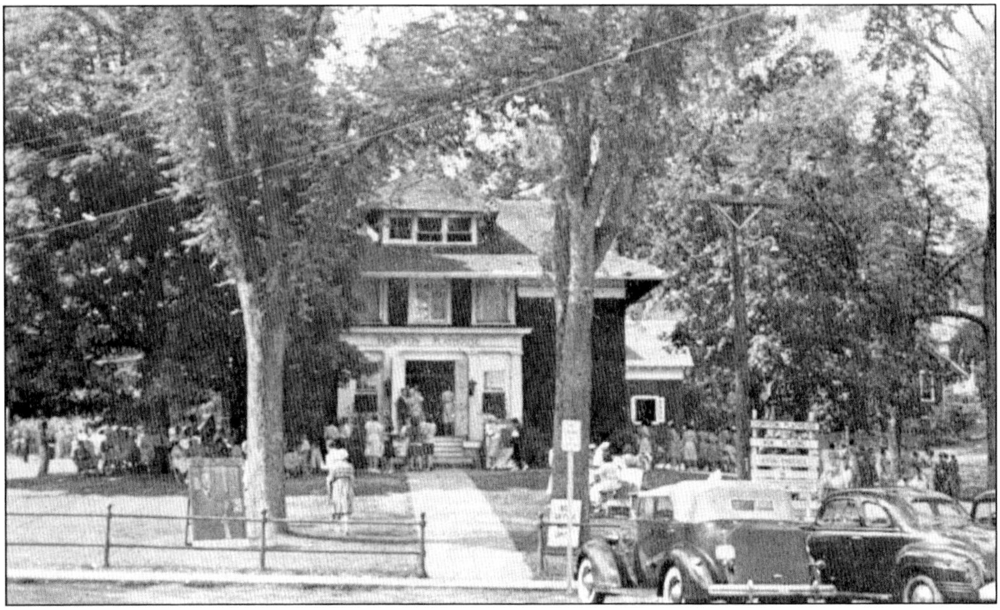

Milton Stiefel's Ivoryton Playhouse. Milton Stiefel literally put Ivoryton "on the map." When he first opened the Ivoryton Playhouse in 1930, the village of Ivoryton was not included on many maps. This proved to be a critical hindrance to ticket sales. With his usual gusto and confidence, Stiefel convinced the AAA' s map department to begin putting Ivoryton on all its new maps. (Photograph courtesy of Ivoryton Library.)

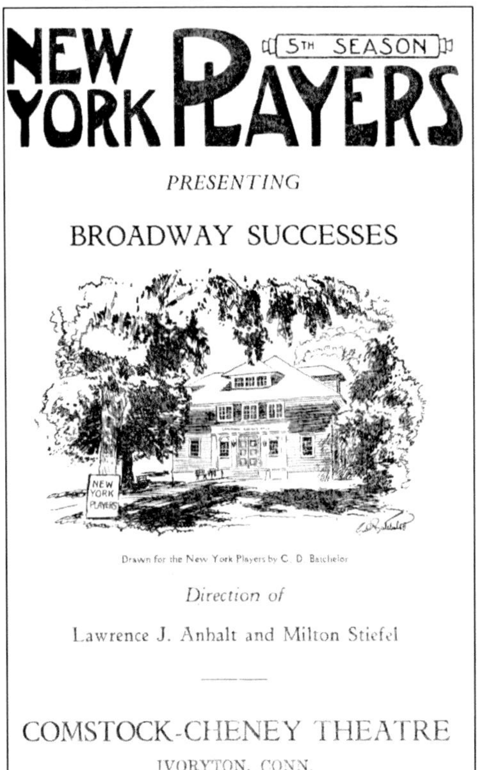

A Playbill Cover, New York Players, Fifth Season, 1934. Milton Stiefel directed and produced many of the Broadway shows that he brought to Ivoryton in the years that he ran the theater, from 1930 until 1976, and was active in an advisory capacity until his death in 1983. Most of the audience came from Essex and surrounding towns. In order to bolster ticket sales, Stiefel put his actors in open-car parades with banners urging crowds to come to the shows. The actors handed out maps with directions to the theater. The Ivoryton Playhouse is the oldest professional self-supporting summer theater in the United States.

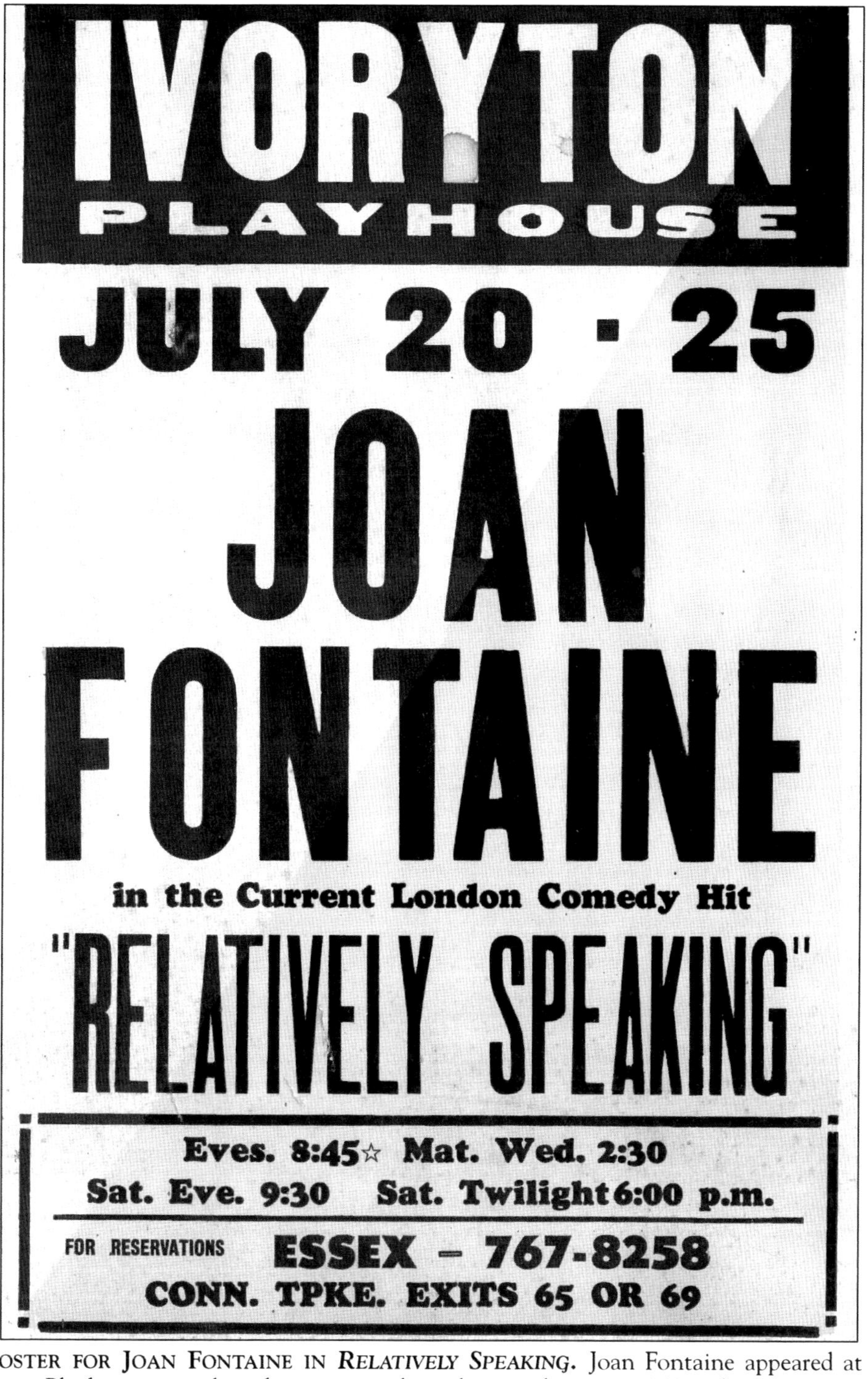

A POSTER FOR JOAN FONTAINE IN *RELATIVELY SPEAKING*. Joan Fontaine appeared at the Ivoryton Playhouse in packaged summer stock productions between 1960 and 1972. Among the plays she did in Ivoryton were *The Spider's Web*, *Private Lives*, and *Dial M for Murder*. Packaged shows toured the East and were guaranteed to bring in audiences because of the celebrity name attached to them. (Photograph courtesy of Ivoryton Library.)

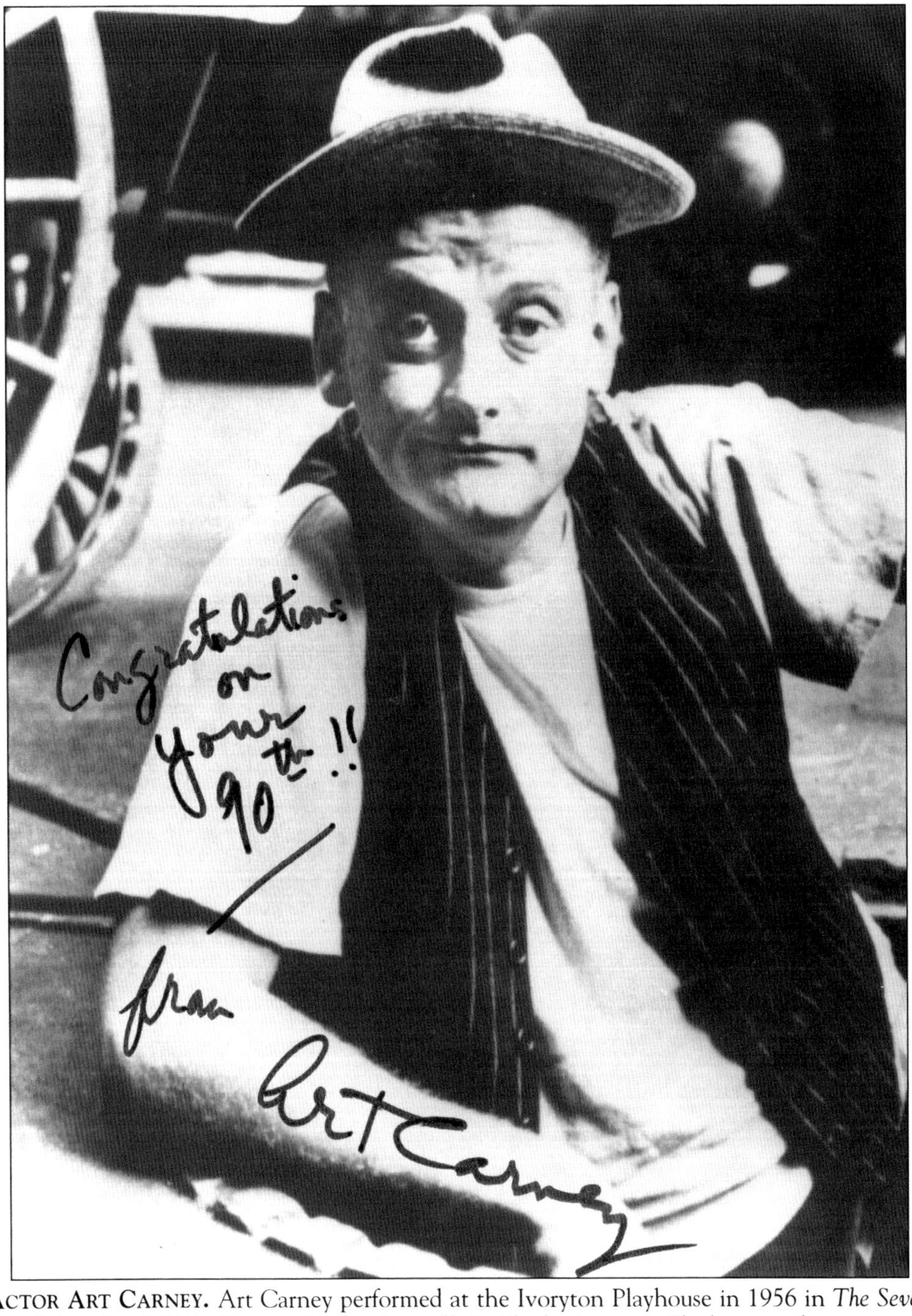

Actor Art Carney. Art Carney performed at the Ivoryton Playhouse in 1956 in *The Seven Year Itch* and in 1957 in *Harvey*. Lining the walls inside the Ivoryton Playhouse today are nearly 100 photographs of actors who trod the boards in the theater's heyday with Milton Stiefel. Actors frequently appeared in more than one play per season here; many returned to appear in plays over the years. Celeste Holm got her start at the Ivoryton Playhouse in 1939 in *The Women* and returned numerous times. Her final appearance at the Ivoryton Playhouse occurred 33 years later in *Butterflies Are Free*. (Photograph courtesy of Ivoryton Playhouse.)

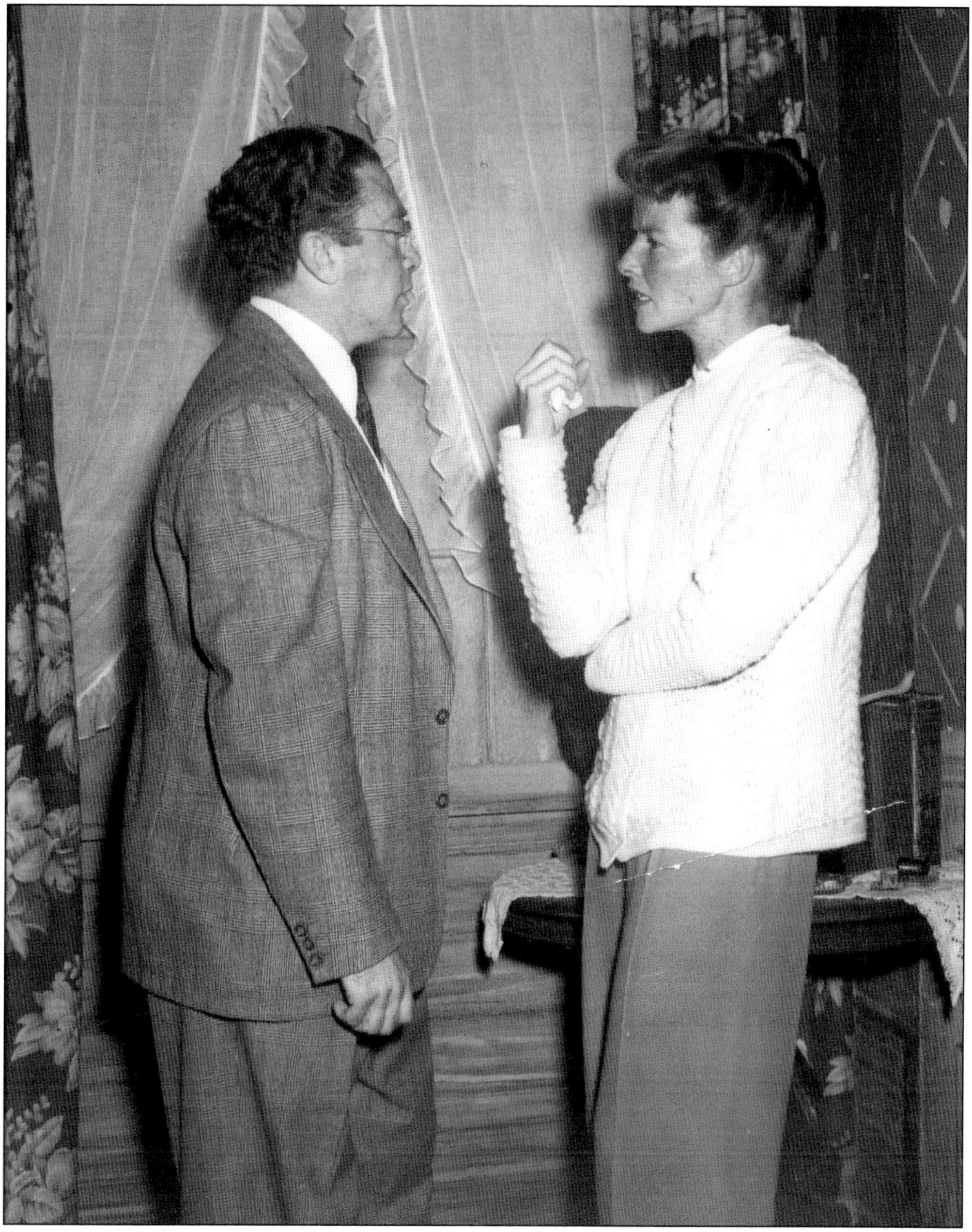

MILTON STIEFEL AND KATHARINE HEPBURN. Legend has it that Katharine Hepburn pestered Milton Stiefel into giving her a chance to act in his Ivoryton productions. Stiefel thought there was something special about the freckled girl, and so he hired her for the summer of 1931. Ticket sales rose as she and her family were from Hartford and had many friends who were curious to see her on stage. She appeared in seven plays that season, including *Just Married*, *The Cat and the Canary*, and *Let Us Be Gay*. She helped increase ticket sales in the first crucial years and, 50 years later, she joined in the efforts to raise funds for renovating the theater. (Photograph courtesy of Ivoryton Playhouse.)

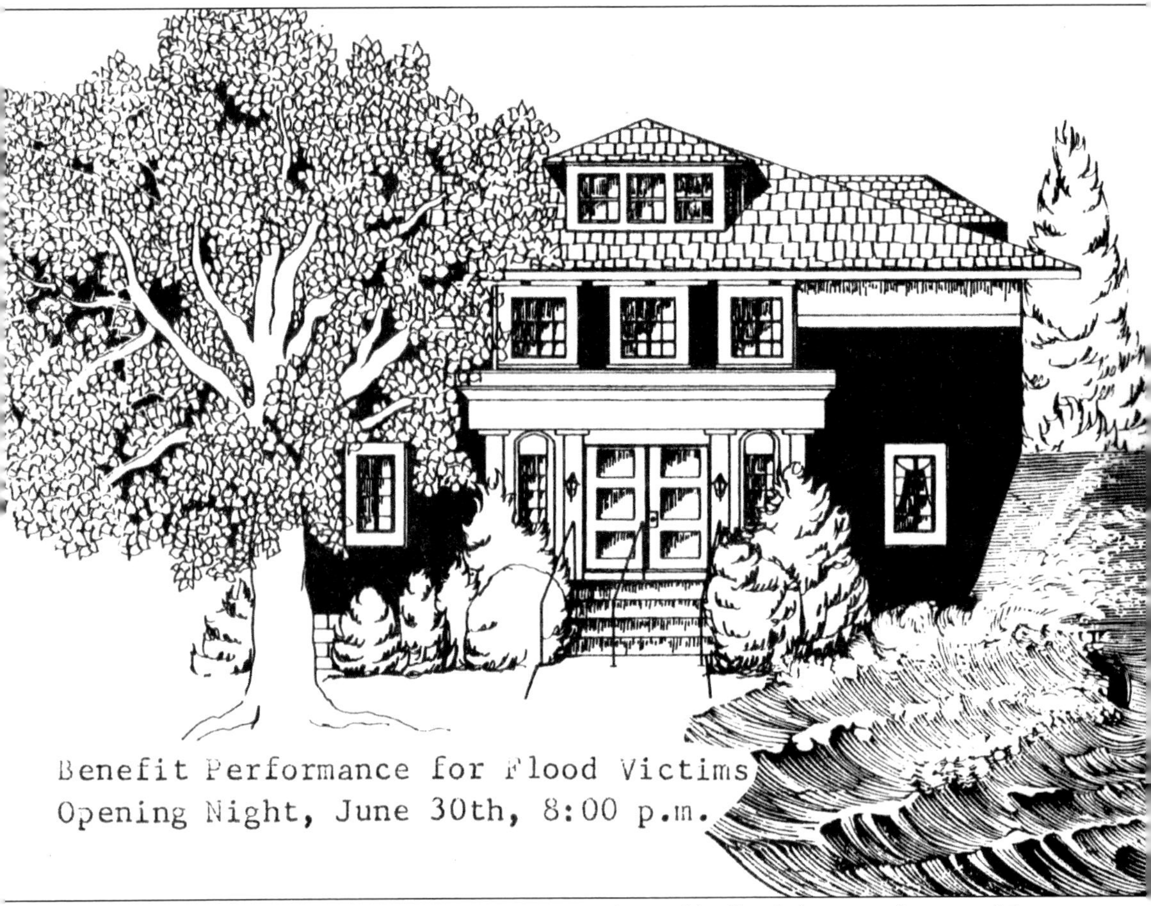

A PLAYBILL, IVORYTON PLAYHOUSE, 1982. A terrible flood devastated parts of Ivoryton in the spring of 1982. This playbill has floodwaters illustrated on its cover and advertises a benefit performance for local flood victims. Ticket sales floundered that year, partly due to the misconception that the theater had been wiped out by the flood. In fact, the Ivoryton Playhouse remained unharmed by the flood due to its setting on a knoll above Main Street. Attempts to draw in bigger audiences after the flood included a last minute decision to bring in the show *Oh! Calcutta!* Publicity and controversy ensued because of the local reaction to nudity in the play.

Six

POTAPOUG POINT, CENTRE SAYBROOKE, AND OYSTER RIVER QUARTER

Three very distinct regions, once called Potapoug Point (Essex village), Centre Saybrooke (Centerbrook), and a portion of Oyster River Quarter (Ivoryton), now form a single town rich in historic beginnings. Essex has become a town of 6,500 residents (2000 census) with three separate post offices (and zip codes), three Congregational churches, two Episcopal churches, and two separate libraries. For historical reasons, the three villages of Essex were distinctly different until the end of World War II. Since 1950, Essex has continued to homogenize, becoming one town rather than three separate entities.

The three Congregational churches were formed for very different reasons. The Centre Brooke (or mother) Church is the oldest, starting in 1722, and was instrumental in the formation of the town. The Essex Congregational Church followed, 130 years later, when 52 people withdrew from the mother church, in a form of rebellion. These people, mostly women, apparently felt that the Centre Brook Church was becoming more interested in making money than saving souls. It had become one of the largest holders of mortgages in town. These 52 parishioners left because of a desire for some old-time Puritan religion. The Ivoryton Congregational Church was formed for an entirely different reason. It was Samuel Comstock's vision to make Ivoryton village the factory and the factory Ivoryton village. This church, built shortly after his death, was on land he had owned and was under the initial direction of his daughter, Harriet. It was known as Comstock Chapel.

The post offices followed a different path. Centre Brooke was the original administrative and social center of Potapoug. With the growth of shipbuilding, this shifted to Essex village, which remained a retail center long after shipbuilding had passed. By the end of the 19th century, Ivoryton had become the economic center of town and, following Comstock's plan, it required its own post office. This situation of three postal services existed when the zip code system was inaugurated. No attempt at consolidation was made, and three zip codes were assigned, one for each village.

There were eight school districts by 1814 in Potapoug. By 1870, under new Connecticut laws regarding schools, a single school board was established in Essex to operate and centralize the school system. After a great deal of study, indecision, and inaction, Essex village eliminated three separate schools and finally built a new brick schoolhouse in 1912. This new building served to educate Essex village youngsters in grades one through eight until 1954. It is now a convalescent hospital, located behind the Catholic church. Centerbrook maintained its independence in this field, replacing its old wooden school building (now the Veterans Hall) with a brick building nearby on Main Street in 1925. This was demolished in 1954, when the centralization took place. The factory philosophy in Ivoryton came into the equation when a new school was needed in 1899, due to the population growth there. The factory did not want to lose control of the work place, socially or economically, and opposed any centralization efforts. As a result, a member of the Comstock family donated land for a new school and Comstock, Cheney & Company provided a majority of the funding for a beautiful new structure, built in

1900. It was located directly across the street from the Ivoryton Library and served Ivoryton until 1954. Why it took until 1954 to finally centralize Essex schools was a reflection of the personalities of the three villages.

The Ivoryton Library Association is the oldest in town. It was formed in 1871, and the library building was erected in 1888. The factory supplied encouragement and financing. The library has remained in the same building for 113 years. In 1889, the Essex Library began in Dr. Russell's home on Essex Square (demolished in 1925 when the Essex Square Theater was built.) In 1898, the library moved to its own building on South Main Street, financed by the estate of Capt. Joseph Tucker. E.E. Dickinson Jr. built a wing on the building in 1940 in honor of his deceased mother. The current library building, on West Avenue, was built in 1980.

The names and the spellings have changed over the course of years. Essex was once known as Potapoug, which has also been spelled Potapaug and Pettipaug. Centerbrook evolved from Centre Saybrooke, into Centre Brooke, Centre Brook, and the current Centerbrook. Ivoryton was once part of Oyster River Quarter and West Centre Brook. The names in this book are consistent with the spelling at the particular time in history.

—Don Malcarne

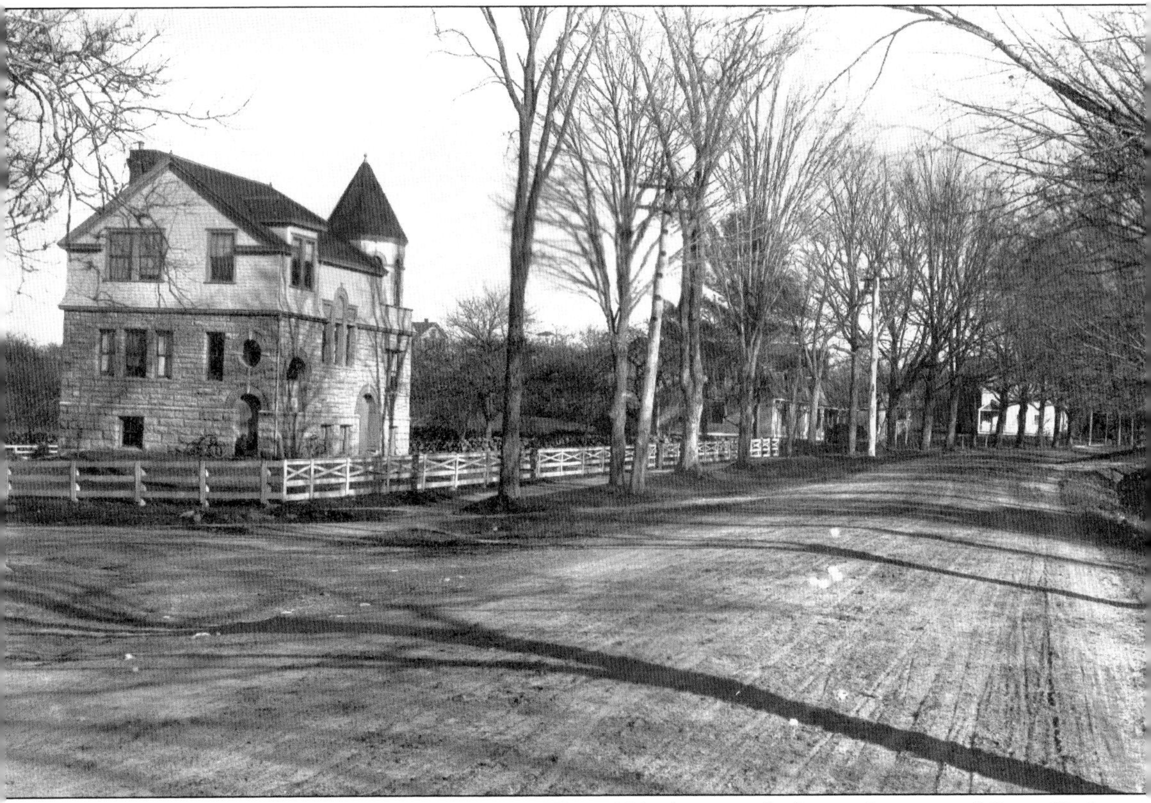

PRATT HIGH SCHOOL, WEST AVENUE. This 1900 photograph shows the original Pratt High School, built in 1894. It burned in 1912 and was rebuilt without the Victorian second floor. It was greatly enlarged in 1922. The funds for the original building came from the estate of Capt. Isaiah Pratt. Pratt willed that the school would be for children whose parents were members of the First Congregational Church of Essex. This was contested and, as a result, Pratt High School was a quasi-public-private school. (Photograph courtesy of Essex Historical Society.)

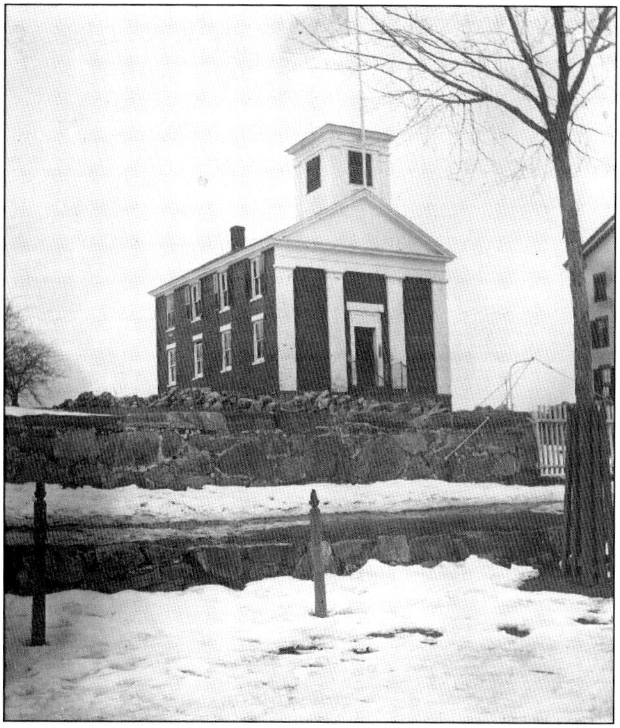

HILLS ACADEMY. Hills Academy, built in 1832 as a private school for grades five through nine, attracted students from many states. In 1849, Lucius Lyon, head of the school, built a seminary or boardinghouse next-door for these students. Hills Academy operated as a private school until the 1870s, and then it served as an adjunct to the nearby Point School. When Pratt High School suffered fire damage in 1912, Hills Academy served in its place for a short time. Today, Hills Academy is owned by the Essex Historical Society. (Photograph courtesy of Essex Historical Society.)

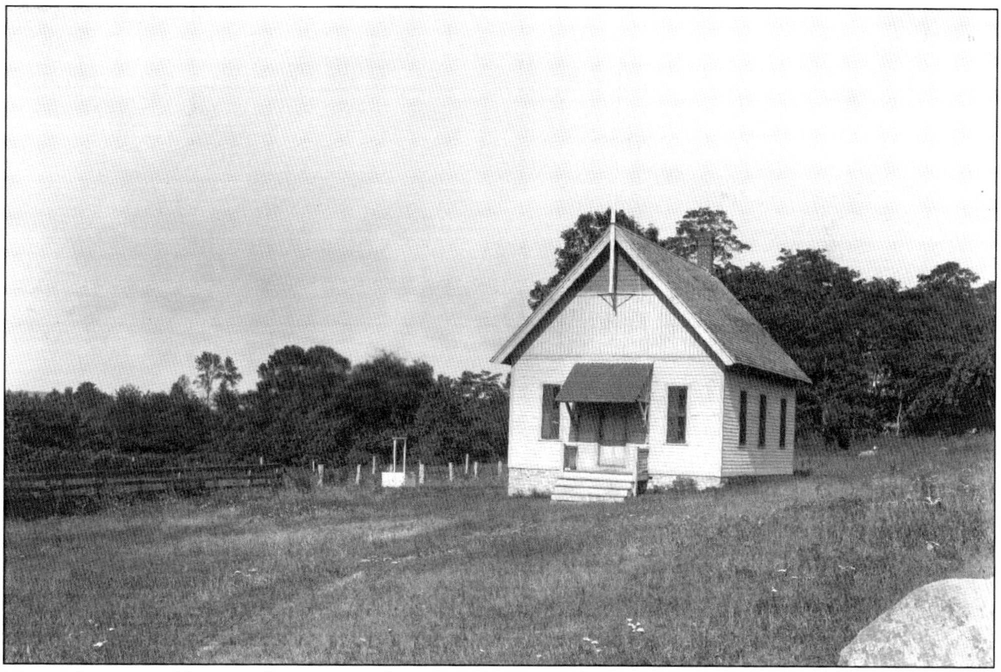

THE MEADOW WOODS SCHOOL. This is a photograph of the Meadow Woods Schoolhouse, just past the intersection of Dennison Road and North Main Street. The original Meadow Woods Schoolhouse was near the intersection of Book Hill and River Road on the east side. The building in the photograph was constructed in the 1880s. (Photograph courtesy of Essex Historical Society.)

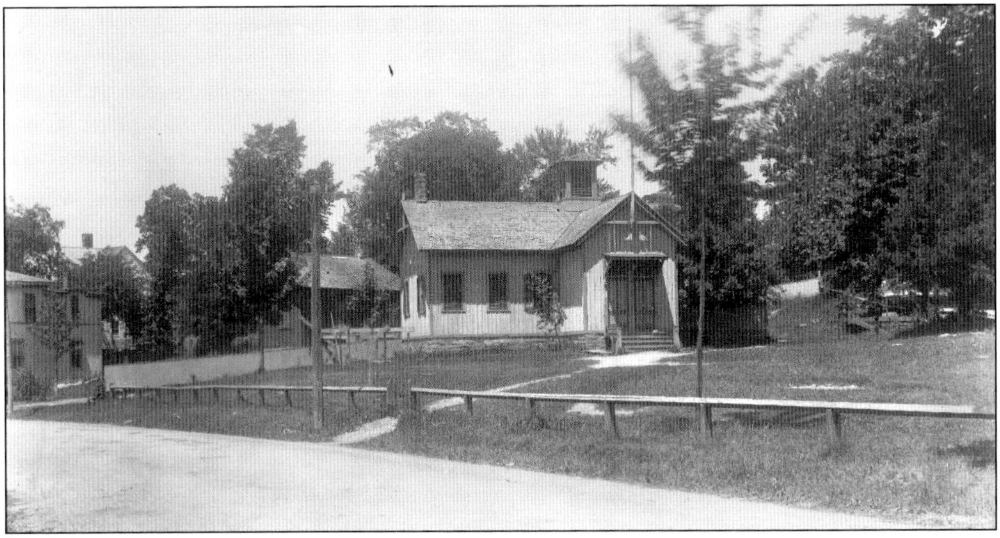

THE COMSTOCK DISTRICT SCHOOL. The old Ivoryton School was a relatively small and unobtrusive building, appearing to have been built in two sections. It operated in Ivoryton until the expanded workforce brought more children and a larger building was needed. The road to the ivory shop is on the left. In front of the school stood the scales used to weigh the ivory or loads of wood from Ivoryton. Ivoryton was beginning to emerge as an industrial force. (Photograph courtesy of Essex Historical Society.)

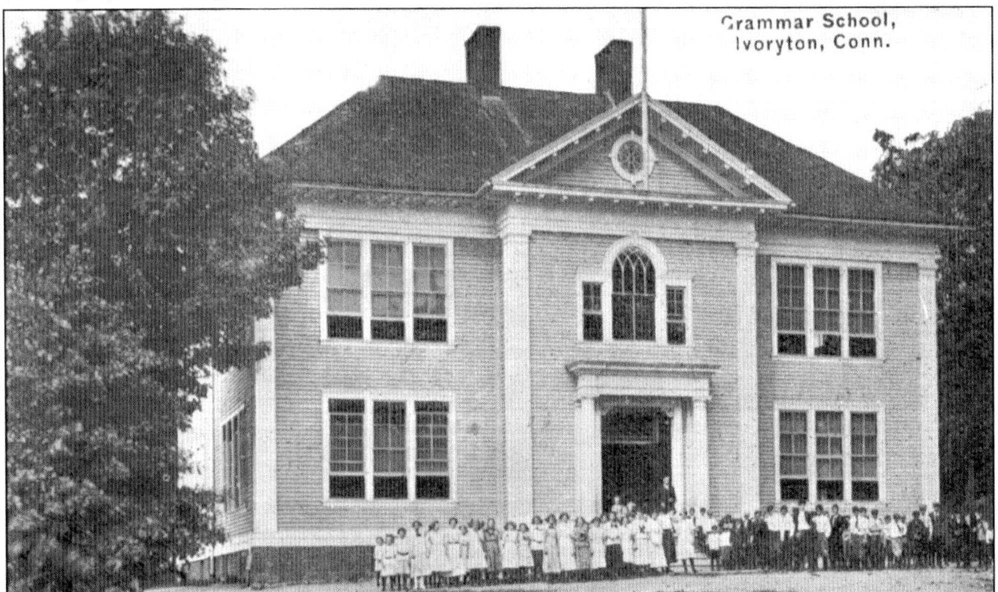

THE IVORYTON GRAMMAR SCHOOL. In 1899, Elizabeth Northrup, wife of the treasurer of Comstock, Cheney & Company and Samuel Merritt Comstock's daughter, donated the property for a new school. The Comstock, Cheney & Company offered half the building cost ($3,000) if the town would match this. A beautiful large structure, architecturally designed as a Palladian-style building with Greek-revival overtones, was built. The school represents a demonstration of the factory's political and economic strength, since at this time Essex was trying to consolidate its school system. (Photograph courtesy of Ivoryton Library.)

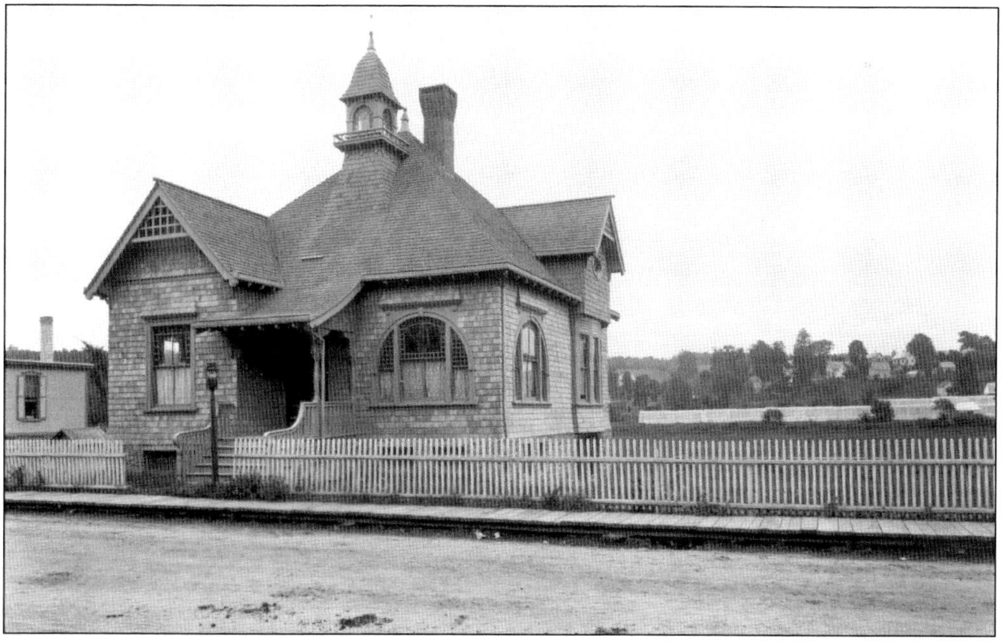

THE IVORYTON LIBRARY. The Ivoryton Library was originally located in the home of Samuel Cheney, on West Main Street in Ivoryton. The Victorian style building pictured here was erected in 1888, funded partially with Comstock, Cheney & Company funds, and has served the village ever since. (photograph courtesy of Ivoryton Library)

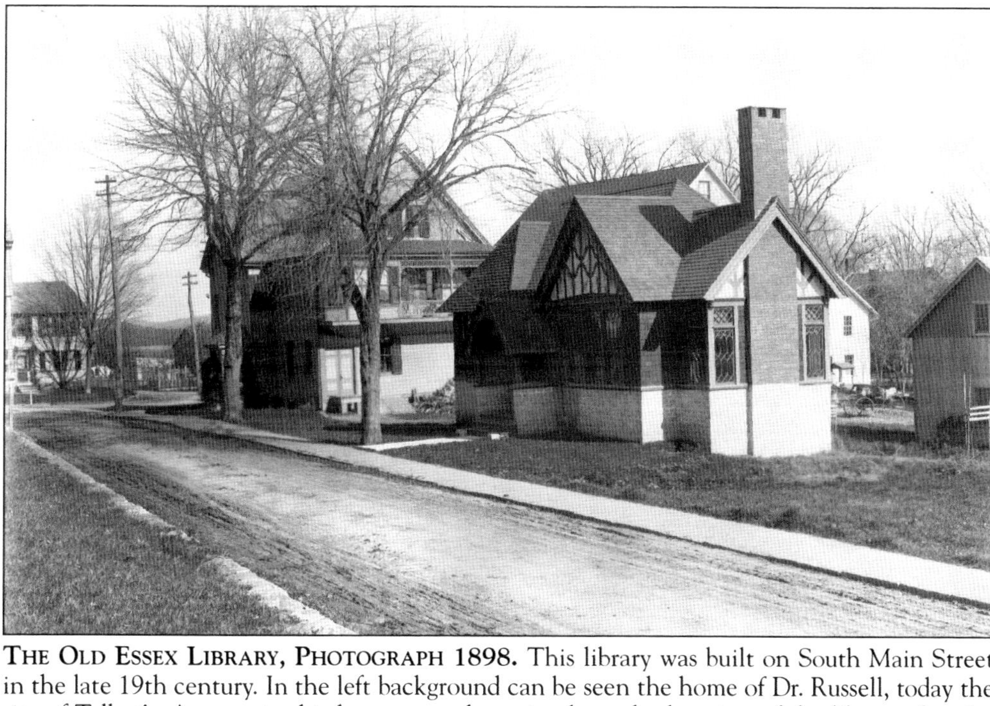

THE OLD ESSEX LIBRARY, PHOTOGRAPH 1898. This library was built on South Main Street in the late 19th century. In the left background can be seen the home of Dr. Russell, today the site of Talbot's. A room in this house served previously as the location of the library after the library association was formed. In 1897, Capt. Joseph Tucker left $5,000 for a new building, as well as several paintings. (Photograph courtesy of Essex Historical Society.)

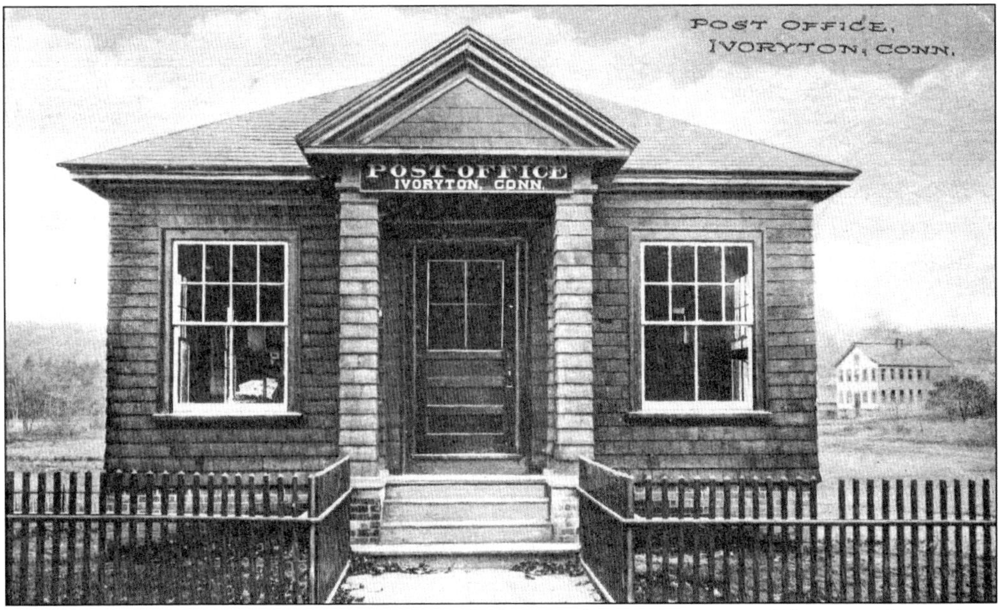

THE SECOND IVORYTON POST OFFICE. The original Ivoryton Post Office was located in the Ivoryton Store. As the town grew, a larger post office was needed, and the building pictured here served that purpose until the 1960s. It is now C.P. Burdick & Sons Office, and the Ivoryton Post Office has been moved east on Main Street. (Photograph courtesy of Ivoryton Library.)

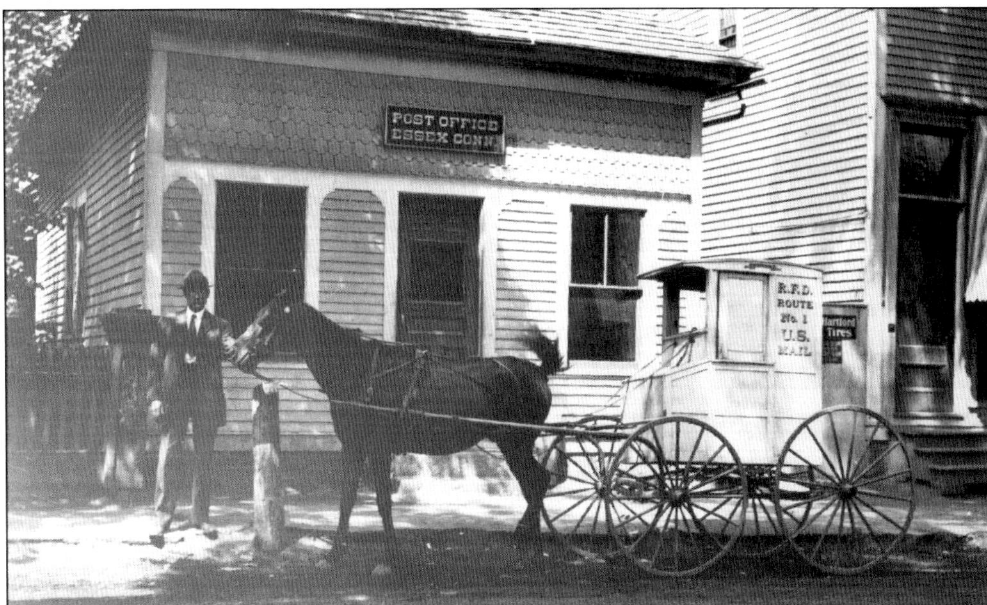

THE OLD ESSEX POST OFFICE, PHOTOGRAPH C. 1910. The post office was located here until 1922, at which time it moved to the new municipal building across the street. It has remained there since, even though the town offices have moved, and the building is now privately owned. Since 1922, the building pictured has housed a goldsmith shop, a liquor shop, and is now the Sew n' So Shop. (Photograph courtesy of Essex Historical Society.)

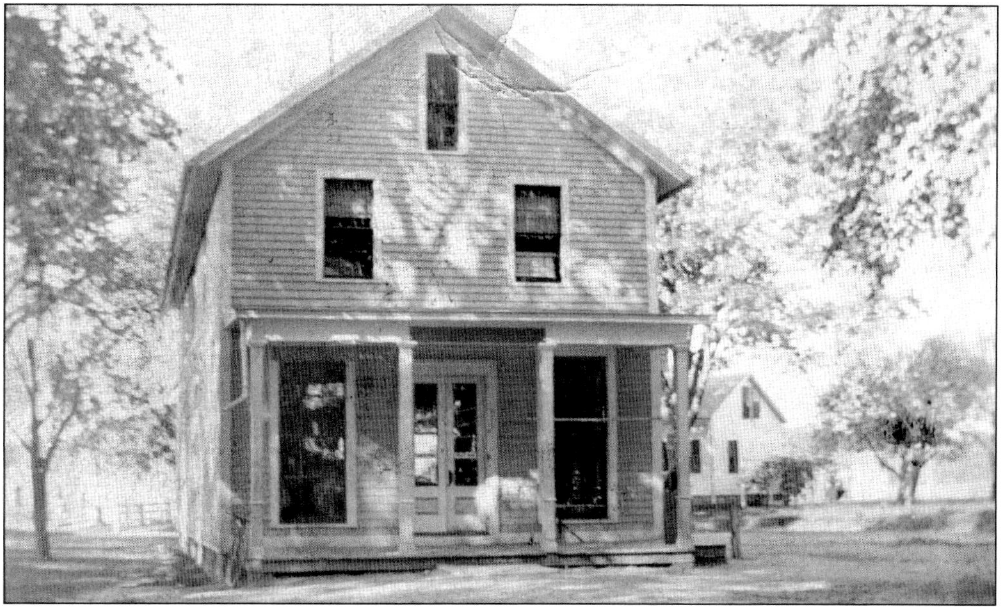

PRANN'S STORE. Pictured is Prann's Store, located where Middlesex Turnpike splits off to the north from the old Pettipaug-Guilford Turnpike, which heads west toward Ivoryton. The Centerbrook Post Office was located in Prann's Store for many years. It was later relocated across the street in a building of its own, where it is today. (Photograph courtesy of Essex Historical Society.)

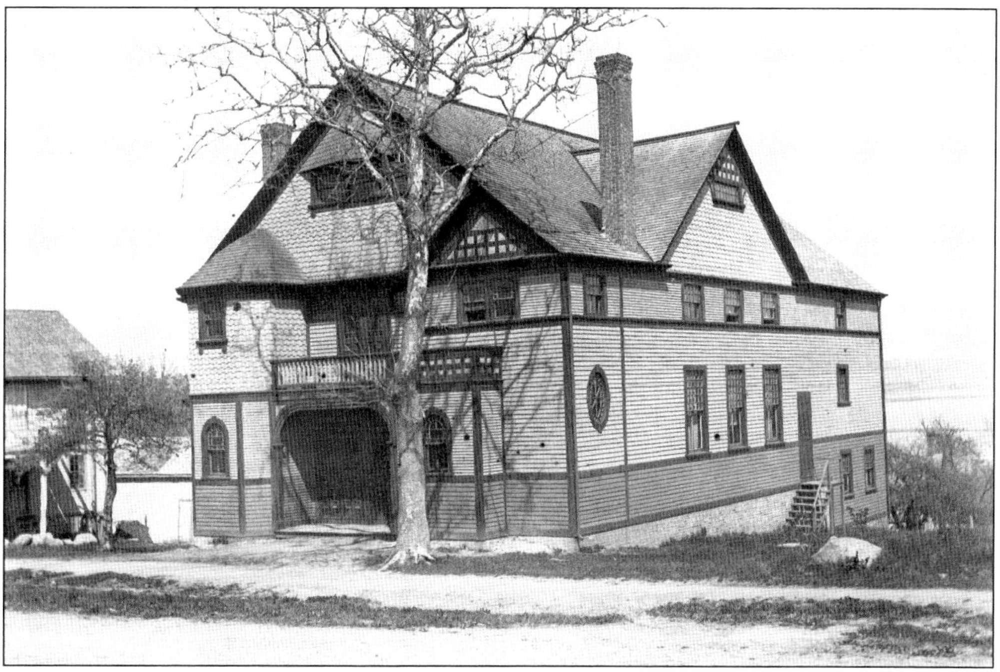

THE ESSEX PUBLIC HALL, PHOTOGRAPH 1895. The Essex Public Hall, built in 1889, was actually a private enterprise until just before the World War I. The town of Essex then took it over, and it remained a public building until sold to a private party in 1962, when it was renovated into an apartment house. (Photograph courtesy of Essex Historical Society.)

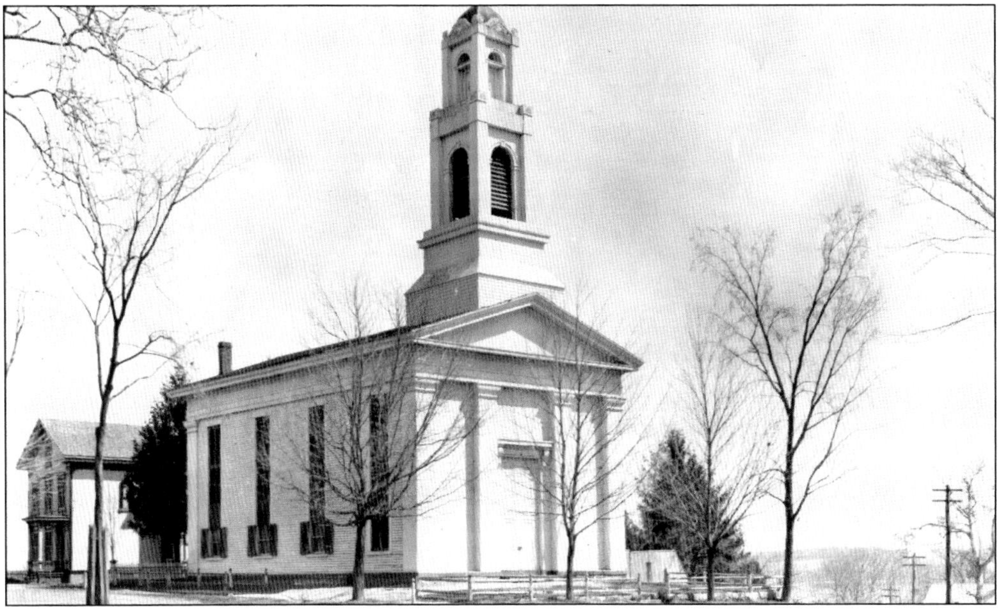

The Methodist Church. This church was constructed in 1849 on Zion (Church) Hill, directly across from the Episcopal church. In 1944, the congregation abandoned this building and it was offered to the town of Essex as a firehouse. That option was not picked up, and it became a warehouse instead, used by companies such as Cheesebrough Pond's and Verplex. Within the past 20 years, the structure was converted to a homestead. (Photograph courtesy of Essex Historical Society.)

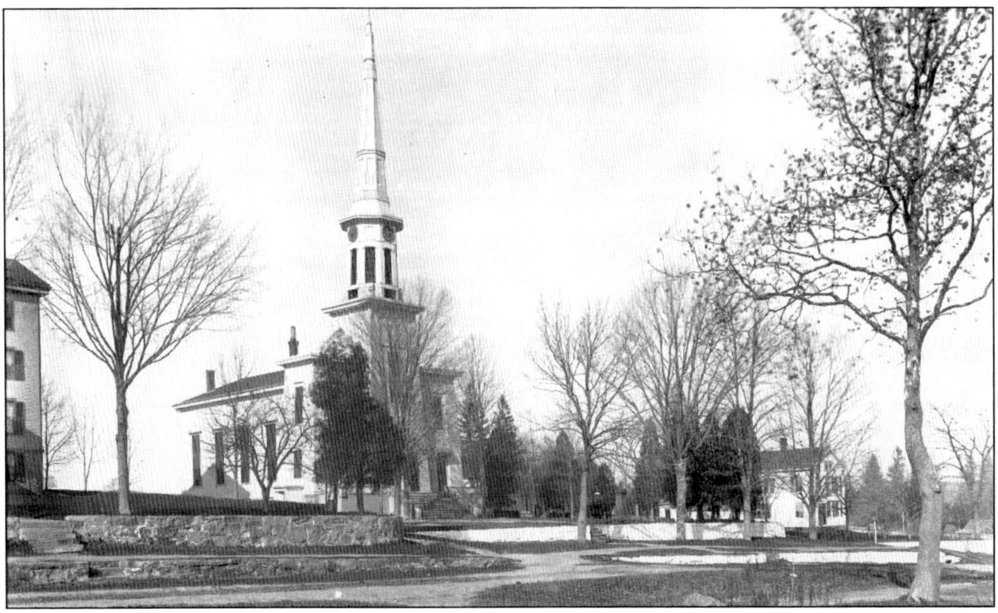

The Baptist Church, Prospect Street. This church was built by Jeremiah Gladwin in 1846 in a unique Egyptian Revival style. It remains the most architecturally sophisticated religious structure in Essex. By the middle of the 19th century, the Baptist Society was the largest congregation in Essex. The parsonage is pictured to the right. (Photograph courtesy of Essex Historical Society.)

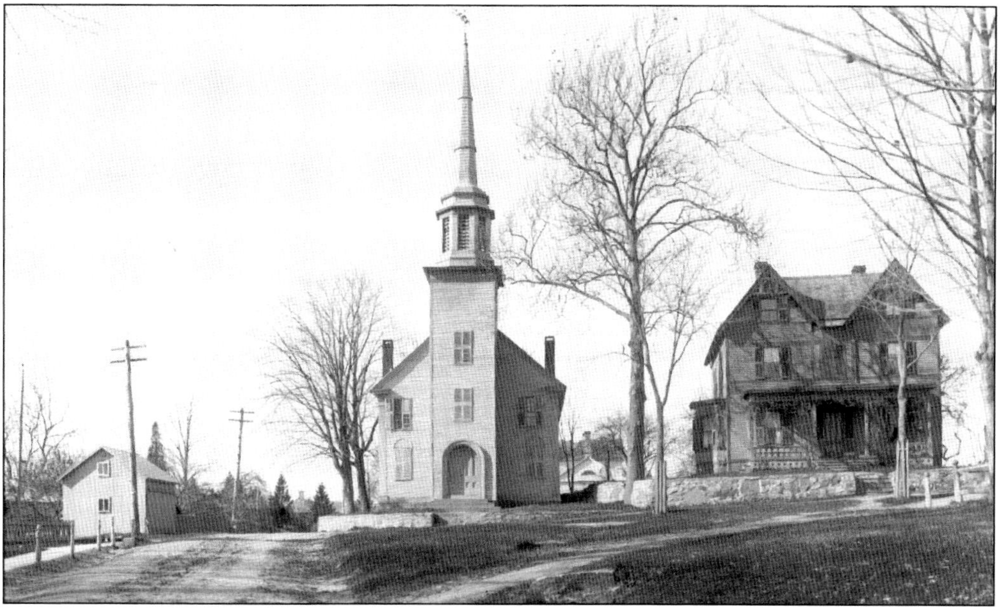

THE FIRST ST. JOHN'S EPISCOPAL CHURCH. This Essex Episcopal church on Zion Hill later became Our Lady of Sorrows Catholic Church. The church and its steeple were very prominent in town. Though not a large church, it was the first church building to exist in Essex village, having been moved *c.* 1800 from its original site in Centerbrook near the train station location of today. (Photograph courtesy of Essex Historical Society.)

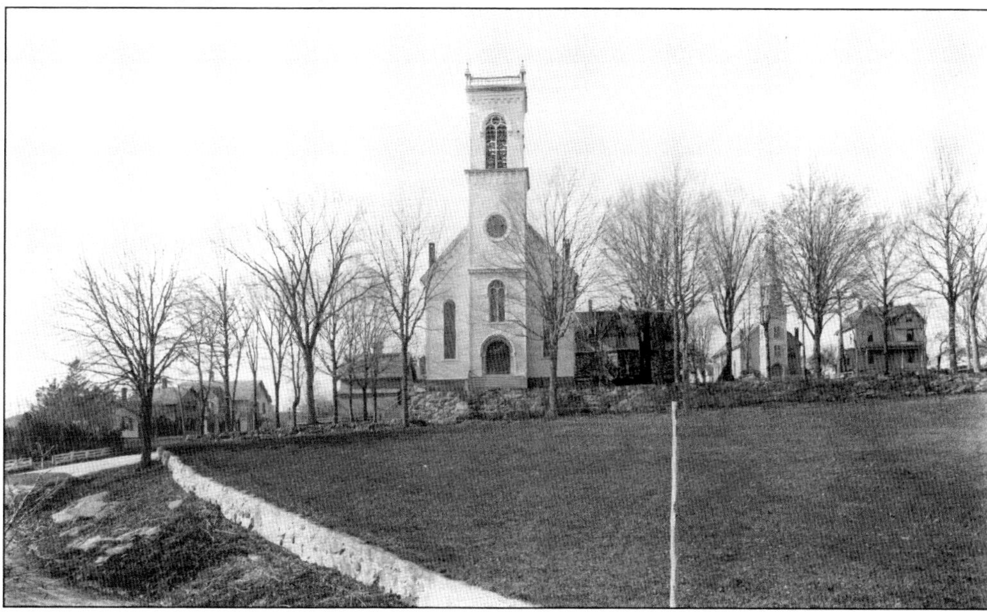

THE 1852 ESSEX CONGREGATIONAL CHURCH. This photograph of the First Congregational Church of Essex was taken from South Main Street in Essex, looking at Zion Hill. Originally, the church had a steeple, but it was removed because it was poorly constructed. The second and third parsonages of the Essex Congregational church are also shown here. The original parsonage was on the north side of Pratt Street in Essex and existed as such from 1856 until the second was built in 1883. (Photograph courtesy of Essex Historical Society.)

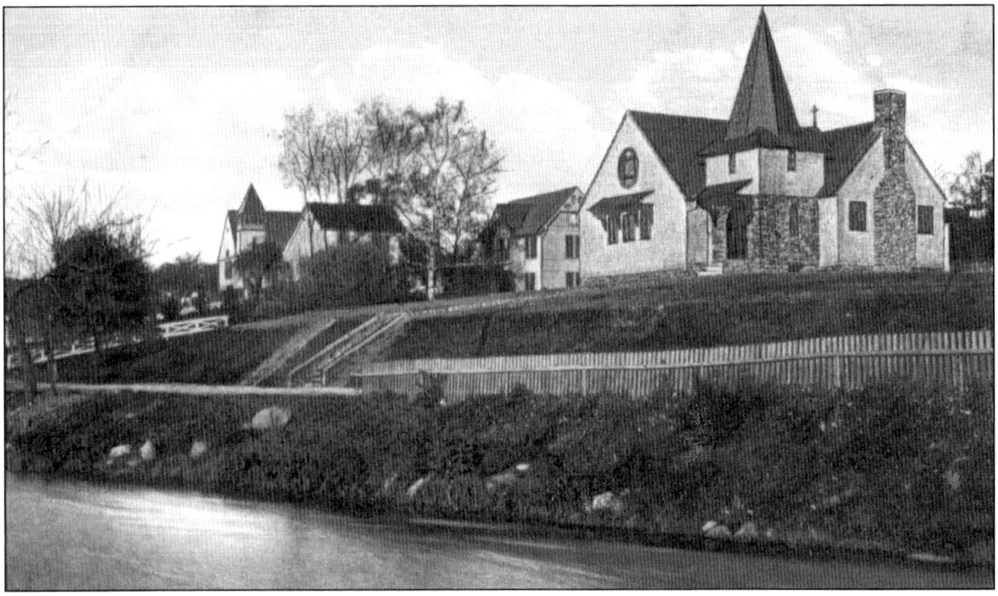

THE IVORYTON EPISCOPAL CHURCH AND THE SWEDISH MISSION. The Ivoryton Episcopal Church (right) is a mission of St. John's Episcopal Church in Essex. The structure was completed in 1905. Comstock, Cheney & Company was not involved in the construction but was interested in having more churches for its workers. Located on West Main Street, the church remains intact today, and the house immediately west served as a rectory for many years. The Swedish Mission (left) was built just before 1898. (Photograph courtesy of Ivoryton Library.)

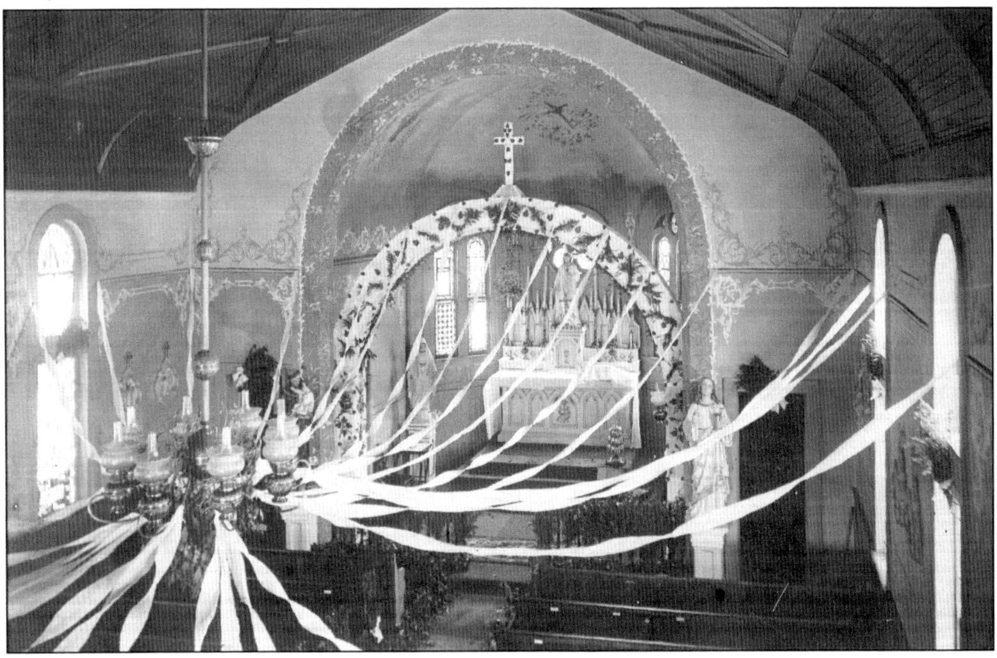

THE INTERIOR OF THE ORIGINAL OUR LADY OF SORROWS CATHOLIC CHURCH, PHOTOGRAPH 1912. This is a rare photograph of a church interior. This church was much smaller than the present Our Lady of Sorrows.

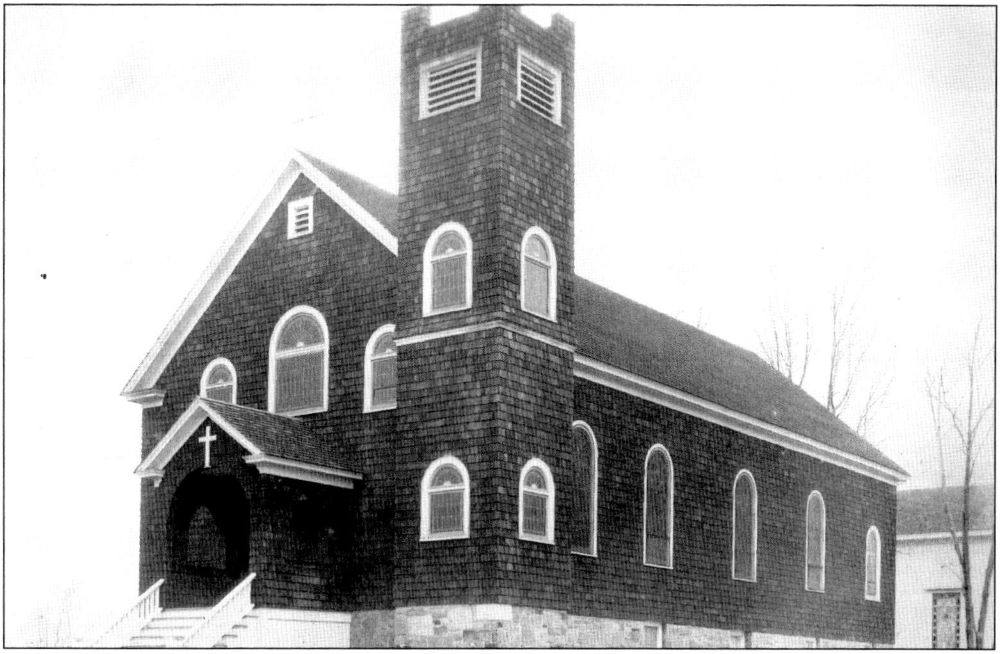

Our Lady of Sorrows Catholic Church, Photograph 1927. Our Lady of Sorrows was relocated here in 1926 after fire destroyed the previous Catholic church, south of here on Prospect Street. This building was once the seminary of Hills Academy, built in 1849 by Lucius Lyon. The church was completely renovated recently. (Photograph courtesy of Don Malcarne.)

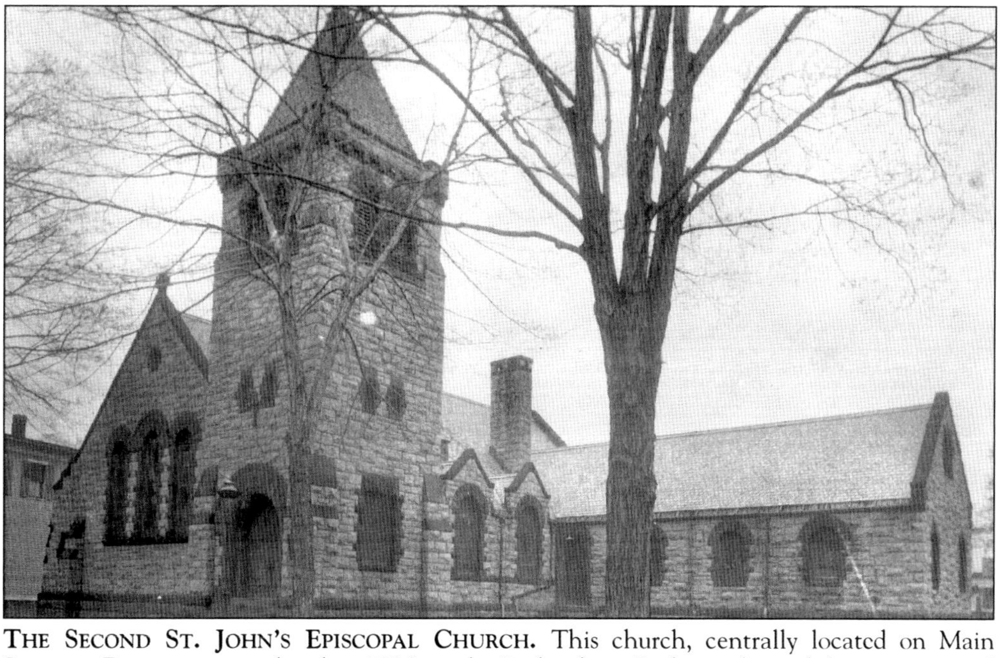

The Second St. John's Episcopal Church. This church, centrally located on Main Street in Essex, was completed in 1896, in the Richardson Gothic style, with brownstone and granite features. It replaced the original church, located on Zion Hill, which was sold by the Episcopalians in 1896 to the Catholics and became Our Lady of Sorrows Catholic Church—the one that burned in 1926. (Photograph courtesy of Don Malcarne.)

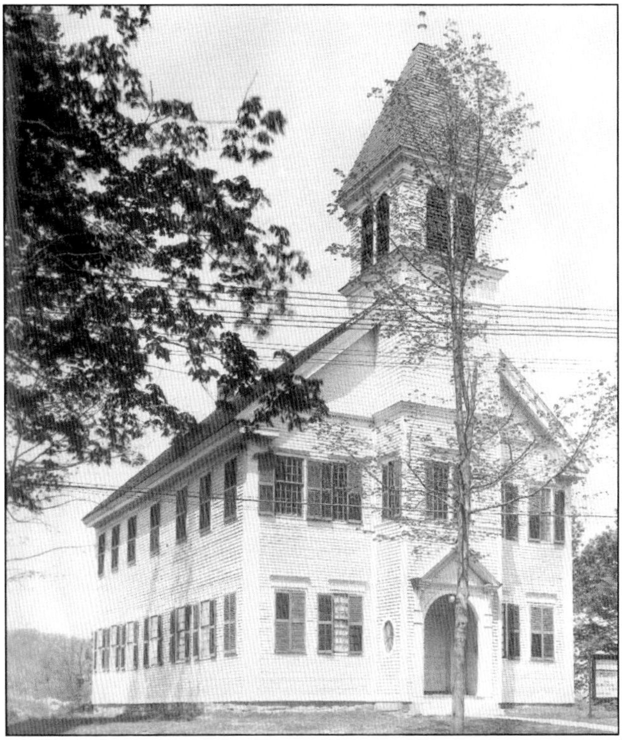

The Centerbrook Congregational Church. The mother church is the Centerbrook Congregational Church. The original church was erected in 1723 and rebuilt in the 1750s. The present-day church was constructed from 1788 to 1790. It remains the oldest church building in Middlesex County still standing. The church originally faced west and now faces south, having been turned in 1839. (Photograph courtesy of Don Malcarne.)

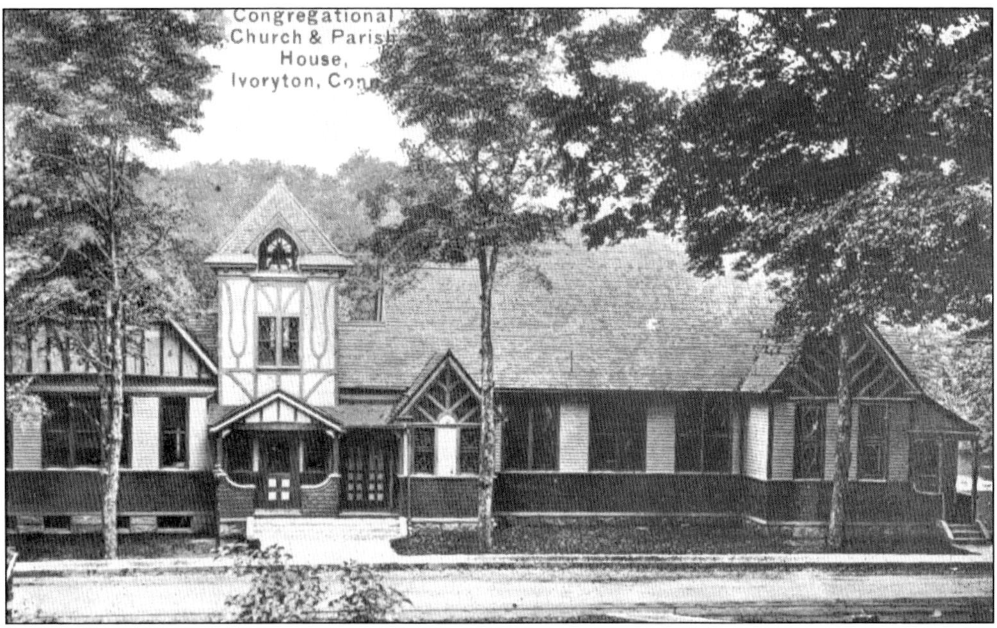

The Ivoryton Congregational Church. The Ivoryton Congregational Church was at first a mission of the mother church in Centerbrook. This building was known originally as Comstock Chapel because it was built on Samuel Comstock's land and was sponsored by his daughter Harriet Comstock. Comstock, Cheney & Company did not deliberately influence the spiritual lives of its employees but did encourage church attendance. (Photograph courtesy of Essex Historical Society.)

Seven

RIVER OF DAMS

The Connecticut River may have been the mainstream, but the Falls River was the lifeline of Essex. This waterway defines the town, from its agricultural beginnings through the Industrial Revolution. There were, at one time or another in Essex, eight dams on this river, which rises in Westbrook. However, by 1850, only six remained. Water was the main source of power in Essex for over 200 years.

The first dam on the Falls River to be used as a single power source was built by the Williams family in 1823 just off the Middlesex Turnpike, about 300 yards north of the Centerbrook Congregational Church. Known locally as the Brush Works dam, this was used by Elisha Comstock only to make ivory combs from 1825 to 1829.

Dam No. 2 (see diagram page 99) was constructed in 1845 on the Denison family property, adjacent to Denison Road. Initially, this powered an ivory comb factory run by Mason Post and Capt. Francis West. Later, A.E. Griswold of Middletown made combs there and, in 1863, Comstock, Cheney & Company purchased the factory. The company owned it for nine months and then sold it. It emerged as a wire goods factory. In all probability, the ivory tools were moved to the company's Ivoryton shop.

The invention of a machine to cut combs by Phineas Pratt in 1790, within a short distance of the site of dam No. 2, was a main reason for the ivory industry to be located in this area.

Dams No. 3 and No. 4 were responsible for Centerbrook's growth of manufacturing. The most important industry at Dam No. 4 was the Connecticut Valley Manufacturing Company, now the site of Centerbrook Architects. This company attracted workers and middle-class jobs to town. A successful enterprise of Dam No. 3 was the Looby Brush Mill. William Looby started the factory in 1888. The Looby factory made dust mops and goblet and gun brushes. It is now the site of a bookstore and an antiques shop. When William Looby, the brush manufacturer died in 1917, he left an estate worth close to $40,000, a considerable amount at that time.

By 1850, the dams generally powered one shop, whereas previously they may have powered both a sawmill and gristmill. The secret to successful manufacturing operations using waterpower was the assurance of an adequate supply of water. Samuel Merritt Comstock recognized this in the first half of the 19th century and developed multiple water sources for his factories.

Water privileges (the right to build a dam) were granted in accordance with location, demand, and needs of the community. When Samuel Comstock wanted to put a dam behind his new ivory shop in 1850, he had to purchase an existing water privilege 300 yards up the Falls River, destroy the existing dam, and rebuild it at his desired location.

In the 20th century, electricity became the primary power source, and dams along the Falls River were largely ignored. On June 6, 1982, a torrential rain fell, depositing up to 15 inches of water on Essex. This put a tremendous strain on the six old dams on this river. The Bushy Hill dam, holding back a feeder stream, and previously a power source for Comstock, Cheney & Company, burst. A torrent of water filled the Falls River, and every dam on it was severely damaged or destroyed. Some have never been rebuilt.

—Don Malcarne and Paula Feder

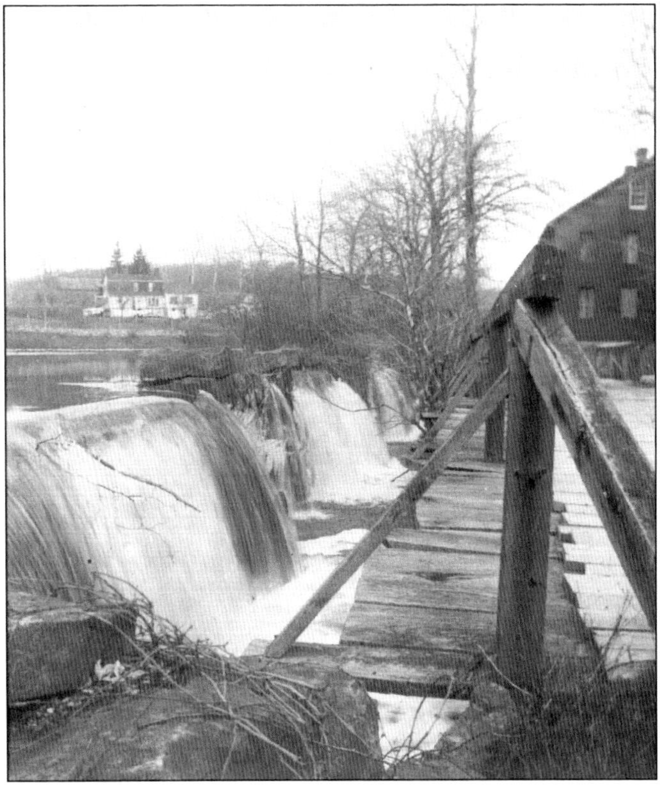

THE WILLIAMS MILL AND THE MEADOW WOODS DAM. This is the three-spillway dam at the mouth of the Falls River, as photographed in 1900. The original dam was constructed in 1689, destroyed by 1730, and rebuilt by the Williams family. It supplied power for the many operations at the Williams complex for about 160 years. The Doane family purchased most of the Williams properties, including the dam, in 1890. (Photograph courtesy of Essex Historical Society.)

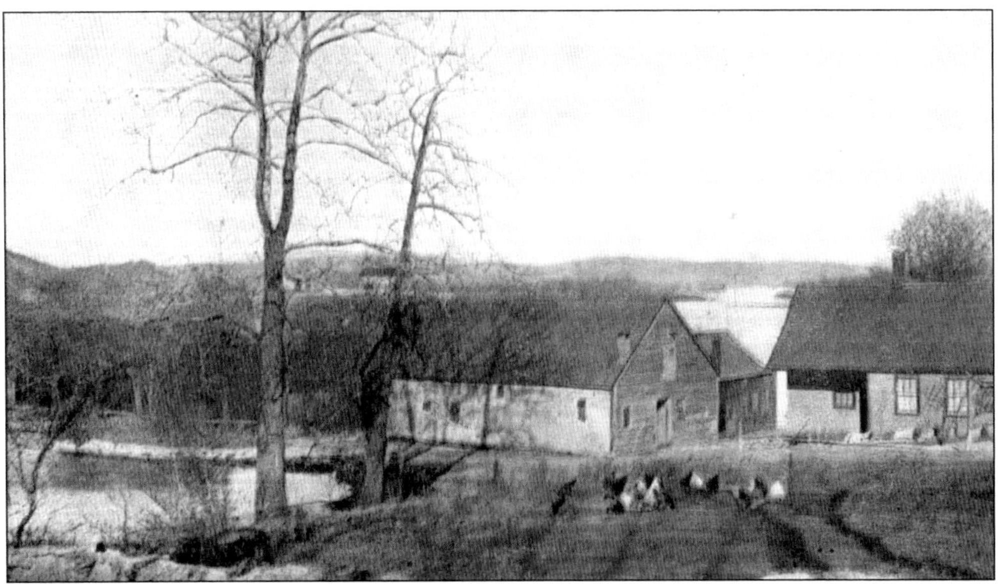

THE OLD GRISTMILL. This 1880s photograph shows the original Williams complex gristmill, defunct by 1885. The building then became the Essex Woodturning Company, which made wooden novelties. It burned down in 1891.

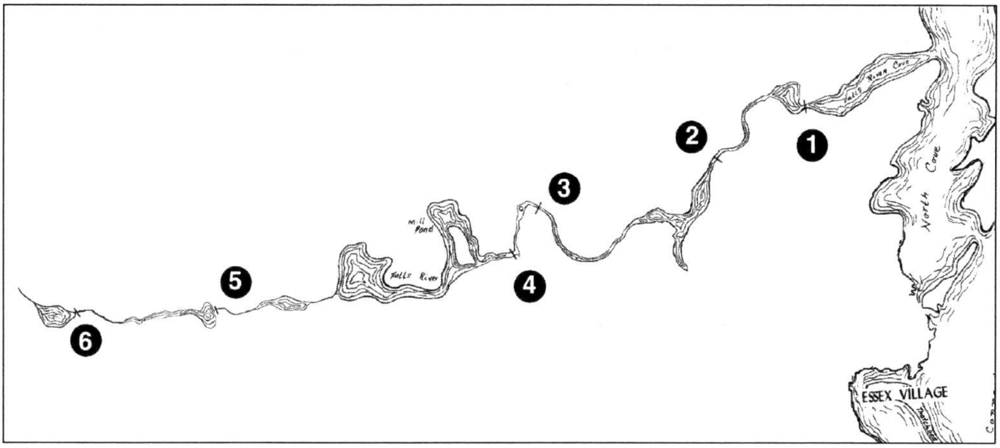

THE FALLS RIVER DAMS. The Hough-Williams dam (1) at the mouth of the Falls River, near the intersection of North Main Street, Dennison Road, and Mill Lane, was built in 1689 and rebuilt in 1730. The Mason H. Post dam (2) on Dennison Road, about one-quarter mile from North Main Street, was built in 1845. The Williams-Elisha Comstock dam (3) in Centerbrook, at the intersection of Route 154 and Old Deep River Road, was built in 1826. The Pratt-Clark-Williams dam (4) in Centerbrook, behind the post office, was built *c.* 1700. The Bull-Comstock-Griswold dam (5) was in Ivoryton, behind the Congregational church. The 1848 Samuel M. Comstock dam (6) was destroyed, but located prior to 1982 across from the Ivoryton Inn. (Photograph courtesy of Ivoryton Library.)

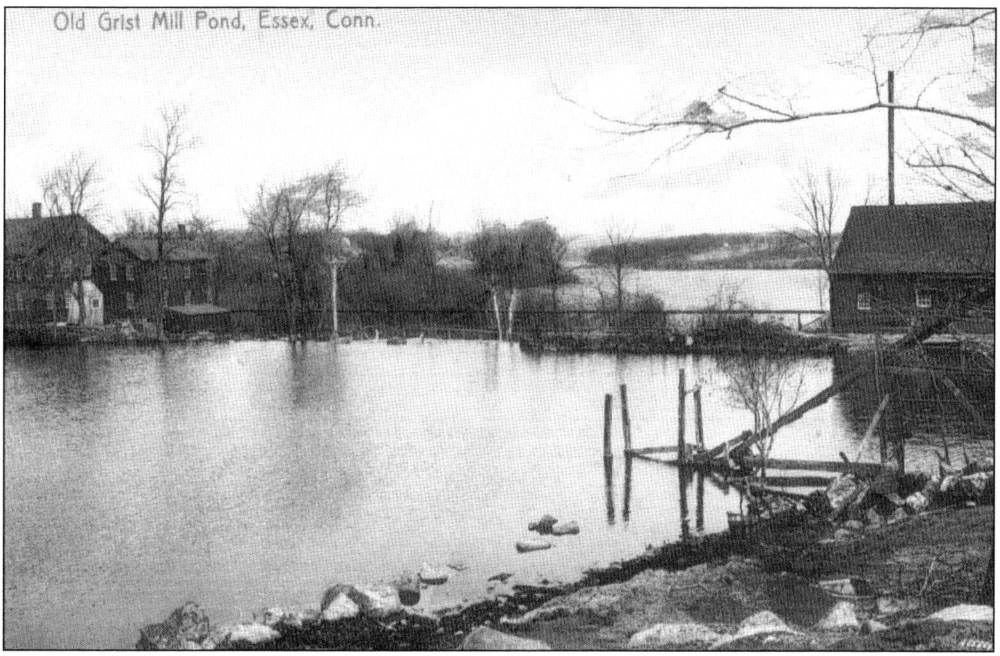

THE OLD GRISTMILL POND. The pond that powered the various operations at the Williams complex is pictured here, with the Williams mill on the left. The Williams shipyard previously was located below the dam in an area now covered by trees, visible in this late-19th-century photograph. (Photograph courtesy of Essex Library.)

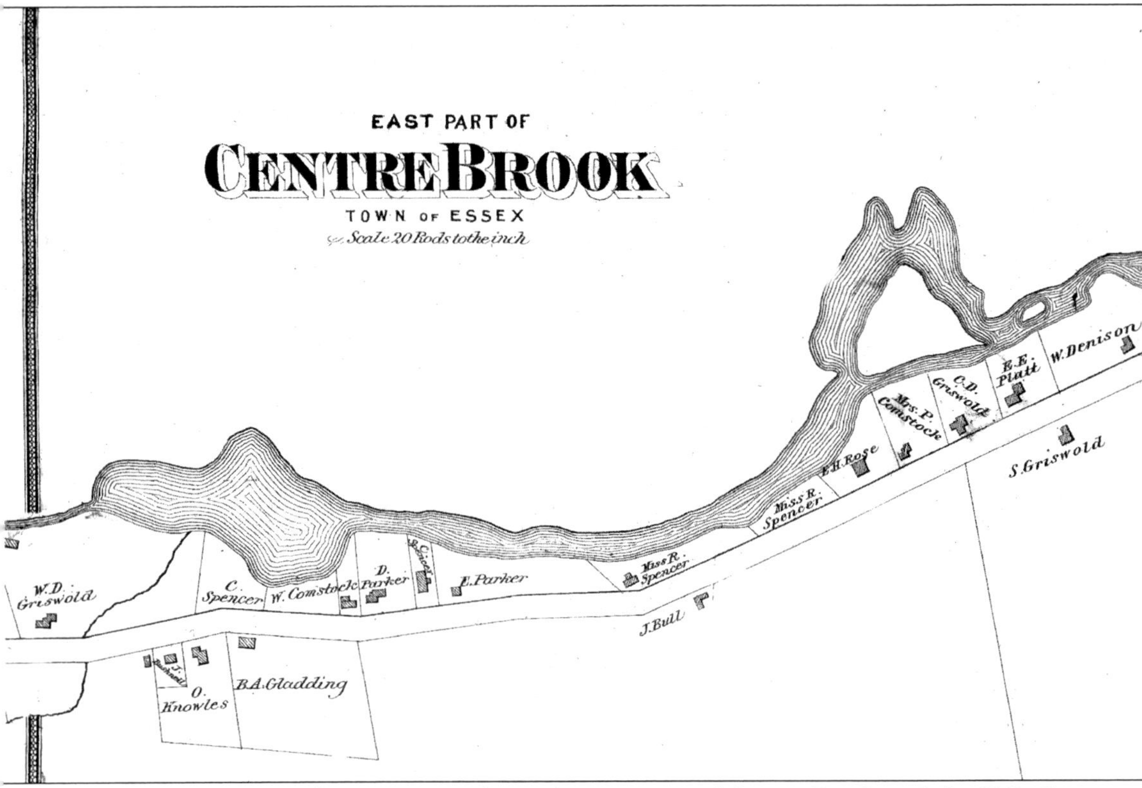

CENTRE BROOK. This 1874 map shows the east part of Centre Brook and the Falls River running through it. Notice the various ponds that were formed by Dams No. 2, No. 3, and

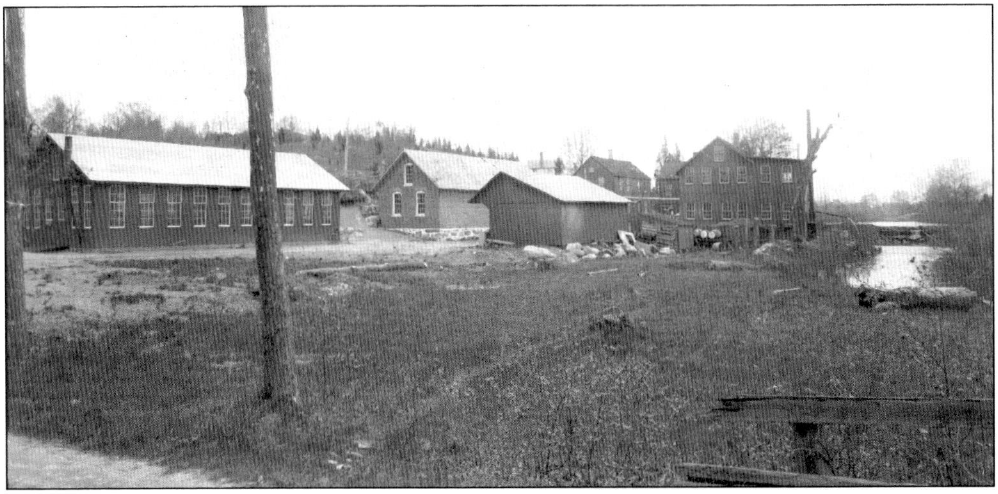

THE DAM ON DENISON ROAD. This *c.* 1895 photograph shows the Tiley-Pratt Company. The dam in the right background was the least severely damaged during the 1982 flood. Originally built in 1845, it powered bone and ivory manufacturing by Mason Hamilton Post and, later, A.E. Griswold. The Tiley-Pratt Company moved to the Middlesex Turnpike after 1900 and continued to produce bicycle spokes, some of which were exported to Japan. At this new location, they also produced an automobile named the Tiley. Between one and two dozen were manufactured. (Photograph courtesy of Essex Historical Society.)

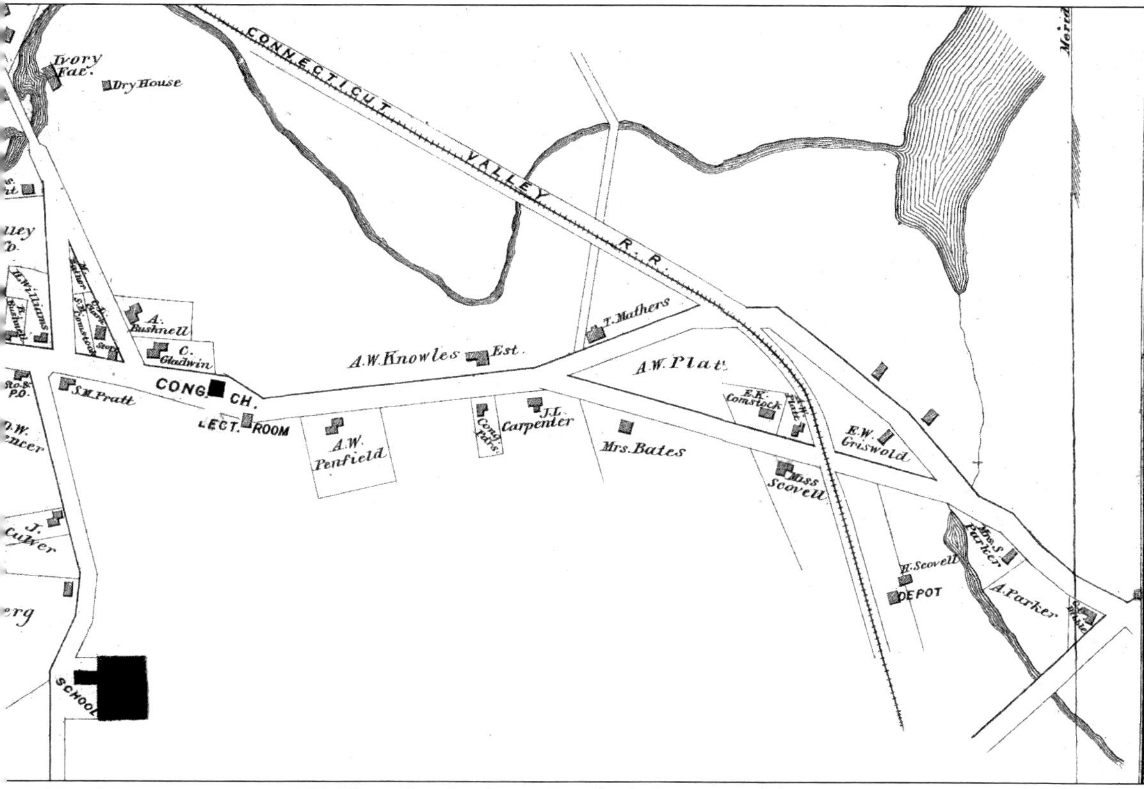

No. 4 (see map on page 99). The island indicated in the left center of the map was created when Dam No. 4 flooded the adjacent land.

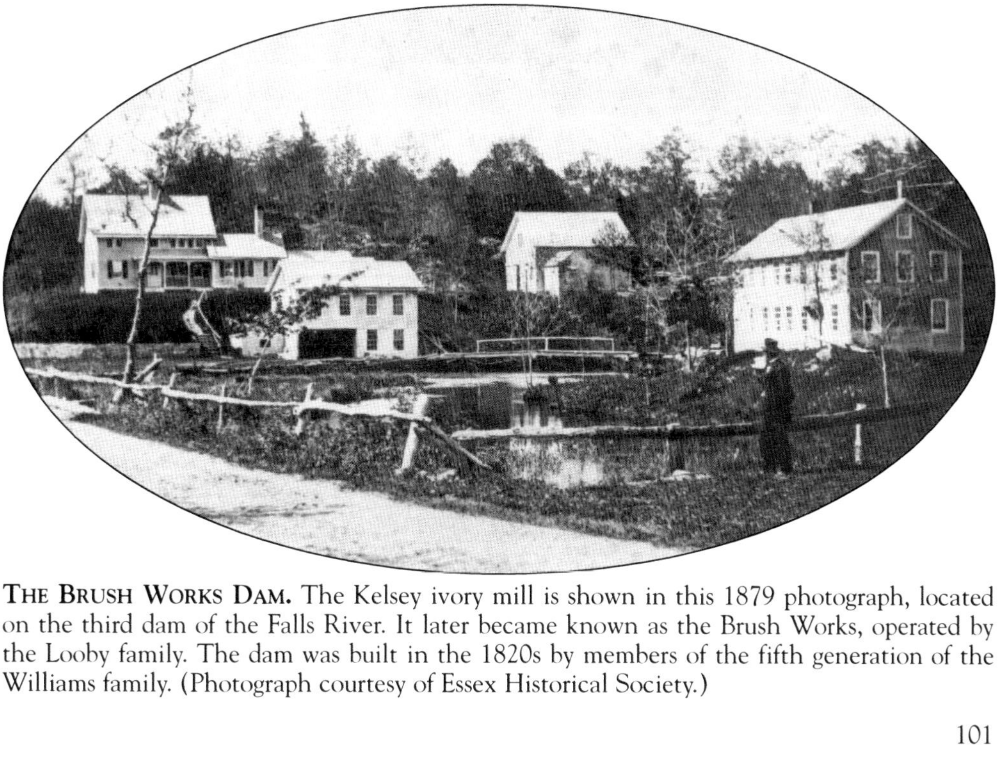

THE BRUSH WORKS DAM. The Kelsey ivory mill is shown in this 1879 photograph, located on the third dam of the Falls River. It later became known as the Brush Works, operated by the Looby family. The dam was built in the 1820s by members of the fifth generation of the Williams family. (Photograph courtesy of Essex Historical Society.)

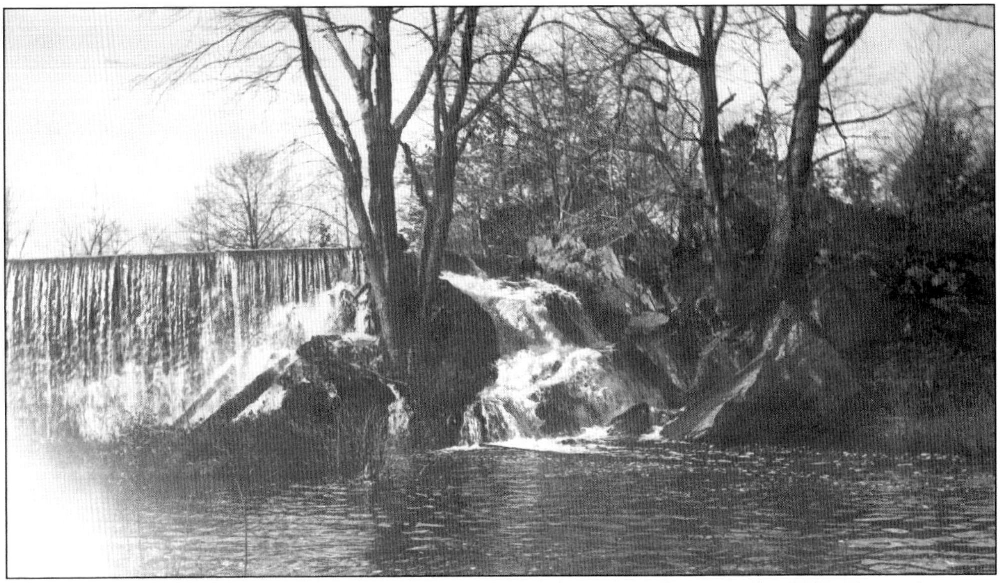

THE BIT SHOP DAM. This is often referred to as the main dam on the Falls River because it is the point of the greatest drop on that stream. From 1700 on, a great deal of industrial activity took place here. First, a gristmill and sawmill were established. Then, an ironworks and triphammer arrived. Perhaps the most famous occupant using the dam was the Connecticut Valley Manufacturing Company, which manufactured drill bits from 1876 to 1969. (Photograph courtesy of Essex Historical Society.)

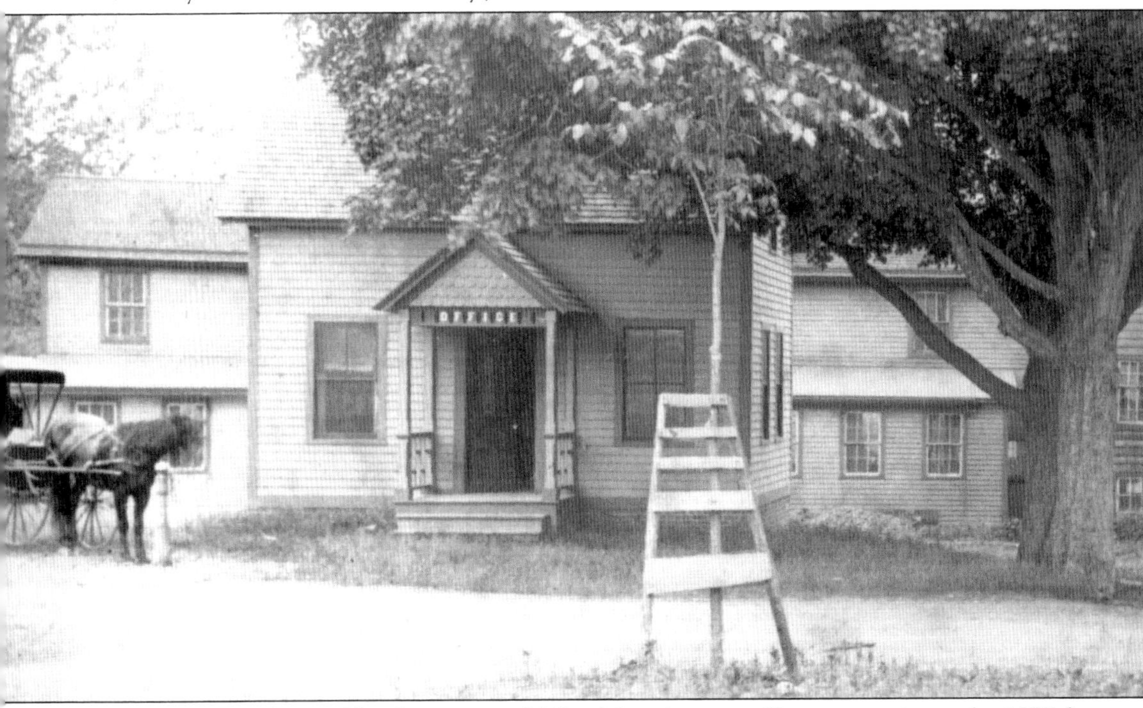

THE OLD BIT SHOP. The Connecticut Valley Manufacturing Company, prior to the 1895 fire, is shown here. Previously, it was the Centerbrook Manufacturing Company, owned by Samuel Merritt Comstock. The Panic of 1873 forced a complete reorganization of the company, and

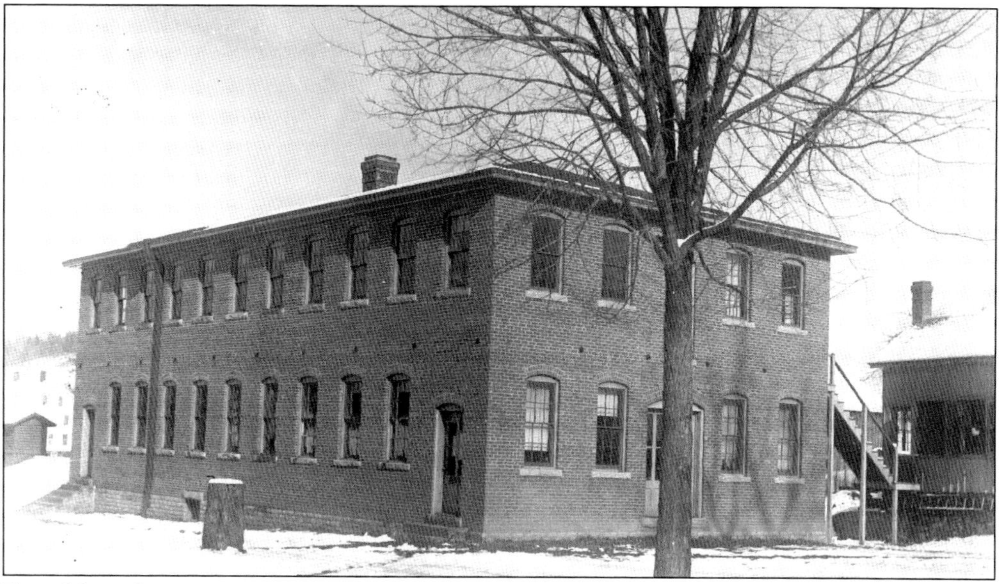

THE NEW CONNECTICUT VALLEY MANUFACTURING COMPANY BUILDING. An 1895 fire destroyed most of the wooden factory buildings of the Connecticut Valley Manufacturing Company. The town of Essex granted the Connecticut Valley a 10-year tax abatement as an incentive to rebuild, and the company rebuilt immediately, using brick as the primary construction material. Today, the above buildings are occupied by the architectural firm Centerbrook Architects. (Photograph courtesy of Essex Historical Society.)

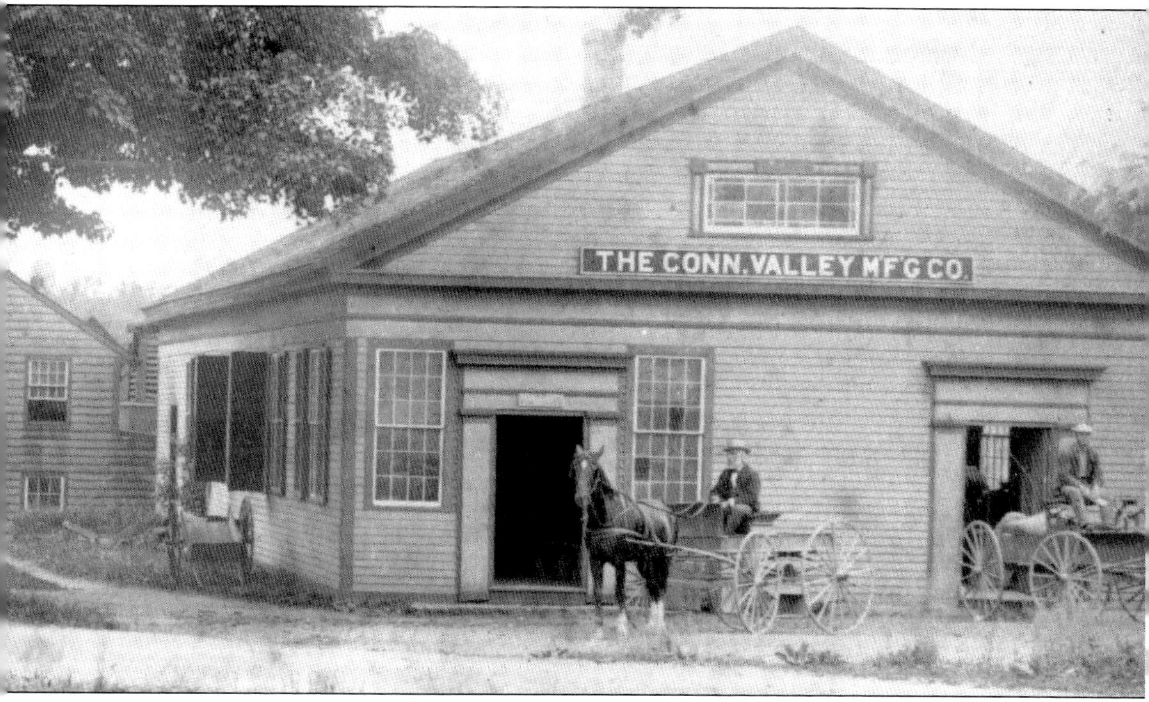

it emerged as the Connecticut Valley Manufacturing Company under the direction of Alfred Wright. (Photograph courtesy of Essex Historical Society.)

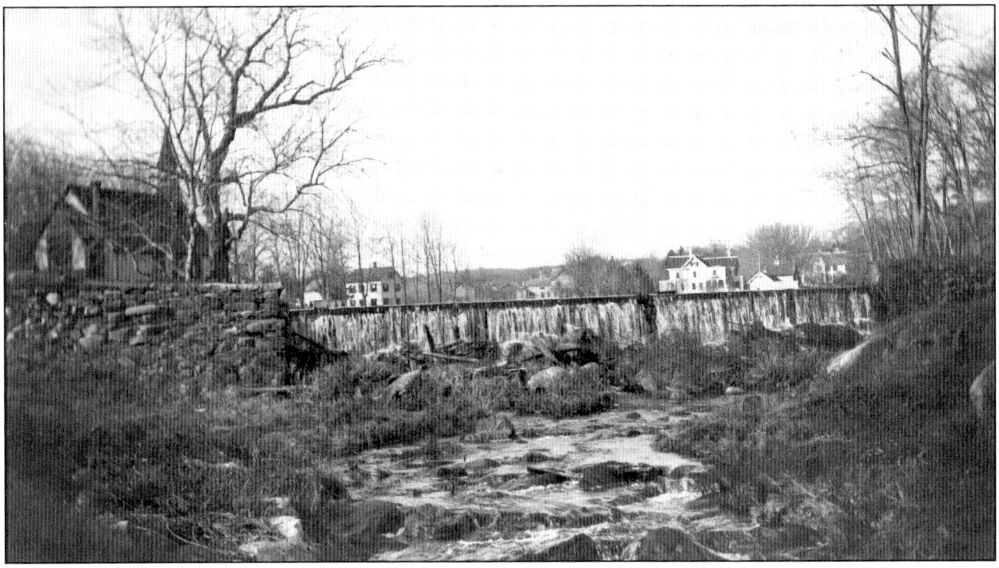

The Bull Family Dam, Photograph c. 1900. Members of the Bull family operated a gristmill, cider mill, and fulling mill here until 1834. At that time Samuel Comstock and Edwin Griswold turned it into a single-function dam for running their ivory comb business. The Ivoryton Congregational Church was built just above the dam, and the R.H. Comstock house can be seen in the center background. This dam was rebuilt after the Flood of 1982. (Photograph courtesy of Essex Historical Society.)

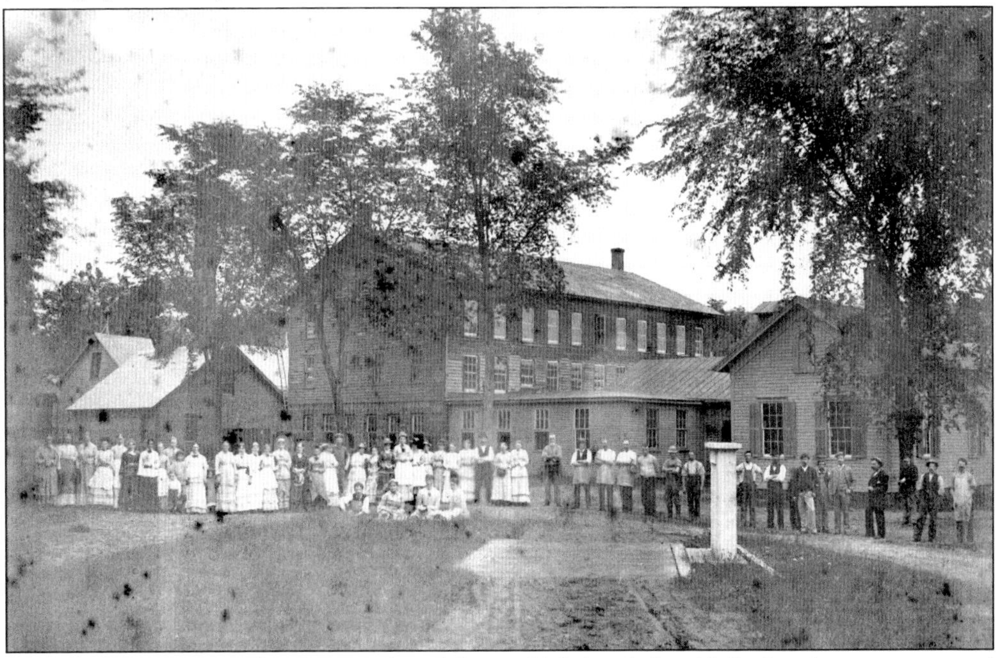

The Bracket Shop. After Comstock and Griswold disbanded in 1848, this shop was occupied by several groups who manufactured axe handles, ivory combs, and wooden novelties. These operations were all powered by the Bull dam. Eventually, the Comstock, Cheney & Company took ownership of the shop and the adjacent water privilege. Iron fittings used in piano parts were produced here. (Photograph courtesy of Essex Historical Society.)

Eight

Bells and Whistles

Main Street, which threads its way west from Essex through Centerbrook and Ivoryton, has connected the villages for over two centuries. In the early 1800s, it was the eastern end of the Guilford-Potapoug Turnpike. Dams on the Falls River—literally the old mill stream that follows the road—provided waterpower for manufacturing. Among the products made by shops here were witch hazel, the folk remedy extracted from the wild local bush of that same name; milled grain and lumber; iron products such as auger bits made for 100 years at the bit shop, the historic brick factory building on the millpond (now home to Centerbrook Architects); and ivory products—from combs and billiard balls to the piano actions of Comstock, Cheney & Company.

The Connecticut Valley Railroad, linking Old Saybrook to the New York-Boston main line to the south and to Middletown and Hartford to the north, arrived in 1871. The original route planned for the line was through the village of Essex, but Samuel Merritt Comstock was on the fledgling railroad's board and had the roadbed rerouted inland through Centerbrook, closer to Comstock, Cheney & Company and Centerbrook Manufacturing Company, both of which he headed. Later a division of the New Haven Railroad, it delivered passengers until 1930 and freight until 1968. Known today as the Essex Steam Train at the Valley Railroad Company, it carries 160,000 passengers annually. At the station in Deep River, passengers can transfer to waiting excursion boats. On certain days, the train also carries people going to a see play at the Goodspeed Opera House in East Haddam, just across the old swinging bridge from the station.

Main Street also provided the roadbed for the trolley. For eight post-Victorian years, a time period spanning World War I, the trolley car bell could be heard on a dozen Main Streets up and down the Connecticut River and the shoreline of Long Island Sound. For a nickel, riders could board a northbound streetcar at the Ivoryton Library and travel in comfort and style to the ivory factories in Ivoryton and Deep River and on to Chester, where the line terminated.

Southbound passengers could ride the three miles to Essex Square and thence, via Old Saybrook, eastbound across the Connecticut River and on to Old Lyme, Niantic, and New London, and Westerly, Rhode Island, on the tracks of several older established local lines. The line also ran west, parallel to the shoreline, into New Haven.

The Essex trolley was part of the ill-fated Shore Line Electric Railway Company. Built with top-of-the-line quality, for which it paid top dollar in a period of inflated prices, the line never could charge enough in fares to service its debt and turn a profit.

The decision in 1910 to serve Ivoryton may have been one of many factors contributing to the line's demise. Instead of running straight from Essex to Deep River, the loop through Ivoryton servicing the factory and its workers was an expensive add-on to build, yet was disappointing in passenger traffic revenue.

If making a profit was a recurring problem for the trolley company, so was its keeping employees on the job for too many hours at a stretch.

Just before 5 p.m. on August 13, 1918, in North Branford, the motormen of two oncoming trains dozed at the controls. The westbound engineer failed to pull into the siding at North Branford, according to procedure, to allow the eastbound train to pass. The westbound engineer, in fact, admitted later that he illegally taped his throttle in the full forward position before dozing off. He claimed, also, to have been on the job 16 hours.

Fifteen people, including the other engineer, lost their lives as the trains telescoped into each other. An additional 35 people were seriously injured. It was the worst streetcar accident in all of New England streetcar annals. In the ensuing lawsuit, plaintiffs sought $1.4 million, a staggering sum in those days.

The new line salvaged from the financial wreckage excluded service to towns north or east of Old Saybrook. Yet, even this greatly compressed system fell victim to buses and the Model T Ford. The last trolley ran from Guilford to New Haven in 1930.

At the village line on Main Street between Centerbrook and Ivoryton, an automobile dealership stands today. It is near the location where there was a tollgate for the turnpike in 1836 and exactly where there was a bicycle shop in 1900. The bright new vehicles on display serve as a reminder of how constantly evolving modes of transportation have displaced the picturesque stagecoaches with their teams of four and the elegant and comfortable trolleys, both of which, in their respective eras, passed here several times daily.

—Dan Nesbett

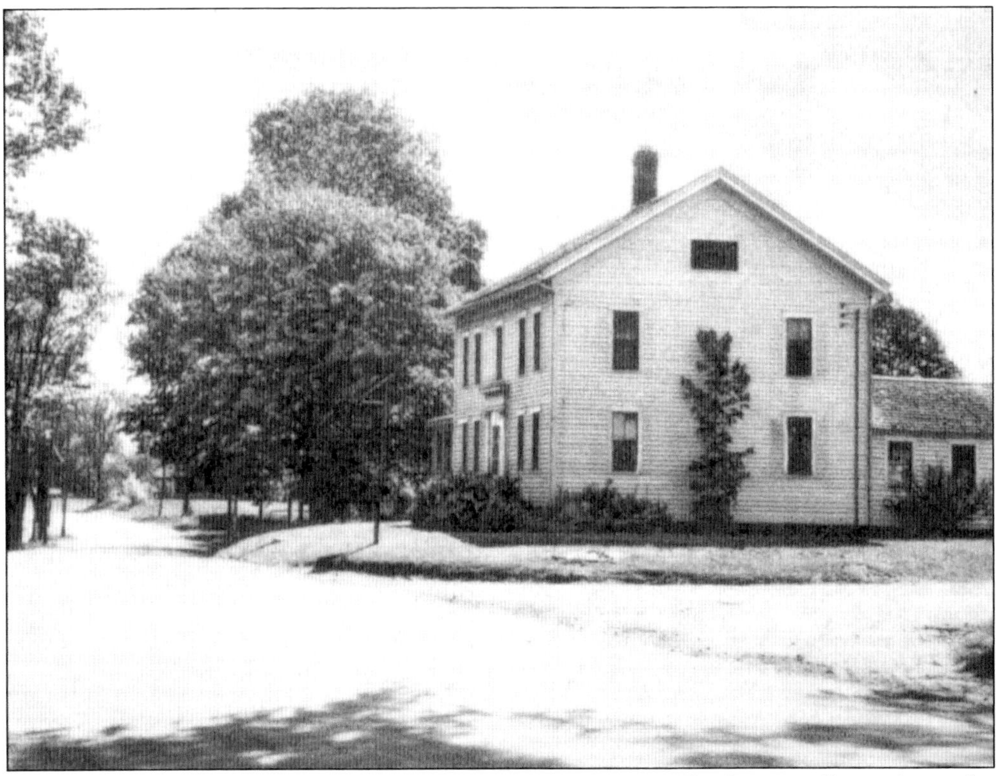

THE TOLLHOUSE ON THE GUILFORD-POTAPOUG TURNPIKE. The house still stands on the south side of Main Street near the Ivoryton-Centerbrook village line. In earlier times, two stagecoaches traveling in each direction passed daily. Local eastbound cargoes included timber and produce bound for the more populous markets and shipbuilding centers, such as Potapoug, as well as shipping points along the river. (Photograph courtesy of Ivoryton Library.)

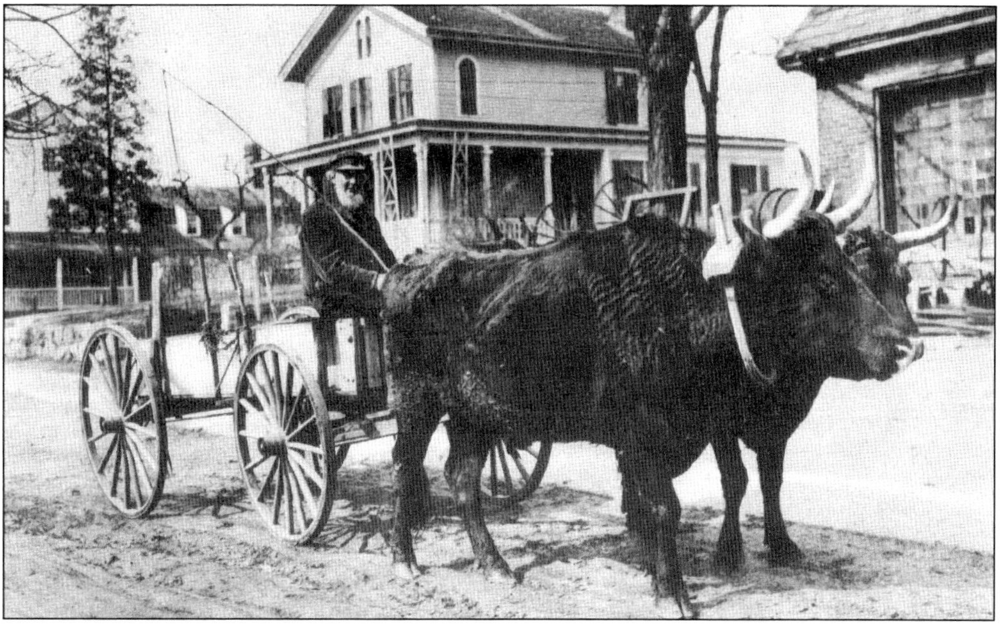

CHAMPLIN SQUARE, ESSEX. Oxen wait their turn at Pratt's Village Smithy in Essex, *c.* 1905. Oxen were more popular than horses because of their ability to pull heavier loads. Two white clapboard Pratt houses appear in the background. The one at the far left is currently owned by the Essex Historical Society. (Photograph courtesy of Essex Library.)

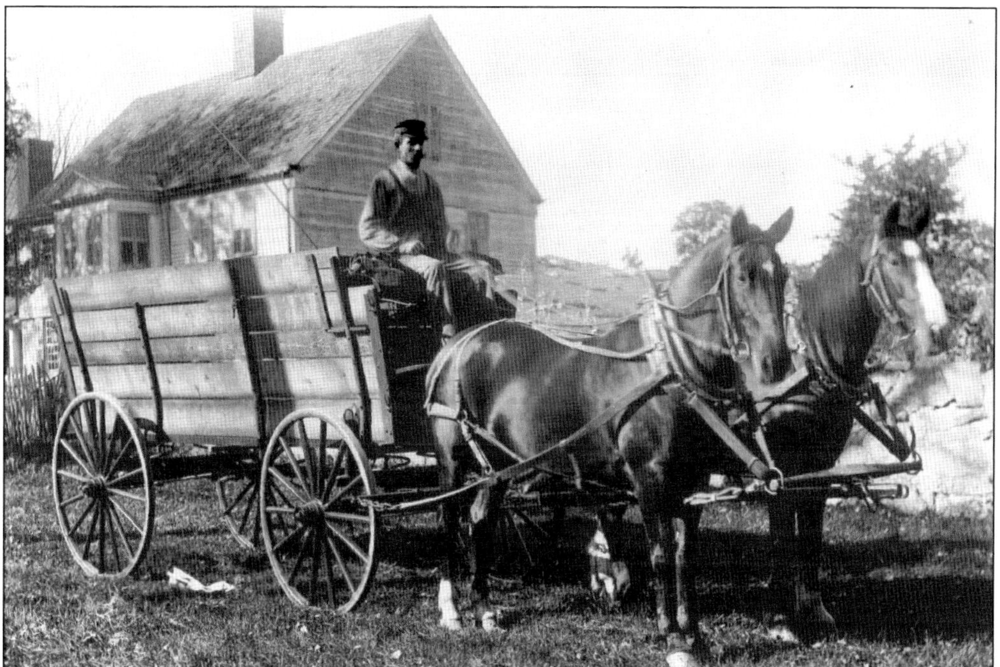

THE CHARCOAL MAN, WEST AVENUE. Horses did a lot of the work in the early decades of the 20th century. These two are delivering a load of charcoal to the Parker homestead on West Avenue. However, as the automobile gained popularity, the rural landscape changed. (Photograph courtesy of Essex Historical Society.)

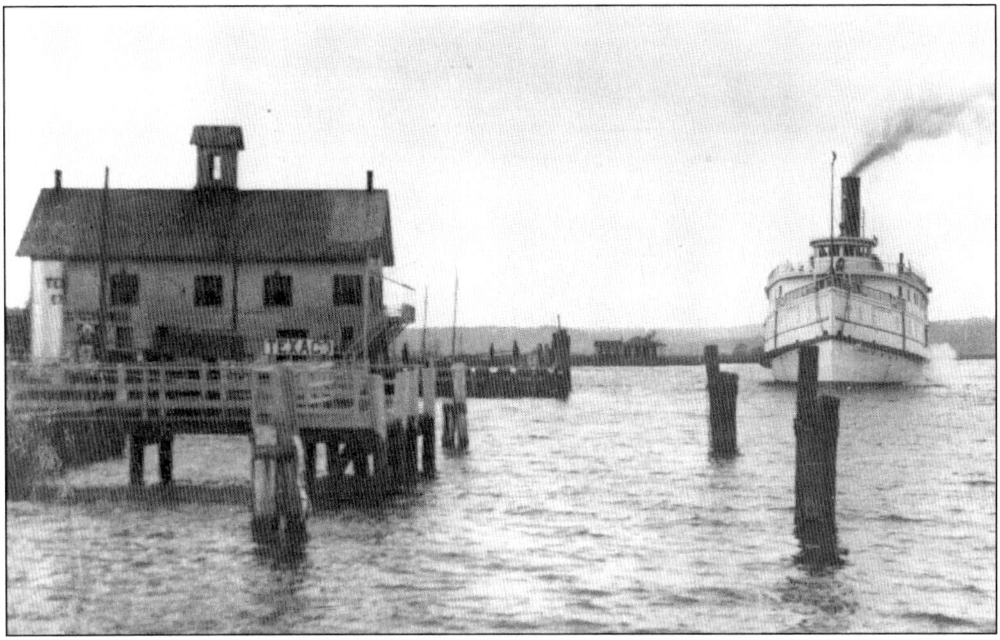

AN ARRIVING STEAMBOAT. En route from Hartford to New York, the *City Of Hartford* arrives at Steamboat Wharf in Essex in 1910. The steamboat service lasted until 1930 as a leisurely and pleasant mode of transportation. Regular service on the river started with the small steamer *Experiment*, which succeeded to the extent that it was followed in 1824 by the elegant *Oliver Ellsworth*, a 112-foot side-wheeler of 230 tons that made three round trips weekly between Hartford and New York. (Photograph courtesy of Essex Historical Society.)

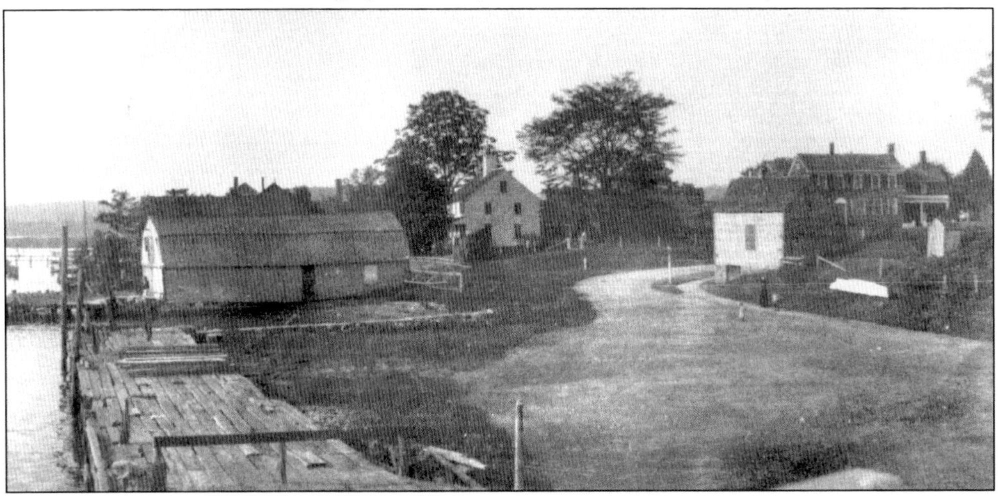

THE ESSEX WATERFRONT, C. 1890. This photograph of the foot of Main Street in the late 1800s shows the deterioration of the once bustling waterfront, brought into decline by the end of Potapoug's dominance in building wooden sailing ships and by the commercial competition of the railroad starting in 1871. Early steamboats stopped at the long shed, next to what today is the town boat launch. The Uriah Hayden house (center) was once a tavern and today is the Dauntless Club. At this location in 1776, it took Hayden less than five months to build the famous Connecticut warship *Oliver Cromwell*. (Photograph courtesy of Connecticut River Museum.)

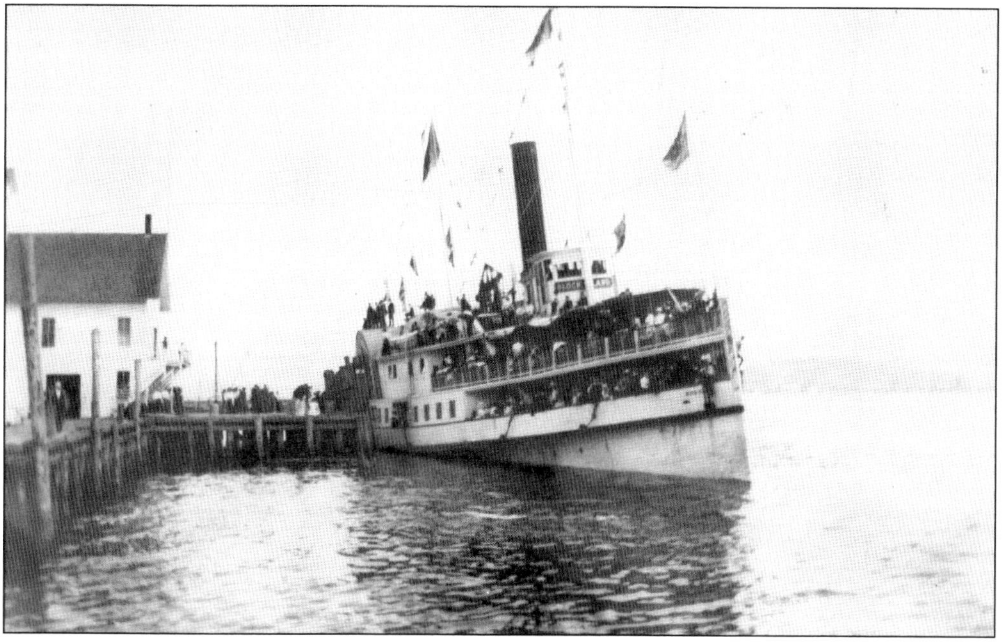

"ALL ABOARD THAT'S GOING ABOARD." This September 1898 photograph shows passengers bound for Block Island, Rhode Island, boarding the steamer at Steamboat Dock in Essex. The building and its location are preserved today as the home of the Connecticut River Museum, dedicated to its mission of educating the public in "the history, culture and environment of the Connecticut River Valley, and the use of the Connecticut River for commerce, natural habitat, and recreation." (Photograph courtesy of Essex Historical Society.)

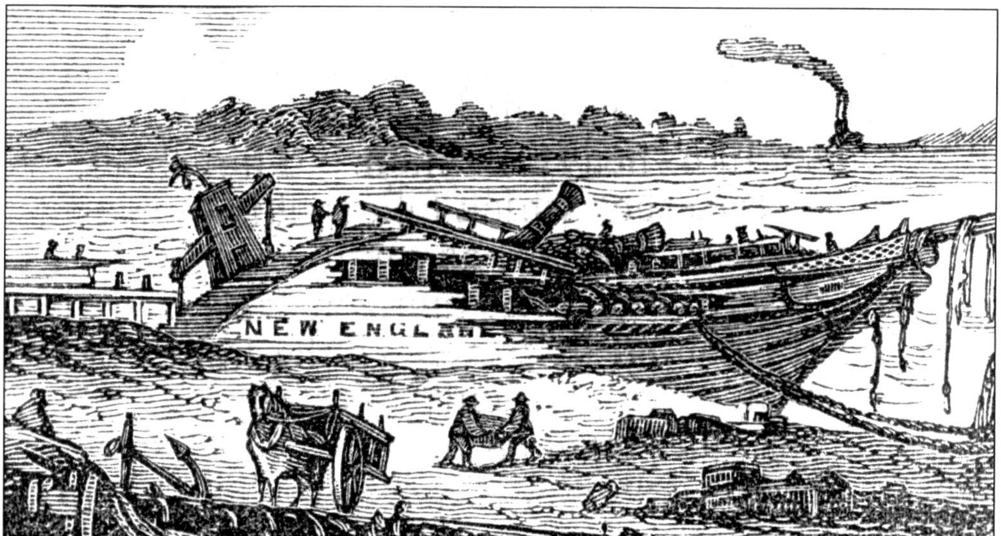

THE WRECK OF THE STEAMSHIP *NEW ENGLAND*, ESSEX HARBOR, OCTOBER 1833. This lithograph shows the destruction when the boiler exploded on the steamer. Fifteen people died as a result and, shortly thereafter, a similar tragedy occurred near Fishers Island, New York. Boiler explosions were a common occurrence until the development of an efficient steam boiler safety valve. Still, passengers were undeterred due to the speed, convenient schedules, and luxury the steamboats offered. (Photograph courtesy of Connecticut River Museum.)

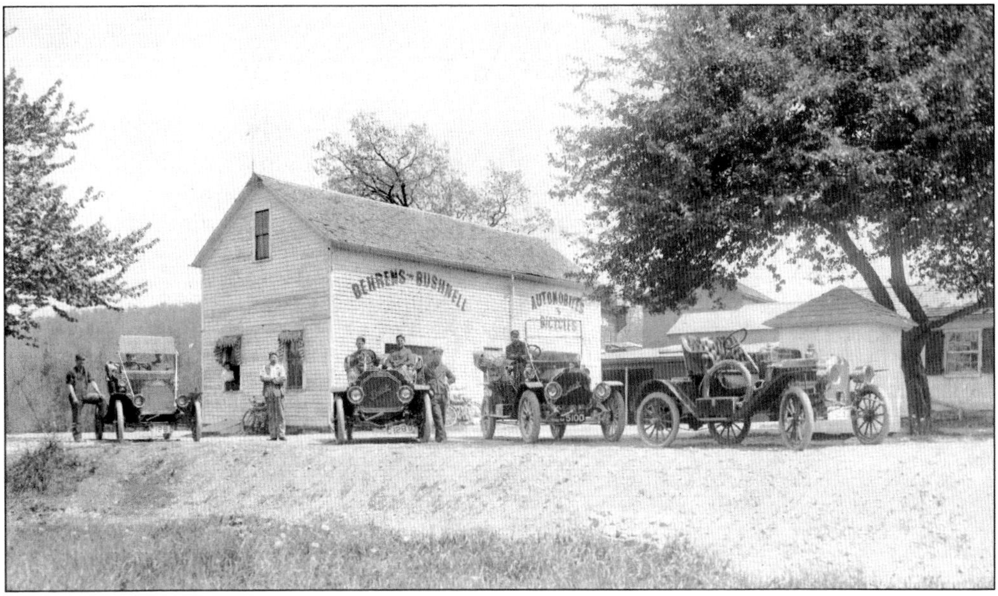

THE BEHRENS AND BUSHNELL BICYCLE AND AUTOMOBILE REPAIR SHOP, PHOTOGRAPH 1905. This business was located on Main Street at the Ivoryton-Centerbrook border. It sold both bicycles and automobiles. Early automobile technology owes much to the bicycle. Even the Wright Brothers built much of the first successful airplane in 1903 at their bicycle shop in Dayton, Ohio. (Photograph courtesy of Ivoryton Library.)

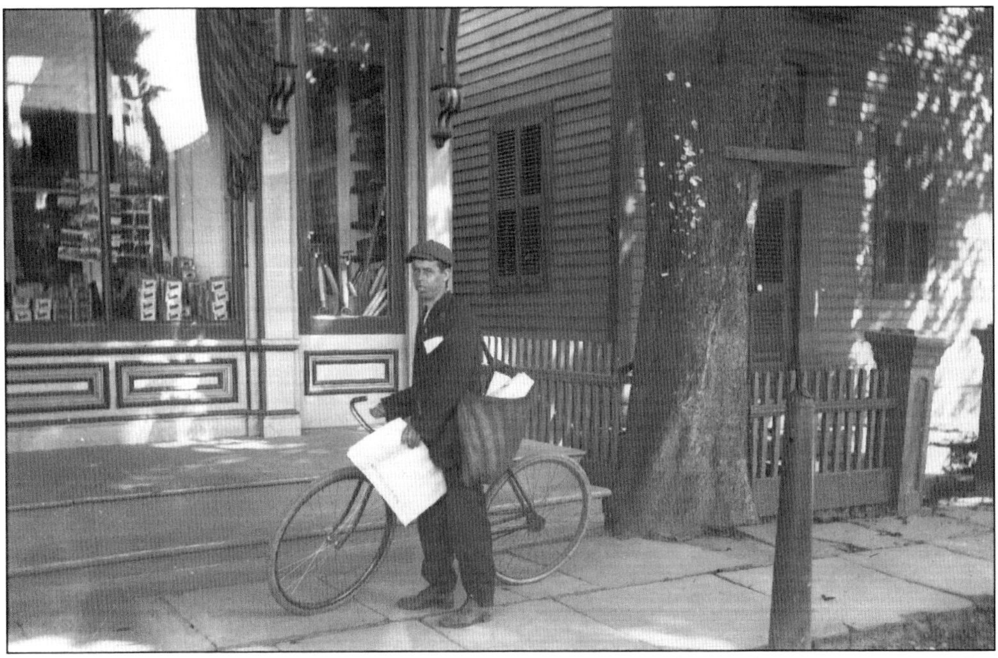

A PAPER BOY ON MAIN STREET, ESSEX. Jimmy Wallace delivers the *Penny Press* on his Columbia Safety Bicycle, made in Hartford. He is standing in front of Burrows' Store, located across from the present post office. During the national bicycle craze of 1895 to 1900, the Ivoryton Wheel Club had many members, most of whom worked at Comstock, Cheney & Company. (Photograph courtesy of Essex Historical Society.)

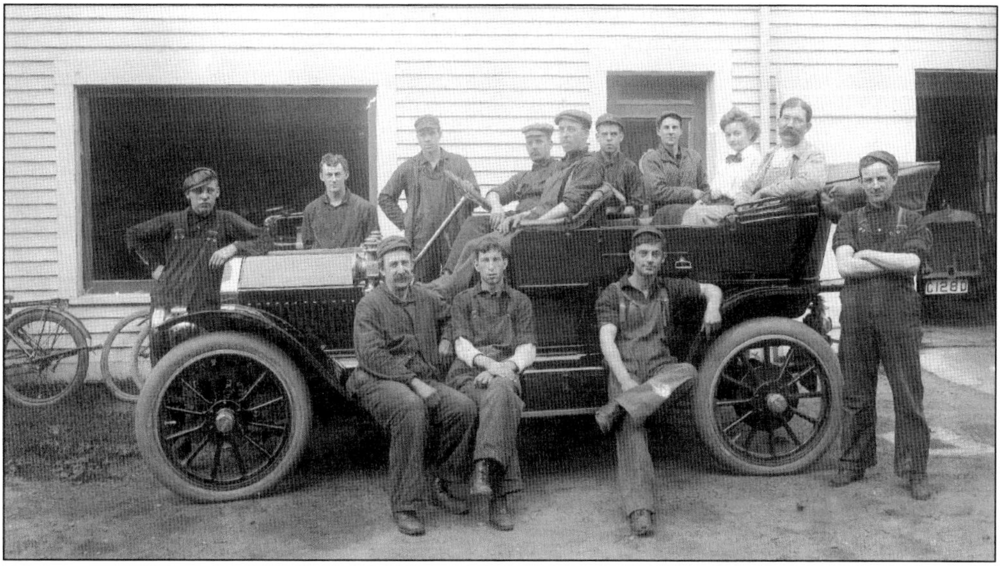

Behrens and Bushnell, 1905. The first car this firm sold was a 1901 Oldsmobile. Most of the early automobiles came unassembled in cartons and had to be put together at garages. Over the years, Behrens and Bushnell sold many brands, including Oldsmobile, Locomobile, Winton, and Ford. They are best known, however, for being Buick and Cadillac dealers. (Photograph courtesy of Ivoryton Library.)

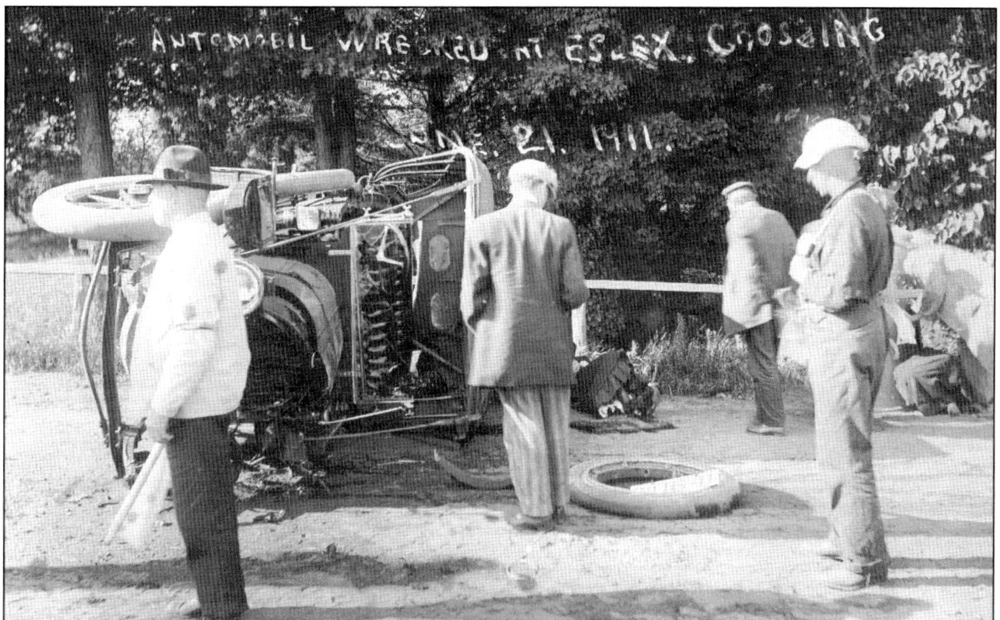

An Accident at the Railroad Crossing, June 1911. Transportation modes frequently collided, particularly while automobile brakes were still primitive. This car was hit by the train at the Main Street railroad crossing in Centerbrook. The railroad had been here for 40 years, but cars for just 10. Leading citizens in large and small towns across the country competed to have the latest, most advanced automobiles, which only their mechanics and hired chauffeurs truly understood. (Photograph courtesy of Essex Historical Society.)

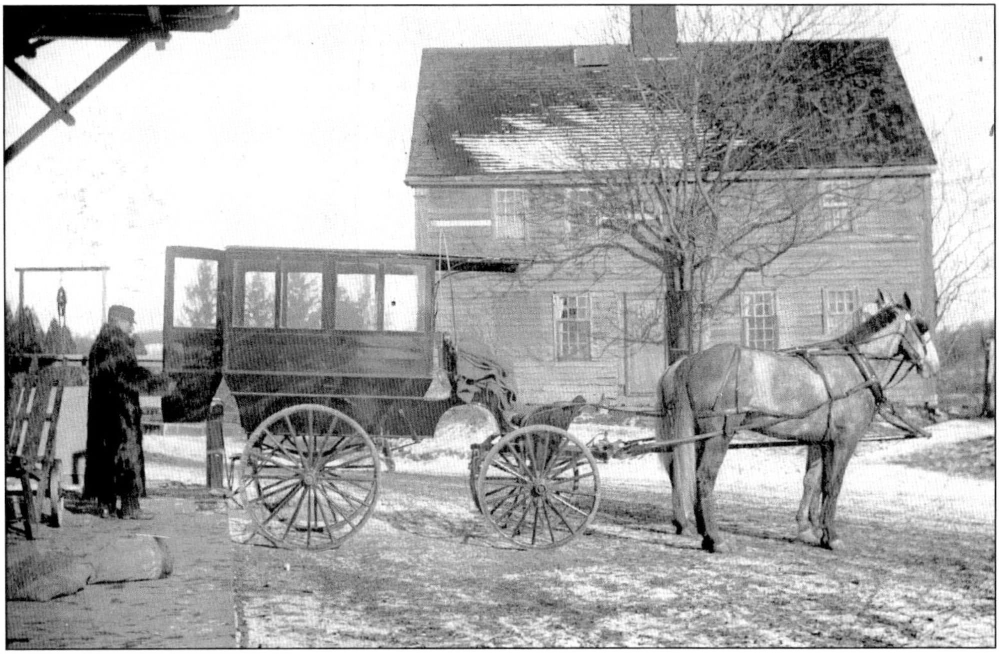

The Local Limousine Meeting the Train. In 1873, five trains were scheduled in each direction, northbound and southbound. Two of the trains were passenger only, two were freight, and one was a combination of both. Likewise, today there are five departures daily of the Essex Steam Train during the warm weather months, with four connecting in Deep River for a boat ride. Special trains with dinner in the dining car and a trip with Santa are offered. The 50-year-old Scoville House (background) was torn down in 1915. (Photograph courtesy of Max Miller.)

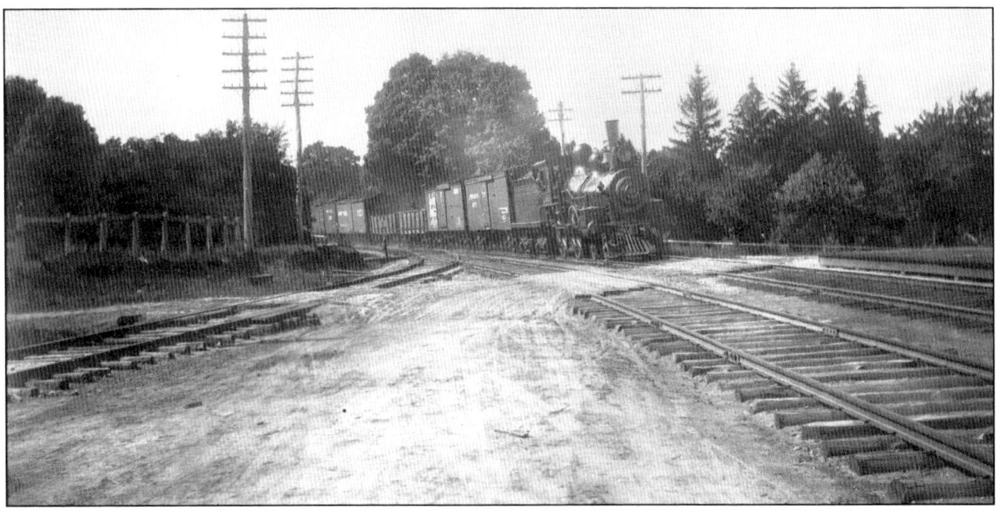

Arriving in Essex. A southbound freight train arrives in 1896 at the Essex station, which actually is in Centerbrook. The railroad, like turnpikes and trolleys, was late in coming to the valley. There never was the population density and commercial activity to warrant them. The Connecticut Valley Railroad started running trains from Old Saybrook to Hartford in 1871, but the first trains had started operation elsewhere in the state in 1843 and had become profitable by the Civil War. (Photograph courtesy of Essex Historical Society.)

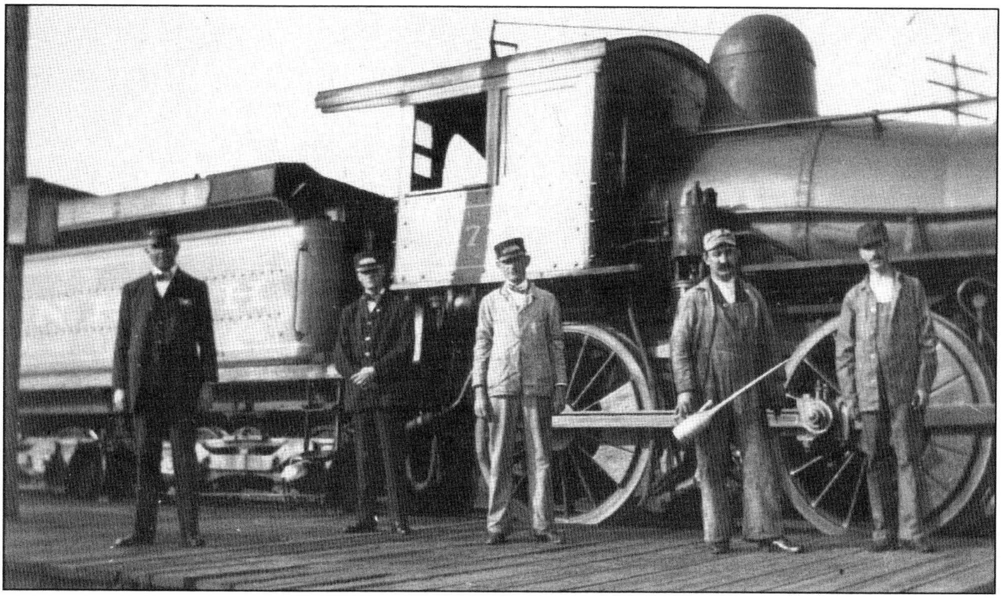

THE ESSEX RAILROAD DEPOT, PHOTOGRAPH 1900. This 1900 photograph could have been taken at the Essex Steam Train today. Miraculously, when the Penn Central Railroad, the successor to the bankrupt New Haven Line, gave up service on the Valley Line in 1968, the state was able to quickly negotiate a deal for the tracks and right-of-way before the rails could be pulled up and sold for scrap. Concurrently, the fledgling Valley Railroad Company was able to muster the necessary capital, equipment, and volunteers to resume operation as a tourist attraction in 1971, 100 years after the Connecticut Valley Railroad first started service. Today, some 160,000 passengers are served annually. (Photograph courtesy of Essex Historical Society.)

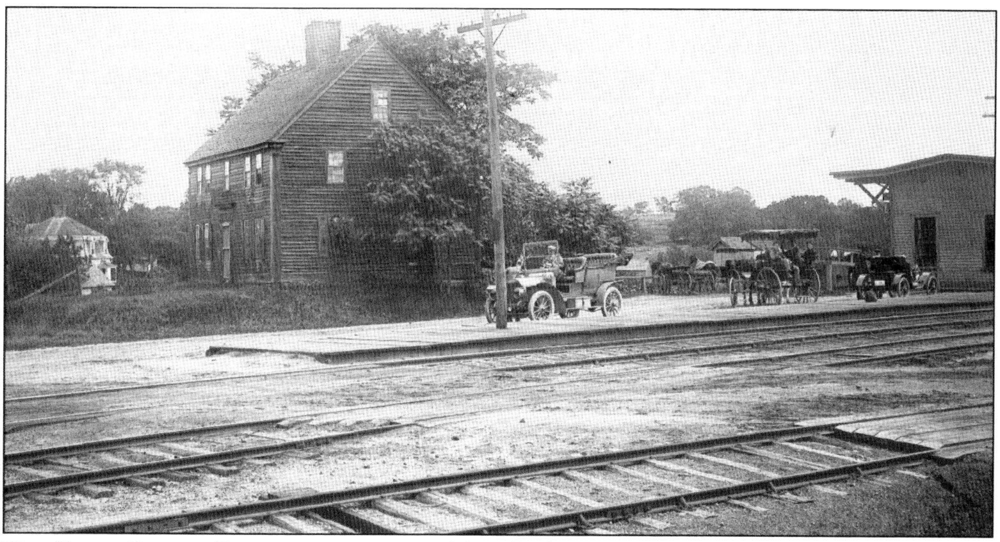

THE ESSEX DEPOT, PHOTOGRAPH 1908. After the beginning of the 20th century, automobiles became a part of the scene at the depot and eventually replaced the horse and wagon, just as trucks and buses eventually replaced regular railroad service. Making a profit was a constant struggle for the railroad in the Connecticut River Valley, where there was never the necessary critical mass of either industry or population. (Photograph courtesy of Essex Historical Society.)

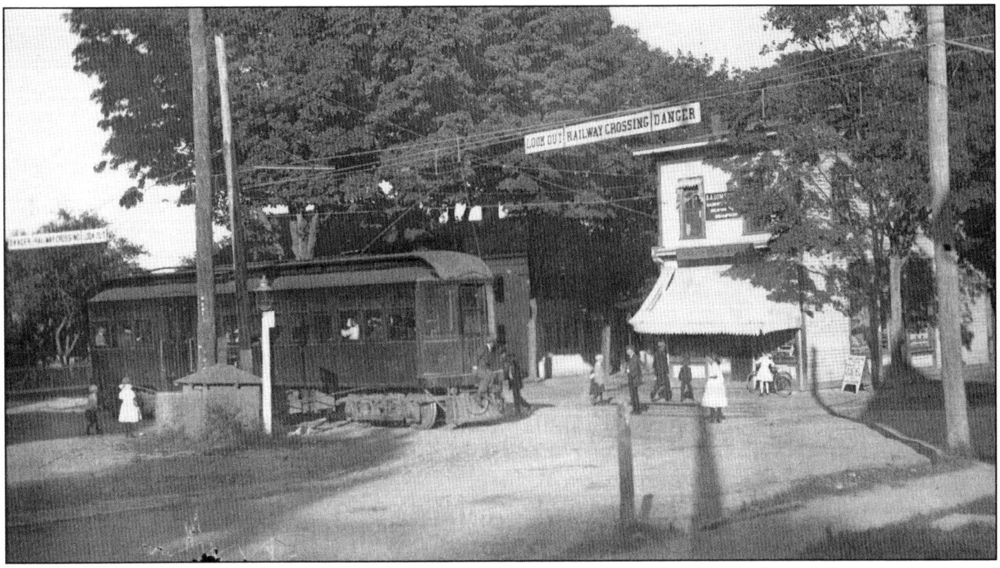

THE TROLLEY IN ESSEX SQUARE, PHOTOGRAPH 1911. The Shoreline Electric Railroad Company commenced service from Old Saybrook north in 1910. Originally designed to go to Middletown, it went as far north as Chester. A "silent policeman," or dummy officer, stands today in the center of the square, replacing the telephone pole shown here. Poor cost controls, disappointing profits, lawsuits stemming from accidents, and a labor strike plagued the trolley line. The untimely death of the line's visionary benefactor, millionaire Morton Plant, added to the line's woes, and it shut down in 1919. (Photograph courtesy of Donald Malcarne.)

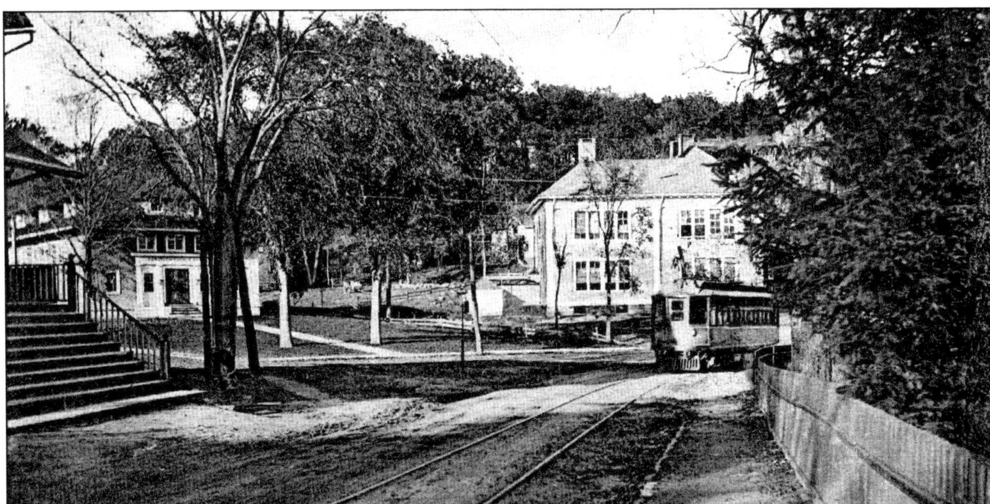

THE TROLLEY IN IVORYTON, PHOTOGRAPH 1911. The trolley makes the turn on Main Street in Ivoryton Center in front of what today is the Ivoryton Playhouse. The building on the right is the now-demolished grammar school, standing where the town green is today. The luxurious, heavy (34-ton) trolley cars, painted a dark Brewster green, had two compartments, one of which was for smoking. The cars were capable of speeds up to 80 miles per hour. That speed could never be attained on actual runs, due to the winding nature of the route. It is said of the engineer who laid it out that wherever there was not a curve, he made one. (Photograph courtesy of Ivoryton Library.)

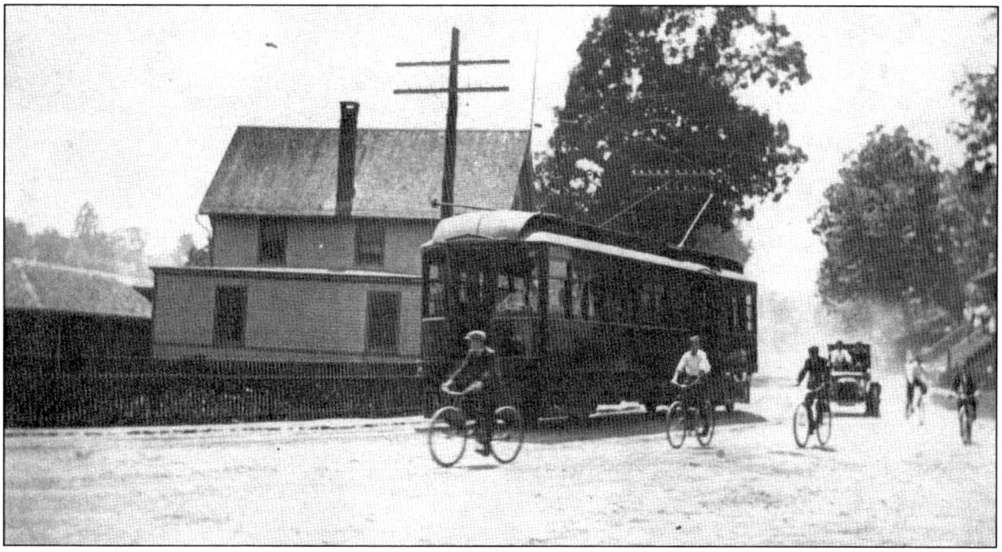

THREE MODES OF TRANSPORTATION. The trolley and its two main competitors, the bicycle and the automobile, were photographed in August 1910 in front of the Ivoryton Wheel Club. Many workers did not commute regularly on the trolley because its 5¢ fare was more than their limited wages could support. Many did pedal to work, however, and Comstock, Cheney & Company provided sheds for the storage of bicycles during the long workday. (Photograph courtesy of Ivoryton Library.)

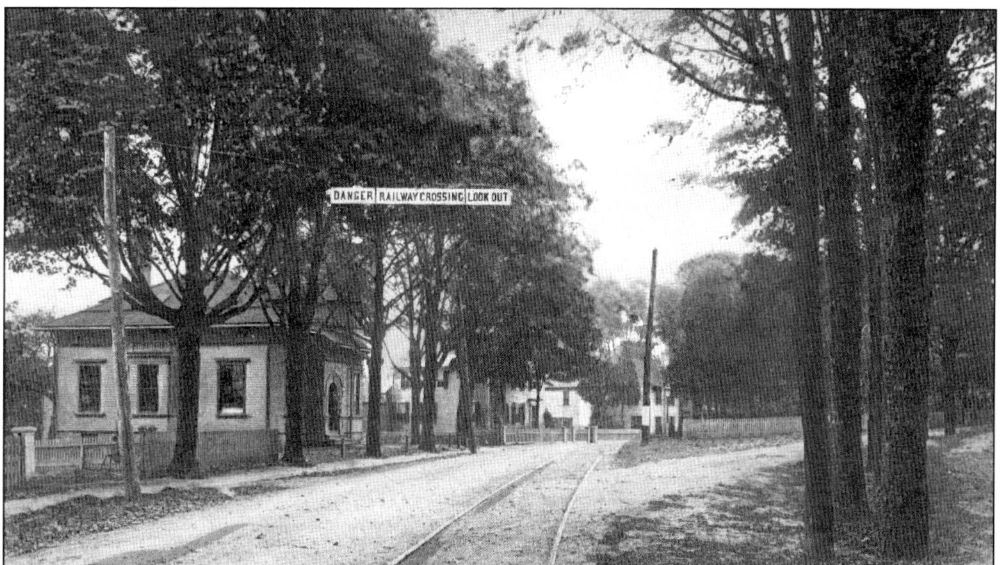

THE TROLLEY ON NORTH MAIN STREET, PHOTOGRAPH 1911. This photograph shows a route along North Main Street with the old E.E. Dickinson Company office building on the left and the E.E. Dickinson residence in the background. The line continued north and west from here through Centerbrook and Ivoryton and on to Deep River and Chester. According to a 1911 account in the *Deep River New Era* newspaper, the route traversed "wild woods, formidable ledges of rock . . ., some little spaces of open country at intervals . . ., and a very pretty sheet of water (just north of Ivoryton), several primitive country roads crossing the tracks and a few humble dwellings of work people here and there." (Photograph courtesy of Essex Library.)

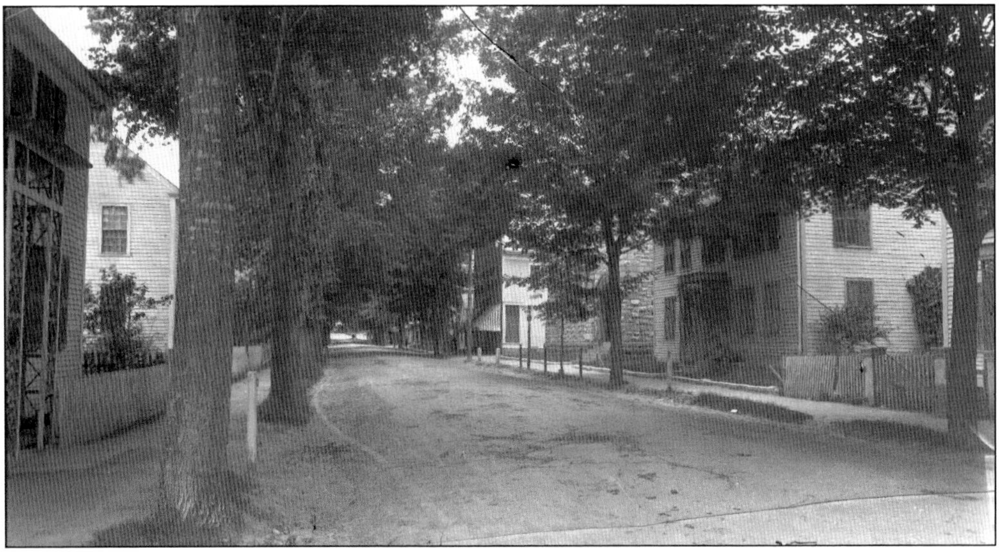

MAIN STREET, ESSEX, PHOTOGRAPH C. 1900. Hitching posts for horses are seen here on sleepy Main Street, Essex, around the beginning of the 20th century. Note the fence on the right in need of repair. Poverty, as they say, preserves. This once prosperous shipbuilding and shipping town has been preserved because there was no commercial incentive to tear down the old structures and rebuild new ones, nor could the owners afford to make extensive repairs or alterations. Prosperity had shifted to the industrial centers of Centerbrook and Ivoryton. In short, the picturesque Main Street, Essex, of today, owes a large measure of its state of historical preservation to being bypassed by the Industrial Revolution. (Photograph courtesy of Essex Historical Society.)

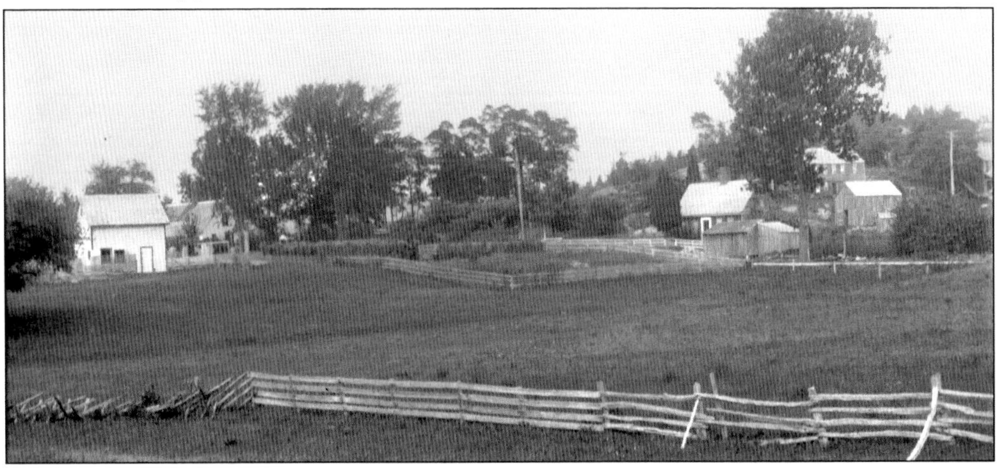

PHELPS CORNER, PHOTOGRAPH 1898. This historic area of Essex vanished en masse in 1965 when the Route 9 Interchange (Exit 3) was constructed. Twenty-six homes and outbuildings adjacent to Phelps Corner (above) were demolished. It was in this area that Phineas Pratt's home and shop were located, where he invented the machine for cutting combs out of horn or ivory. This technology allowed factories in Ivoryton and Deep River to develop as the world's leading manufacturers of ivory products, including buttonhooks, billiard balls, and piano keys. This also was an important intersection on Middlesex Turnpike, which opened in 1801 as a toll road, becoming the main north–south artery in Middlesex County. (Photograph courtesy of Essex Historical Society.)

Nine

Child of the River

The Connecticut River has always defined Essex to a major extent, with the ships built along the shore and the ivory unloaded at the docks. Unlike most of places in the valley, Main Street of Essex village runs straight for the river. Surrounded by water on three sides, the peninsula that was once Potapoug Point has changed over time. The Federal houses remain planted on the edge of the sidewalk, seaport fashion, and the commercial waterfront is still devoted to boats in one form or another. The West Indies Warehouse at the foot of Main Street became the site of E.E. Dickinson's boathouse. Ship launching ways became a marine railway that gave way to a travel lift, and the old sail loft, down on its luck, became Essex Island Marina. At the tip of Main Street, the old Essex Steamboat Dock became the Connecticut River Museum, devoted to preserving the changes in this sea-going village.

The coves and waterfront continue to provide a great variety of marine services, including boat-repair yards, sailmakers, chandlers, boat brokers, marine architects, marine publications, and winter boat storage. Essex is known far and wide as a yachting haven and is home to the Dauntless Club, Essex Yacht Club, Essex Corinthian Yacht Club, Pettipaug Yacht Club, and Essex Motor Boat Club.

Prior to the 20th century, when the prevailing form of transportation was still the river, the town was affected by the ice that formed in the winter. The steamer traffic between Hartford and New York, which also served the small river ports, generally ended in December and did not begin again until the ice went out. The spring freshet of high water, caused by upper Connecticut River Valley snowmelt, also delayed the steamers because of hazardous floating debris that sometimes included doghouses, chicken coops, and whole trees. The Great Flood of 1936, when the river reached its highest crest of 36.6 feet at Hartford, was a combination of March snowmelt and an extra tropical northeaster. Because it was so early in the season, most of the boats were still in winter storage. It is only in recent memory that people have built their homes at the water's edge. Fortunately, there is considerable water storage in the Great Meadow that helps Essex keep its feet dry each spring.

The spring freshet also heralds the arrival of the shad season. For two centuries, this bony herring has been fished in the lower reaches of the Great River. This activity occupied fishermen from the three villages for about six weeks each spring. Shares in small fishing "companies" were so prized that they were handed down in wills. The wooden frame reels for drying and mending the large shad nets were once a common sight at the water's edge. Today, shad is still fished, but by fewer fishermen. The annual Rotary Club Shad Bake is held each June; the tradition is to nail the oily fish to hickory planks and bake them around an open fire.

If fishing has declined over the years, the interest in yachting has exploded. In the summer, the harbor is crowded with beautiful watercraft. For people cruising on Long Island Sound, Essex harbor offers a full range of marine services and a walkable New England village full of shops. The various yacht clubs often invite other clubs for races and rendezvous, and the river is a playground for a growing number of water sports. The Connecticut River Museum hosts Antique, Classic, and Traditional Vessel Weekends that celebrate the town's rich yachting heritage and that pay homage to the private boat owners who are partners in historic preservation.

The fall often brings the best sailing weather. It also brings the hurricane season. Being six miles up river provides some protection, but the combination of high water pushed by southeast winds usually means continual assault for the exposed Essex village and the marinas. The Hurricane of 1938 hit Connecticut on September 21, 1938, after four days of rain. Fortunately, the month had been cool and many sailors had already hauled their boats for the season, but in Essex harbor, a fleet of cutters, yawls, and schooners had assembled for an Off-Soundings cruise. Without adequate warning from the National Weather Service, the extensive damage in the anchorage occurred as the rising river lifted the moorings one by one. The boats crashed into each other and were then lifted over the bulkhead. The river rose six feet in three hours, the barometer dropped like a stone, and the wind climbed to more than 88 miles per hour. When the storm was over, the harbor had been swept clean. Two men were dead, 50 boats were sunk, and another 50 damaged, some smashed to smithereens.

There have been many damaging storms since the Hurricane of 1938 but, today, early warning gives boat owners a chance to flee the open water of the harbor for refuge in Hamburg Cove. Residents themselves have learned to hunker down and to prepare their families and property for the seasonal tropical storms.

Sailboats at anchor, dinghy racing, the occasional crab fisherman, a passing work barge, and perhaps the now infrequent tanker, are, for many, all that is required to make a visit to the Essex waterfront a satisfying experience.

—Brenda Milkofsky

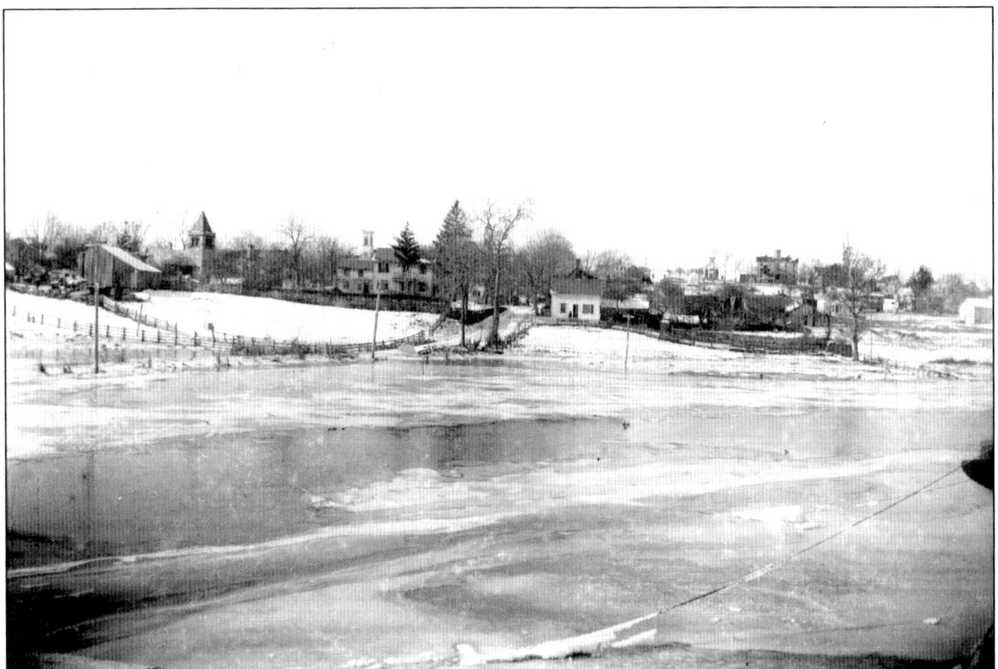

THE ESSEX CAUSEWAY AND PRATT STREET. In the background of the photograph can be seen Hills Academy, Pettipaug Hotel, and the Baptist church. (Photograph courtesy of Essex Historical Society.)

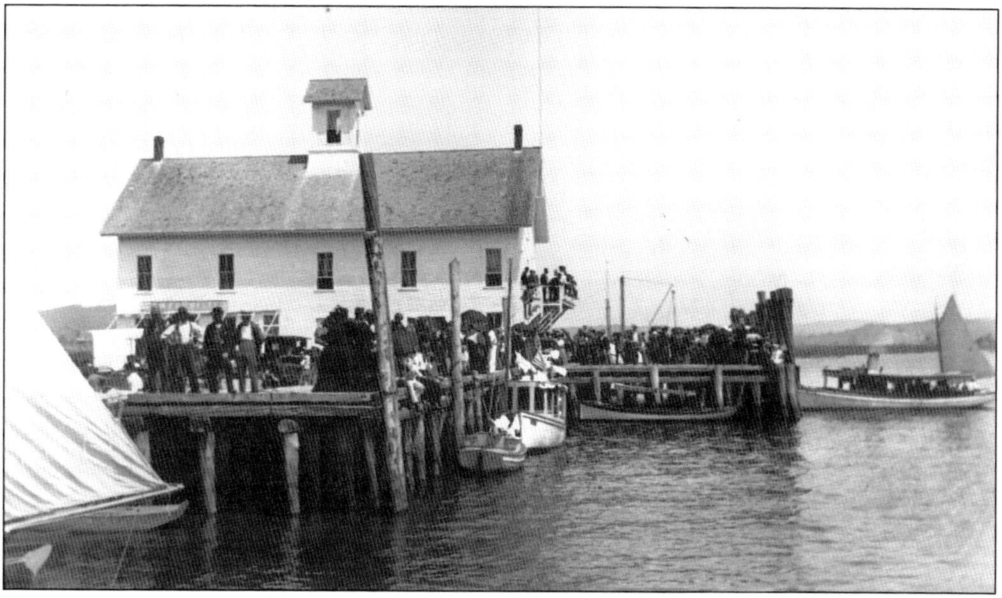

THE ESSEX STEAMBOAT DOCK, WITH CROWD. The Steamboat Dock house, built in 1878 by Phebe Hayden and operated by her nephew William H. Parmelee, was always a great place to view the river. Built to house incoming and outgoing river cargoes, the house had a second-floor porch, which was once accessible by outside stairs. One could watch for steamboats or, as in the case of this crowd, view the weekend sailboat races. Even before the advent of organized yacht clubs, retired shipmasters and fishermen sailed against each other with wagering, prizes, and great anticipation. (Photograph courtesy of Connecticut River Museum.)

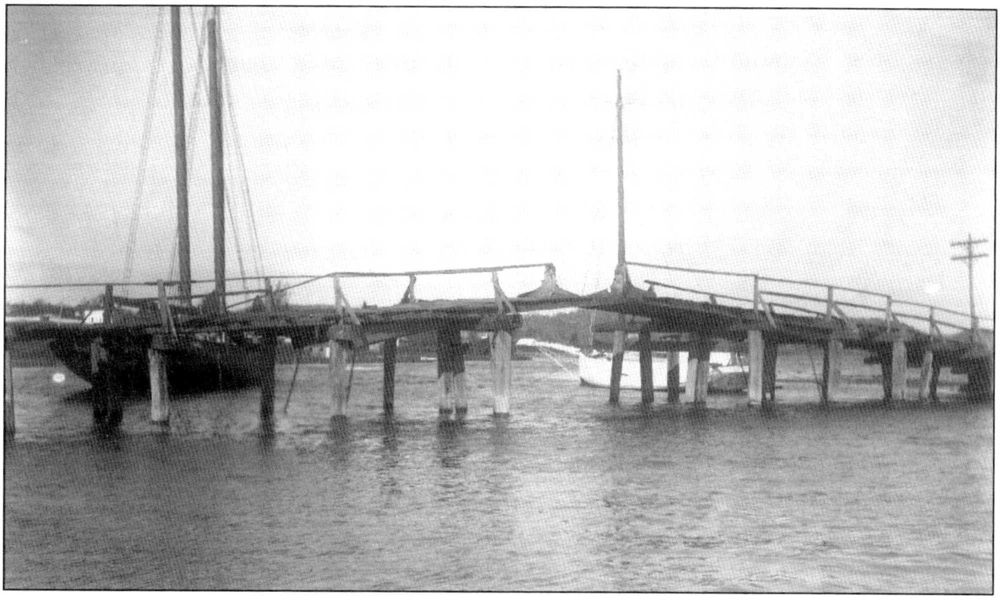

THE ESSEX TURNPIKE DRAWBRIDGE. This bridge connected Essex village to Essex Island at the foot of Ferry Street. Ferry Street was originally named Essex Turnpike, and this street ran up the island and along the meadow at the water's edge to a point opposite Ely's Ferry Landing. A scow ferry delivered passengers across the river to Lyme and on to the road to Norwich and New London. (Photograph courtesy of Essex Historical Society.)

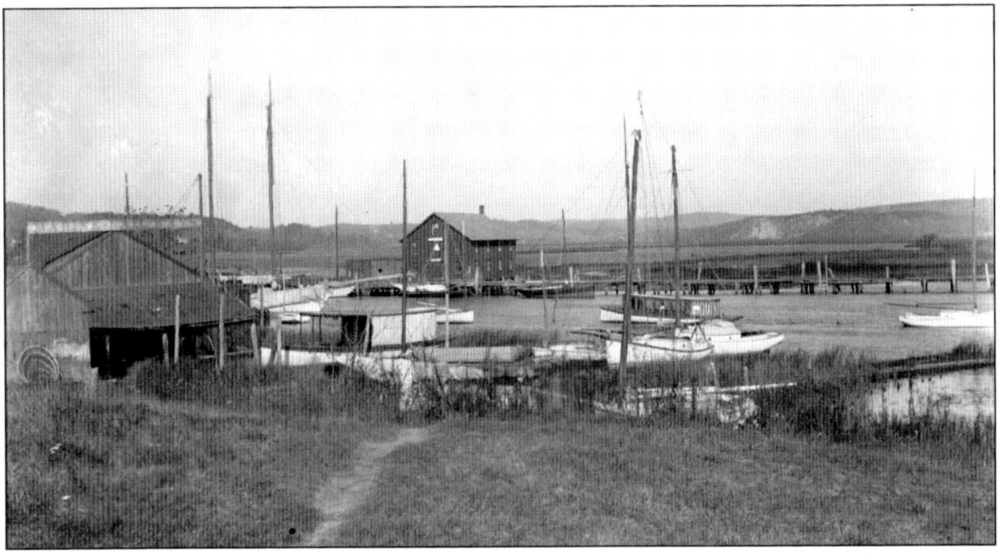

A VIEW OF THE SAIL LOFT DOCK. The Essex waterfront has continually changed in response to the times. This view from north of the Essex Steamboat Dock looks down on what was once the Redfield & Parmelee shipyard. On this site the 1,400-ton ship *Middlesex* was launched in 1851. To the left, the Essex Marine Railway, on the site of the Essex Boat Works, looks across to Braddock's Sail Loft. The long dock running south allowed several large vessels that were fitting out to bend on their sails under Braddock's watchful eye. There is a nice variety of small craft in this view, including a small steamer heading for the drawbridge, with a large schooner just beyond. (Photograph courtesy of Essex Historical Society.)

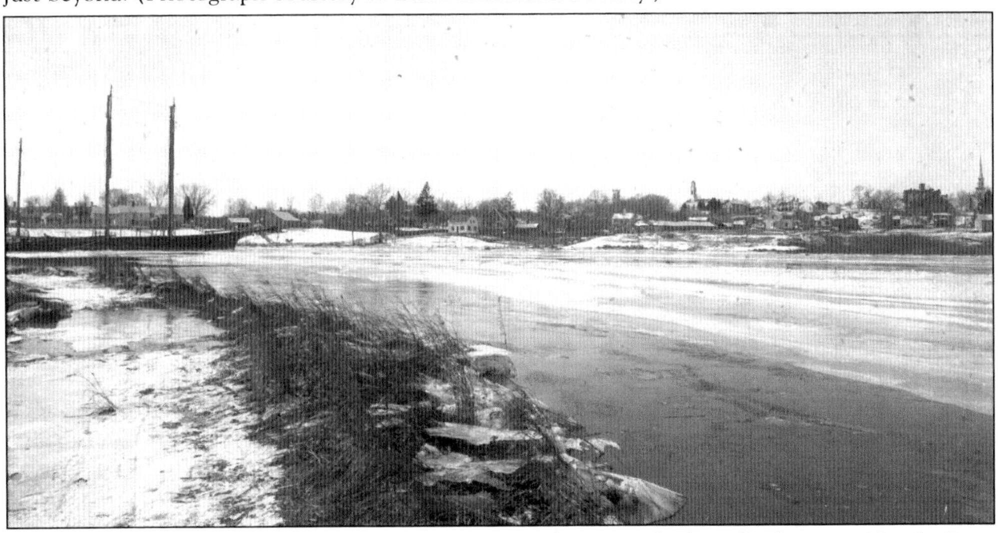

A VIEW OF THE VILLAGE FROM ESSEX ISLAND. In this view, looking back across North Cove from above Braddock's Sail Loft on Essex Island, the familiar Essex landmarks pierce the sky. On Zion Hill, from south to north, are the First Church Congregational, the rounded Methodist church dome, the short Hills Academy, the Pettipaug Hotel, and the once magnificent Egyptian Revival Baptist church. Running down toward the water is the long covered ropewalk, owned by R.W. Robbins during the 1870s. An empty shad reel sits at the water's edge, awaiting spring. The large schooner to the left is the *Dauntless*, with another ship's mast beyond. (Photograph courtesy of Essex Historical Society.)

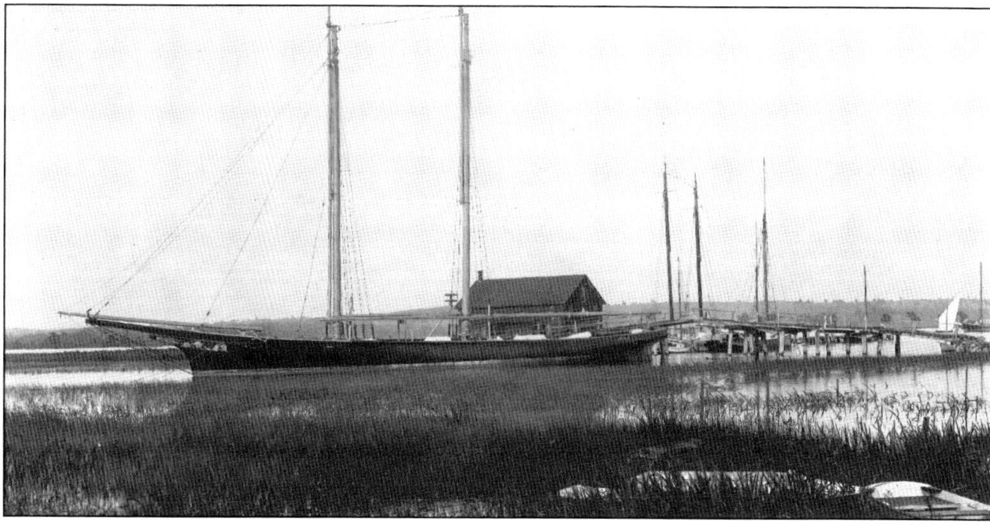

THE *DAUNTLESS*, ABOVE THE BRIDGE IN NORTH COVE. The most famous yacht connected with the town of Essex was the schooner *Dauntless*, owned by Elizabeth and Caldwell Colt (the son of Hartford arms maker Samuel Colt). The 120-foot vessel was built at Mystic in 1865 and was lengthened by 23 feet in the bow when it was owned by James Gordon Bennett, publisher of the *New York Herald* and commodore of the New York Yacht Club. The yacht placed fourth in the America's Cup when Bennett raced her in 1870. Colt purchased the boat in 1882 and competed in transatlantic races. Each fall between 1882 and 1894, the *Dauntless* put into Essex for duck and rail hunting. (Photograph courtesy of Essex Historical Society.)

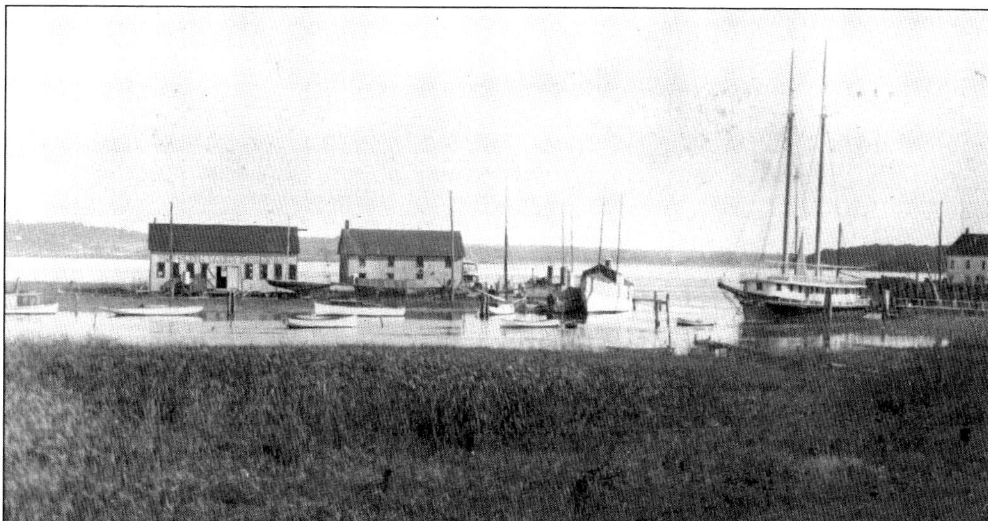

THE *DAUNTLESS* AS A HOUSEBOAT. A playboy, Caldwell Colt died young in 1894, and the *Dauntless* remained a shrine to him until his mother passed away in 1902. The boat was willed to a relative with the condition that it never sail again. Leased to a New York sportsman, who renovated it into a houseboat, it was used for hunting a few weekends a year. Finally in the winter of 1915, lying neglected, the once fabulous yacht sank at her moorings, her seams split, and her deck rotted. This view also includes the Smith Yacht Works and the old sail loft building on the island, but the drawbridge used from 1823 to 1889 is gone. (Photograph courtesy of Essex Historical Society.)

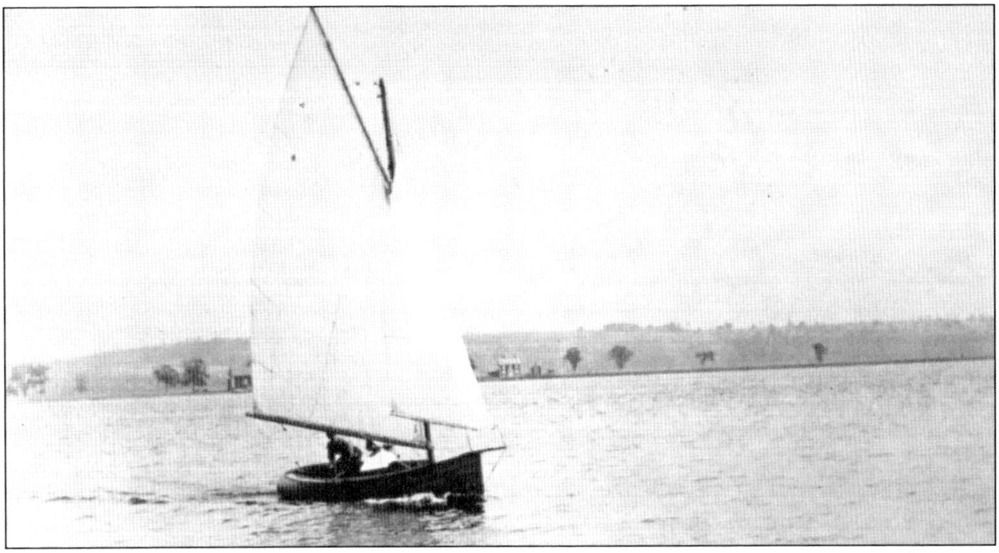

THE NANCY G. It took some time for yachting to develop as a viable industry along the lower reaches of the river. Once shipbuilding ended, land along the waterfront became available for the sometimes marginal practice of boatbuilding. Hartford businessmen often came to Essex for the hunting and, in 1905, they formed a sporting group named the Dauntless Club. It was their interest in the possibilities that Essex offered in this transitional time that once again brought attention to the town as a boatbuilding center. E.N. Way of Hartford designed and built the *Nancy* G for Hartford attorney Charles A. Goodwin. (Photograph courtesy of Connecticut River Museum.)

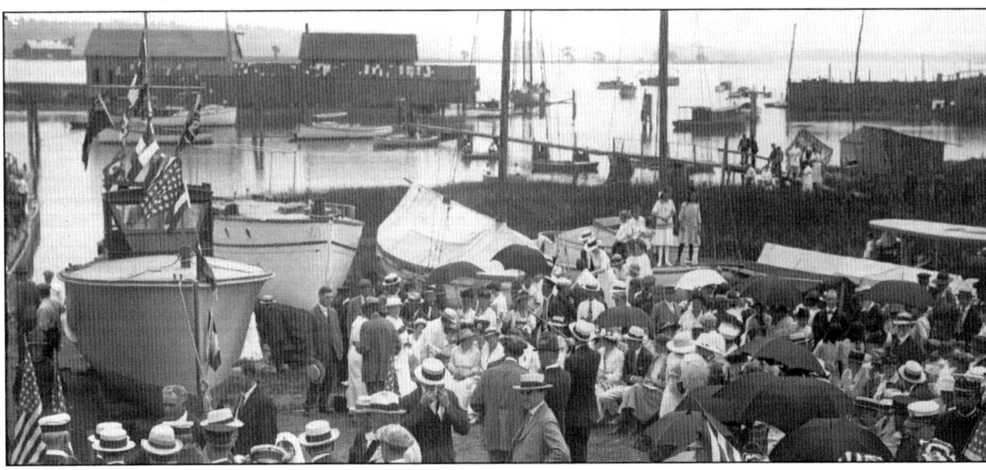

A BOAT LAUNCHING, WITH CROWD. Hartford attorney Charles A. Goodwin, who was interested in politics and yachting, got the Dauntless Club to agree to finance a torpedo patrol boat for the U.S. Navy during World War I. He purchased W. Frank Harrison's boatyard on North Cove and hired Harrison and Lew Mack to build a speedboat designed by Ernest N. Way of Hartford and Essex. Launching Day on July 7, 1917, began with a parade from Ivoryton through Centerbrook to the Essex waterfront. Crowds from Fenwick and Hartford attended to hear speeches, patriotic poems, the firing of the commissioning cannon, and to hear "Columbia, the Gem of the Ocean." The boat was christened *Dauntless* by Barbara Barnes, daughter of Roy T.H. Barnes, the owner who paid for the boat on behalf of the club. (Photograph courtesy of Connecticut River Museum.)

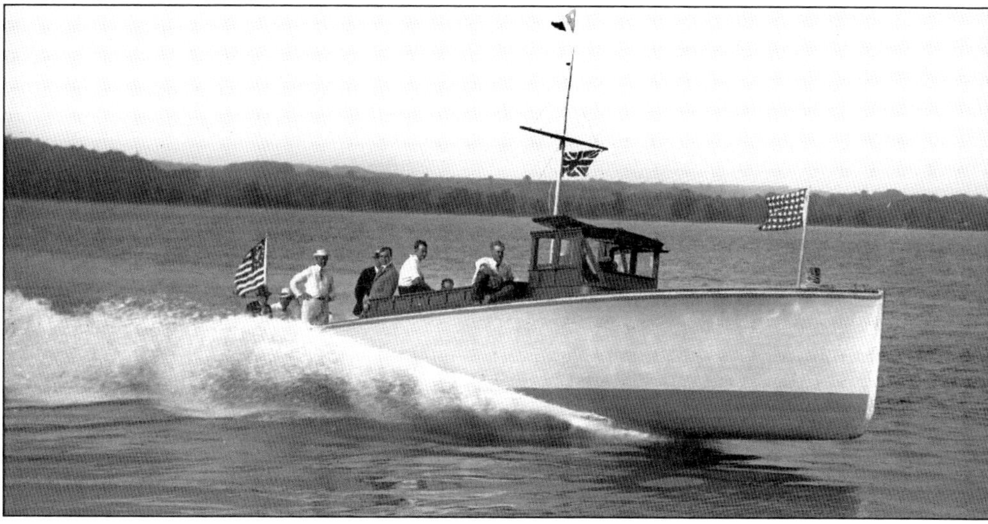

THE TEST RUN. During its trials, the 45-foot *Dauntless* reached 30 miles per hour with its 400-horsepower, eight-cylinder Deusenberg engine. Designed for coastal patrol, the boat had a 210-gallon gas tank, five berths, and a cooking galley. The mahogany brightwork was to be painted battleship gray once the boat was accepted by the government. The *Dauntless* served the government, as did many other private yachts during the two wars, primarily to deliver dispatches and personnel. E.N. Way went on to design a variety of fast and prizewinning powerboats and sailboats for yachtsmen here and at Middletown and Hartford. (Photograph courtesy of Connecticut River Museum.)

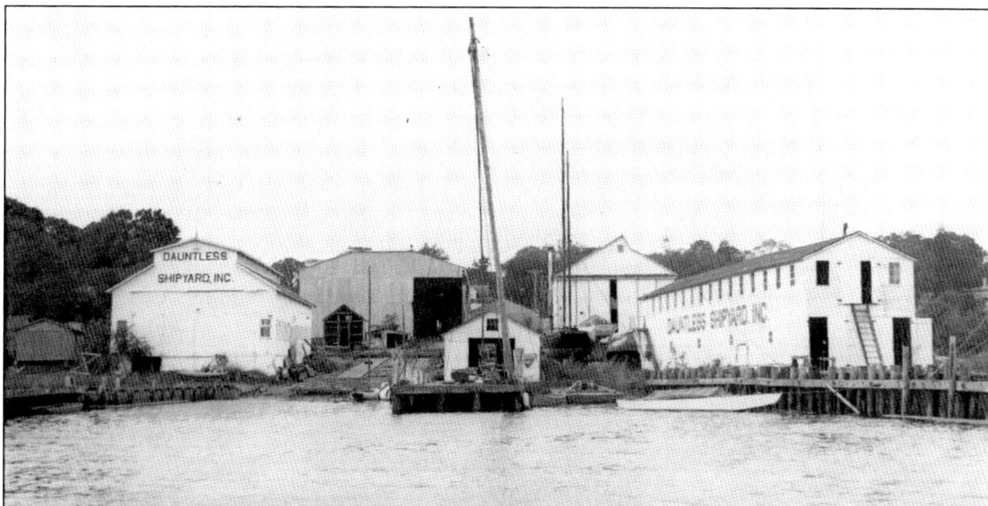

THE DAUNTLESS SHIPYARD. In 1925, the Dauntless Shipyard hired Maj. William Smythe as its superintendent, and subsequently a series of large yachts by nationally known designers came down the ways. The shipyard's owner, Charles A. Goodwin, had built a John Alden design named *Golden Hind.* Alden of Marblehead, Massachusetts, was a frequent visitor to the Dauntless yard, where several of his famous racing-cruising boats were built. The yard also built for Middletown designer Winthrop Warner. During the 1920s, yachting was largely a rich man's sport and the development of marine services here and elsewhere was slow to blossom. This view is from 1934, and the expanded yard appears quiet. (Photograph courtesy of Connecticut River Museum.)

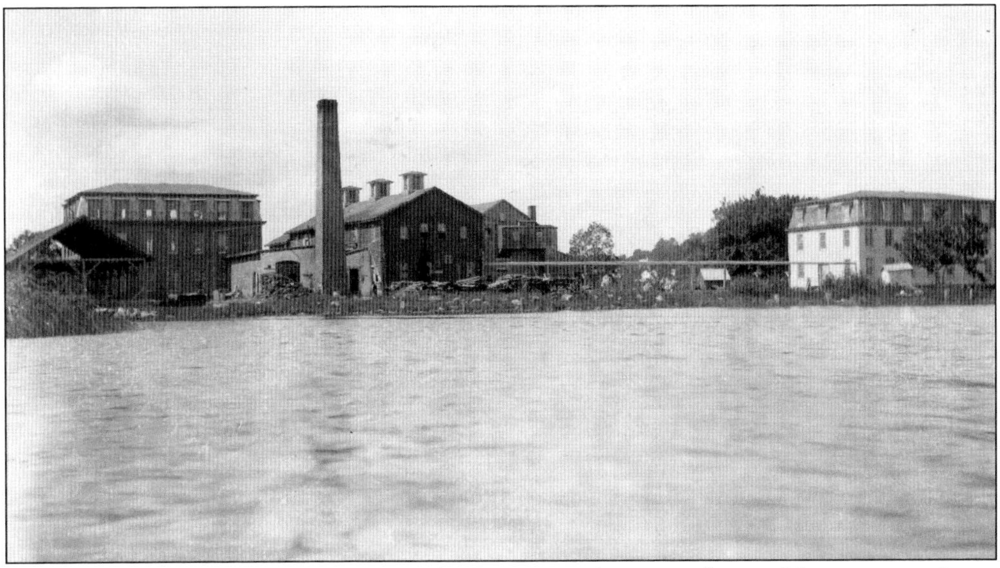

WOOD TURNING, OLD SHODDY MILL. The Essex waterfront was also used for various industry unrelated to shipbuilding or other marine activities. The Middle Cove Shoddy Factory, shown here, was once owned by Thomas N. Dickinson, who went on to found the Dickinson Witch Hazel Company. The entire complex burned down before 1900 and, today, the site houses the Essex Yacht Club, Essex Corinthian Yacht Club, and Novelty Lane.

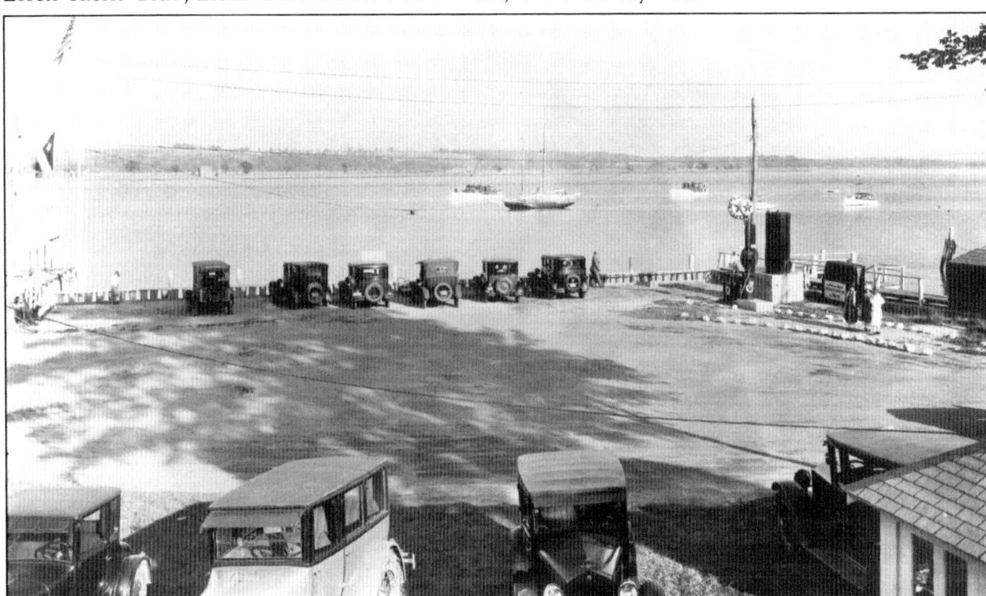

THE PARKING LOT AT THE ESSEX STEAMBOAT DOCK. The Essex waterfront, at the Essex Steamboat Dock and elsewhere, was extended by fill from the natural bank to deeper water. The site has had a variety of uses over the years, including a parking area for people using the wharves. The Hartford Yacht Club, with its burgee flying below the colors, used the second floor of the dock house as a downriver station after the club's Fenwick-on-the-Sound station at Saybrook Point burned in 1917. The Middletown Yacht Club used the other half of the upper floor for activities. (Photograph courtesy of Connecticut River Museum.)

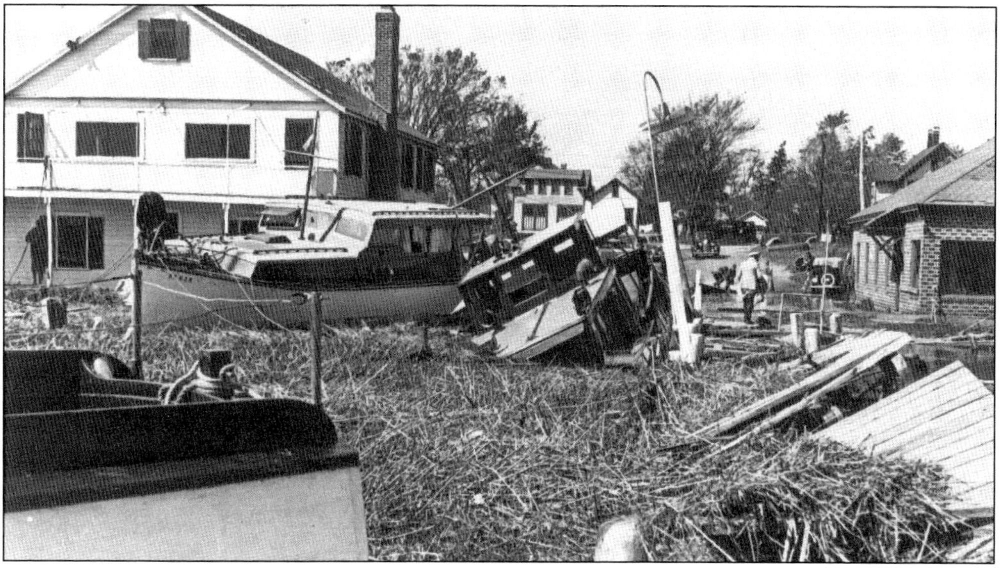

THE SHORE, AFTER THE 1938 HURRICANE. The Hurricane of 1938 blew into Essex on September 21, 1938. Powerboats, as well as sailing craft, were carried ashore by the more than 88-mile-per-hour winds and horizontal rain. Essex Paint and Marine Company, the brick building on the right, had just recently (1936) built and leased the building on the left to the new Essex Yacht Club, now the home of the Essex Corinthian Yacht Club. The force of the storm is also evidenced by the meadow grass in the middle ground, which was torn by its roots from the islands. (Photograph courtesy of Donald Malcarne.)

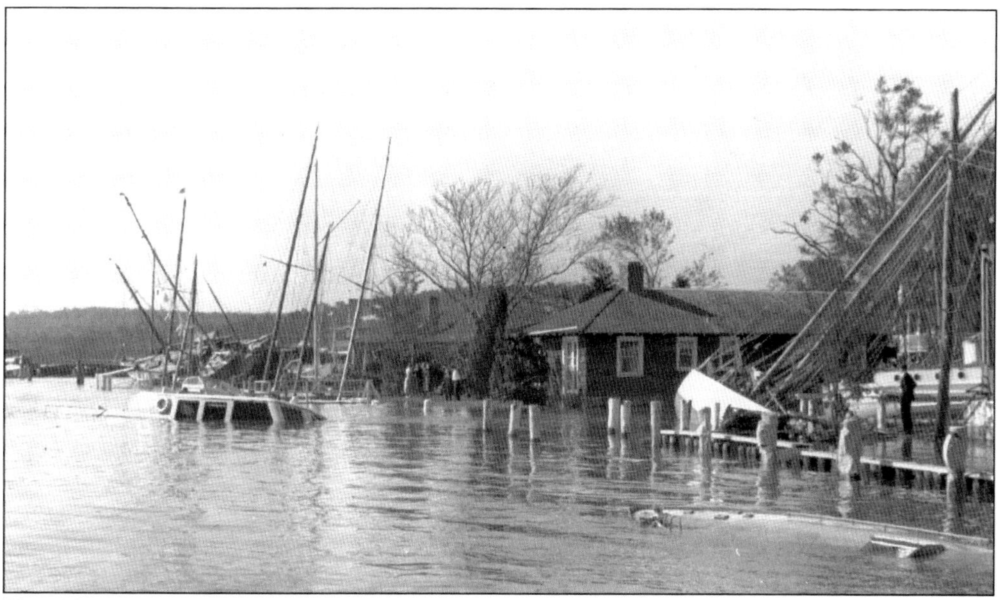

THE HARBOR, AFTER THE 1938 HURRICANE. At Essex, some 50 vessels were sunk in the anchorage and another 50 were damaged, mostly by going ashore. This view of the harbor at the foot of Main Street shows a flooded Dickinson boathouse (center) with boats ashore everywhere. Loggers from as far away as Maine came down to cut up the fallen debris, and small salvage operators worked for months to clear the waterways of sunken and damaged vessels. (Photograph courtesy of Donald Malcarne.)

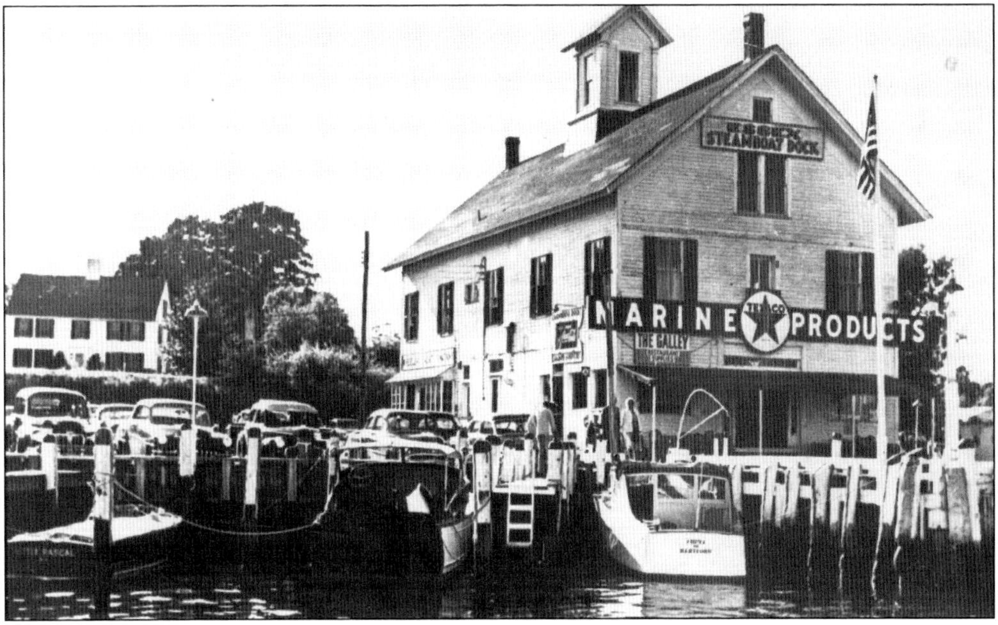

The Essex Steamboat Dock, with a Sign. In 1931, the steamer traffic on the river ended. Jim Parmelee, nephew of William Parmelee who operated the Essex Steamboat Dock from 1878 on, set about developing the site to service yachtsmen. He repaired the docks, added finger piers, and painted the tops of the pilings white for nighttime visibility. He restocked the building with marine items and got a franchise to sell Wheeler Cabin Cruisers and Fair Form Flyers. The view from the porch was obscured by the Texaco sign, and the second floor was rented as apartments. (Photograph courtesy of Connecticut River Museum.)

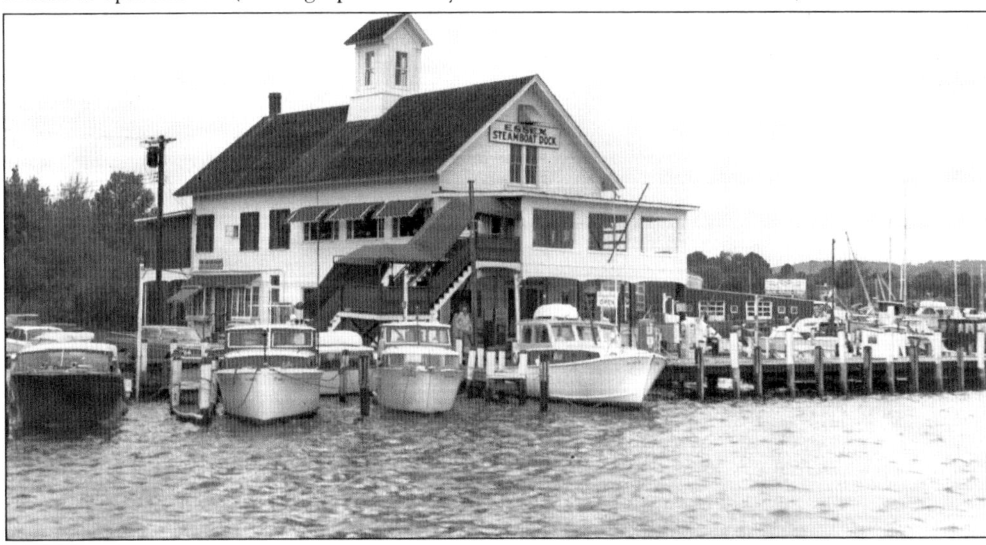

The Essex Steamboat Dock, with Awnings. By the 1950s, a restaurant had been added to the upper floor of the Essex Steamboat Dock, as Essex became a destination for tourists, as well as yachtsmen. The porch was closed in and eventually became a cocktail lounge. The Cheese Shop, in the rear, occupied the old Parmelee Store. Beyond the dock, the old Essex Boat Works can be seen. This building burned along with many boats during a disastrous fire in 1962. (Photograph courtesy of Connecticut River Museum.)

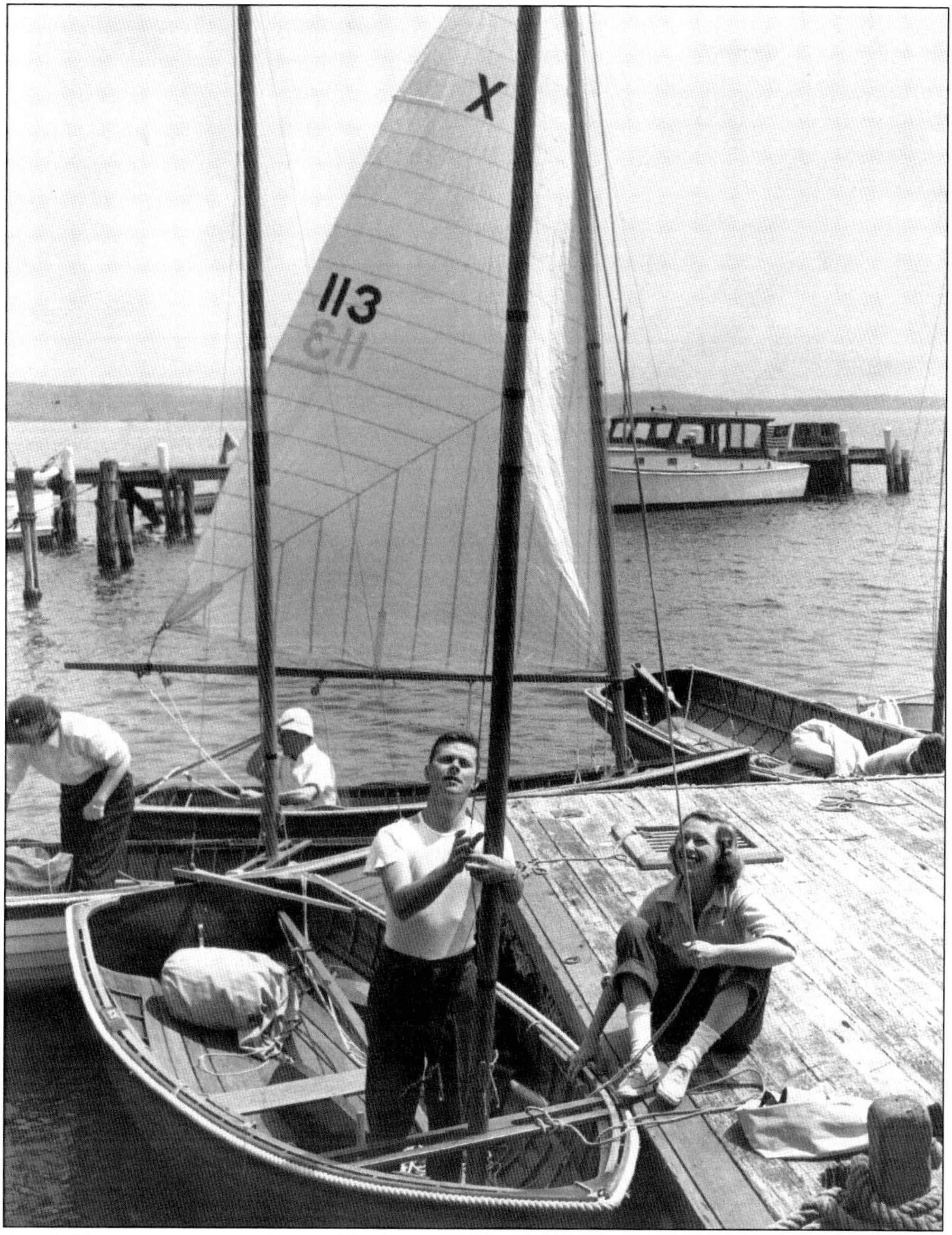

AN X-DINGHY AT THE DOCK. Charlotte and Peter Comstock (who was later president of Pratt Read & Company in Ivoryton) pose while rigging their X-dinghy for a race in 1937. In 1933, the Essex Yacht Club was formed to promote frostbite dinghy racing in the off-season. Club members met at the Essex Steamboat Dock, until they rented quarters just south of Essex Paint & Marine. Although small, these boats made for deadly serious racing. Frostbite sailors are rarely out in weather that permits T-shirts. (Photograph courtesy of Connecticut River Museum.)

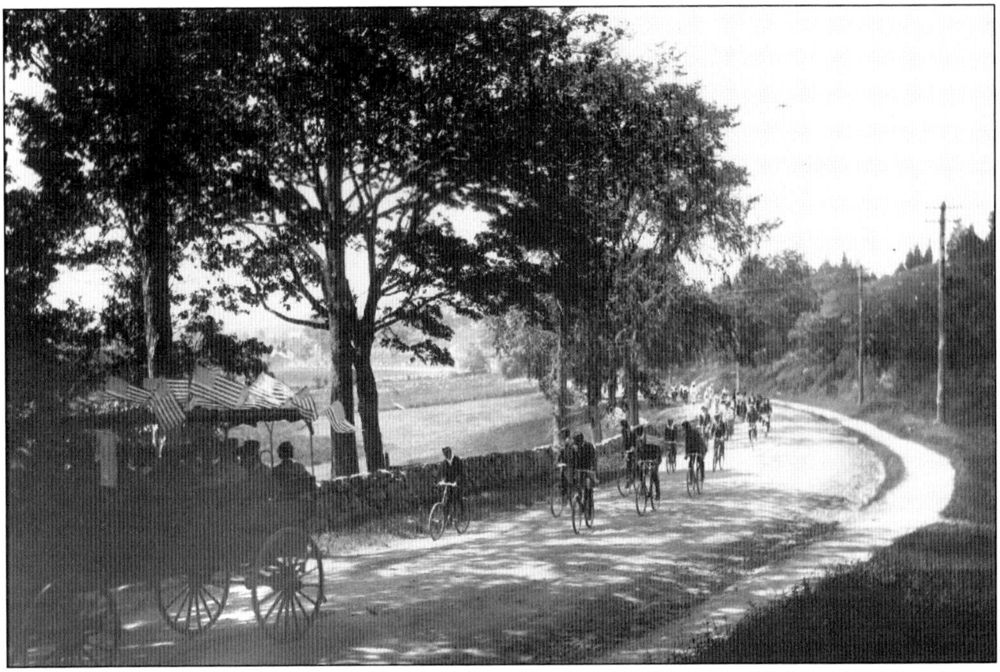

ESSEX LOVES A PARADE. Essex village celebrates either the Fourth of July or Memorial Day with a parade on West Avenue *c*. 1900.

Winter Audubon Society Eagle Festival
EHS-CRM-sponsored Trees in the Rigging
Groundhog Day

Spring Essex Garden Club May Market
Ivoryton Day Parade
Memorial Day Parade
Rotary Club Shad Bake
Sailing Masters Parade, celebrating the ships that were burned in 1814

Summer EHS Good Old Summertime Fair
Farmers Market
Firemen's Golf Tournament
Hot Steamed Jazz Festival
Lions Club Golf Tournament
Lions Club Lobster and Steak Bake
Park and Recreation Concerts in the Park
Rotary Club Golf Tournament

Fall Connecticut Valley Railroad Thomas the Train Weekends
Firemen's Breakfast
Firemen's Halloween Parade
Park and Recreation Family Day Town Picnic
Pumpkin Festival at the Ivoryton Gazebo
Rotary Club Bluefish Bake